ANTIETAM

The Photographic Legacy of America's Bloodiest Day

WILLIAM A. FRASSANITO

ANTIETAM

The Photographic Legacy of America's Bloodiest Day

CHARLES SCRIBNER'S SONS / NEW YORK

Copyright © 1978 William A. Frassanito

Library of Congress Cataloging in Publication Data

Frassanito, William A.
    Antietam: the photographic legacy of America's
bloodiest day.

    Includes index.
    1. Antietam, Battle of, 1862.   I. Title.
E474.65.F7   779'.9'9737336   78-2336
ISBN 0-684-15659-8 (cloth)
ISBN 0-684-17645-9 (paper)

The photograph on page 168 is reprinted from *The Photographic
History of the Civil War*, Francis T. Miller, ed.
[New York: Review of Reviews Co., 1911] by permission of
A. S. Barnes & Company, Inc.

3 5 7 9 11 13 15 17 19   Q/P   20 18 16 14 12 10 8 6 4 2

Printed in the United States of America

To a scholar and a friend, Mr. William C. Darrah

CONTENTS

ACKNOWLEDGMENTS

This book could not have been written without the aid of numerous institutions and individuals. The author wishes to thank, first and foremost, Mr. Jerry L. Kearns of the Prints and Photographs Division, Library of Congress, for his invaluable cooperation in allowing me to undertake a detailed examination of the library's original Antietam glass-plate negatives. Thanks are also due to two private collectors, Gordon D. Hoffman of Green Lake, Wisconsin, and John L. McGuire of Burbank, Illinois, both of whom generously entrusted with me all the Antietam material in their extensive assemblages of original Civil War stereo views and album cards.

Living and writing in Gettysburg, Pennsylvania, I had at my disposal several fine Civil War libraries, including those of the Gettysburg National Military Park, the Adams County Public Library, and Gettysburg College. I am greatly indebted to the personnel at all three institutions, and particularly to Anna Jane Moyer and the staff at the Schmucker Library, Gettysburg College. Additionally, I would like to extend a note of personal gratitude to Dan Mangan, News Bureau Director of Gettysburg College, for his understanding and cooperation regarding my use of the college's darkroom facilities.

National Park Service personnel at the Antietam National Battlefield Site likewise showed a great interest in my work, and I would especially like to thank Betty Otto and Mike Mastrangelo for placing at my disposal the park's research holdings. Additionally, resources at the Fredericksburg National Military Park, Fredericksburg, Virginia, proved to be surprisingly helpful in my Antietam research, much of this material being brought to my attention by staff members Robert Krick, Stuart Vogt, and my good friend Dave Lilley.

The efforts of Sandra Groover, Georgia Department of Archives and History; Patricia Hudson, Monroe County (Michigan) Historical Commission; Rosemary Philips, Chester County (Pennsylvania) Historical Society; Les Jensen, Museum of the Confederacy, Richmond, Virginia; Frederic Ray, Jr., Harrisburg, Pennsylvania; Joyce H. Znamierowski, East Hartford, Connecticut; James V. Murfin, National Park Service, Harpers Ferry Center; Benjamin B. Rosenstock, Frederick, Maryland; and the staffs at the National Archives; New York Public Library; Washington County (Maryland) Historical Society; Maryland Historical Society; Valentine Museum, Richmond, Virginia; Burton Historical Collection, Detroit Public Library; and the U.S. Army Military History Research Collection (Mike Winey, curator; Dr. Richard Sommers, manuscripts), Carlisle, Pennsylvania, are likewise greatly appreciated. The latter collection at Carlisle contains a veritable gold mine of information pertaining to all aspects of American military history. Its Military Order of the Loyal Legion, Massachusetts Commandery, collection of Civil War photographs is without question one of the most important such collections ever assembled.

Many others made integral contributions to this study by providing helpful leads, documented tidbits of information, a roof over the author's head while on research jaunts, et cetera. They are Phil Chen, Chicago, Illinois; Bob Sullivan, Baltimore, Maryland; Dr. H. K. Henisch and Dennis Lowe, State College, Pennsylvania; Bill Horwitz, Huntington, New York; Josephine Cobb, Cape Elizabeth, Maine; Peggy Linvill, Media, Pennsylvania; Mr. and Mrs. Minor Wine Thomas, Cooperstown, New York; Phil and Stephanie Hostetter, Herndon, Virginia; Bill Curtis, Gettysburg, Pennsylvania; Steve Evans, Scott Lange, Karl Thallner, and our fellow brothers of the Eta Phi chapter of Alpha Chi Rho Fraternity at Gettysburg College.

ANTIETAM

The Photographic Legacy of America's Bloodiest Day

PART ONE

THE QUEST FOR REALITY

1

BRINGING THE WAR HOME

It was October in New York City. Broadway appeared much as it had the year before and the year before that. The sidewalks were crowded, the streets filled with carriages and omnibuses as pedestrians, eager to cross the busy thoroughfare, waited at corners for breaks in the traffic. Business seemed as usual; shoppers could be seen here and there gazing into store windows, inspecting the latest fall fashions. Aside from the presence of an occasional soldier there was little indication that the country was in the throes of civil war. The year was 1862.

An unknown reporter for the *New York Times*, whether on assignment or by chance, noticed as he approached Mathew Brady's prestigious photograph gallery that crowds of passersby were filing in and out of the studio entrance. The reporter's curiosity mounted as he walked up to the doorway and glanced at the small placard announcing Brady's latest series of war views, "The Dead of Antietam." Upstairs in the exhibition room hushed groups of potential buyers stood around the small album cards, bending down to examine the details as if under some strange spell.

The reporter, a sensitive man, could not help but admit to himself and his readers that these photographs were morbidly captivating, for the views that attracted the greatest attention depicted clusters of bloated corpses stiffened in grotesque positions. With the aid of a magnifying glass the very features of the lifeless, swollen faces could be distinguished. It bothered the reporter that these scenes should have been repulsive but were instead terribly fascinating.

The article written as a result of this visit to Brady's gallery appeared in the *New York Times* on October 20, 1862, approximately one month after the battle of Antietam and nearly a year and a half after the war had begun. It is one of the most pensive commentaries ever written concerning a series of war photographs. The following excerpts (eliminating the passages describing the views in detail) convey a message that, though dated in style and particulars, is tragically timeless in content.

> The living that throng Broadway care little perhaps for the Dead at Antietam, but we fancy they would jostle less carelessly down the great thoroughfare, saunter less at their ease, were a few dripping bodies, fresh from the field, laid along the pavement. There would be a gathering up of skirts and a careful picking of way; conversation would be less lively, and the general air of pedestrians more subdued. As it is, the dead of the battle-field come up to us very rarely, even in dreams. We see the list in the morning paper at breakfast, but dismiss its recollection with the coffee. There is a confused mass of names, but they are all strangers; we forget the horrible significance that dwells amid the jumble of type. The roll we read is being called over in Eternity, and pale, trembling lips are answering to it. Shadowy fingers point from the page to a field where even imagination is loth to follow. Each of these little names that the printer struck off so lightly last night, whistling over his work, and that we speak with a clip of the tongue, represents a bleeding, mangled corpse. It is a thunderbolt that will crash into some brain—a dull, dead, remorseless weight that will fall upon some heart, straining it to the breaking. There is nothing very terrible to us, however, in the list, though our sensations might be different if the newspaper carrier left the names on the battle-field and the bodies at our doors instead.
>
> We recognize the battle-field as a reality, but it stands as a remote one. It is like a funeral next door. The crape on the bell-pull tells there is a death in the house, and in the close carriage that rolls

away with muffled wheels you know there rides a woman to whom the world is very dark now. But you only see the mourners in the last of the long line of carriages—they ride very jollily and at their ease, smoking cigars in a furtive and discursive manner, perhaps, and, were it not for the black gloves they wear, which the deceased was wise and liberal enough to furnish, it might be a wedding for all the world would know. It attracts your attention, but does not enlist your sympathy. But it is very different when the hearse stops at your own door, and the corpse is carried out over your own threshold— you know whether it is a wedding or a funeral then, without looking at the color of the gloves worn. Those who lose friends in battle know what battle-fields are. . . .

Mr. Brady has done something to bring home to us the terrible reality and earnestness of war. If he has not brought bodies and laid them in our door-yards and along streets, he has done something very like it. . . .

[But] there is one side of the picture that the sun did not catch, one phase that has escaped photographic skill. It is the background of widows and orphans, torn from the bosom of their natural protectors by the red remorseless hand of Battle. . . . Homes have been made desolate, and the light of life in thousands of hearts has been quenched forever. All of this desolation imagination must paint— broken hearts cannot be photographed.

These pictures have a terrible distinctness. . . . We would scarce choose to be in the gallery, when one of the women bending over them should recognize a husband, a son, or a brother in the still, lifeless lines of bodies, that lie ready for the gaping trenches. For these trenches have a terror for a woman's heart, that goes far to outweigh all others that hover over the battle-field. How can a mother bear to know that the boy whose slumbers she has cradled, and whose head her bosom pillowed until the rolling drums called him forth—whose poor, pale face, could she reach it, should find the same pillow again . . . when, but for the privilege of touching that corpse, of kissing once more the lips though white and cold, of smoothing back the hair from the brow and cleansing it of blood, stains, she would give all the remaining years of life that Heaven has allotted her—

how can this mother bear to know that in a shallow trench, hastily dug, rude hands have thrown him. She would have handled the poor corpse so tenderly, have prized the boon of caring for it so dearly— yet, even the imperative office of hiding the dead from sight has been done by those who thought it trouble, and were only glad when their work ended.[1]

Other articles describing the startling Antietam series appeared in such popular journals as *Harper's Weekly* and the *Atlantic Monthly*.[2] These articles invariably focused their attention on the death studies, with *Harper's* reproducing several of the views as woodcuts. In fact, more contemporary media attention was paid to the Antietam photographs than to any other single photographic series recorded during the entire four years of warfare. Why the outstanding publicity? Although fully two-thirds of the initial collection of Antietam views to reach the market depicted typical battlefield landscapes and group portraits of prominent participants, Antietam was the first battlefield in American history to be covered by cameramen before the dead had been buried. It was the remaining third of the photographs, the scenes showing human wreckage, that thrust the Antietam series into the public limelight like no other series before or after.

The battle of Antietam, called by Southerners the battle of Sharpsburg, began at dawn on September 17, 1862. The fighting soon spread over twelve square miles of countryside adjacent to the small Maryland village of Sharpsburg and along the banks of Antietam Creek. By sunset of that day twenty-six thousand Americans, both Northern and Southern, were dead, wounded, captured, or reported missing in action. Although the military results of the engagement proved indecisive in terms of the final outcome of the Civil War, September 17, 1862, achieved immortality as the bloodiest single day in the history of the United States.[3]

This book focuses not on the strategy and tactics employed by the opposing armies during the Maryland campaign, nor on the engagement's political overtones, though these will be discussed. Nor is it the intention to explore the personalities of the leading generals and politicians whose careers were influenced by the battle's outcome, for these traditional subjects have been covered many times during the past century. Instead, this book will focus on the series of photographs recorded shortly after the battle by a team of two cameramen,

ANTIETAM

Alexander Gardner and his assistant, James F. Gibson. The views these men produced at Antietam included scenes that would open the country's eyes and highlight a new era in the visual documentation of war.

My goals in the following presentation of the Antietam photographs may be broken down into several categories. First, it is my desire to establish Antietam's significance as a landmark event in the history of photography by placing that event in the perspective of what had gone before. Second, I have attempted to document the Antietam series as extensively as possible, determining the precise location and subject identification of each view, the date the view was taken, and the name of the specific cameraman (in this case either Gardner or Gibson) who recorded the original negative. All aspects of documentation are presented in perspective with the events of the battle itself, thereby enhancing the immediacy of each scene as it relates to the historical record.

Third, in an effort to reduce much of the anonymity that surrounds these photographs of nameless corpses, I have sought to acquaint the reader with the personal lives of a number of common soldiers for whom Antietam was more than just another battle, another word in a stuffy history text. To do so I have included photographic portraits, together with vignette biographies, of some of the individuals who fought and, in many cases, were either maimed or killed at Antietam. These names and faces have a tendency to become abstract with the passage of time; common soldiers (enlisted men and junior officers) frequently take a back seat in our rush to analyze and make heroes or villains of the generals and other high-ranking leaders. I have chosen to highlight the common soldiers not for the sake of color or to exploit nostalgic anecdotes but because it is they who are the subjects of most of the Antietam death studies.

War is a dangerously easy thing to glorify. Vivid accounts of battles and campaigns frequently make war seem exciting, even attractive as a vicarious adventure, especially for those far removed from the actual sights, smells, and pain of a freshly scarred battlefield—far removed from a home that has just received a telegram prefaced with the words, "We regret to inform you. . . ." By reducing war to its most fundamental elements of personal human tragedy and suffering and by interpreting this one battle through the photographs, I fervently hope that the reader will achieve a better understanding of the scenes recorded by the cameramen at Antietam, as well as a more realistic appreciation for photography's role and limitations in the documentation of historical events.

2

THE EVOLUTION OF
EARLY WAR PHOTOGRAPHY

War photography, though still in its pioneering stages in 1862, was not without precedent. During the Mexican War, and nearly sixteen years before Antietam, an American cameraman recorded a series of ten daguerreotype scenes in or about the city of Saltillo, Mexico, some 175 miles southwest of Laredo, Texas. Only four of these images, taken either in late 1846 or early 1847, are military in nature. They depict scenes of Gen. John E. Wool and staff on horseback, a Virginia regiment, [Joseph D.?] Webster's battery, and a group of Mexicans with Lt. [Abner?] Doubleday. Although important today as the world's first known war photographs, their significance as an influence in the development of war reportage diminishes when one considers that they came to light only within the last fifty years. They therefore had no impact on the course of early war photography in either the United States or Europe.

The cameraman who recorded the Saltillo views, an amateur from Texas, did so by means of a process which, though capable of producing a fine image, could not be mass-produced. The daguerreotype was a direct positive photograph on a silver-coated copper plate. It did not entail a negative. Although woodcuts based on the images could be mass-produced, these scenes were apparently taken for the artist's personal amusement.[4]

The first war scenes that could be reproduced from a negative were not taken until 1852. The photographer was a surgeon in the British army named

John MacCosh, a professional army officer who had taken up the study of photography as a hobby. MacCosh's first military experiments with the calotype process, which produced a paper negative, took place while he was serving in India during the Second Sikh War in 1848 and 1849. At this early date his output was limited to formal portraits of friends and high-ranking officers. But by the Second Burma War of 1852–53, MacCosh, then assigned to the Fifth Bengal Artillery, had advanced his skills to include outdoor photographs. Those views that have survived show primarily buildings, statues, and captured artillery pieces. MacCosh's work was little known at the time, was not mass-produced, and probably had a minimal effect, if any, on the efforts of later cameramen.[5]

Not until 1854 and 1855, during the Crimean War, would there occur any photographic coverage of a military conflict that can be termed extensive. Without question the most famous of all Crimean War photographers was an Englishman named Roger Fenton, a professional cameraman who spent nearly four months, from March 8 to June 26, 1855, on the Crimean peninsula, producing a series of 360 glass negatives. Fenton's stay in the area occurred during a period of relative military stagnation, the fighting, with few exceptions, being confined to abortive allied assaults and the monotonous routine of siege warfare. Most of the conflict's greatest battles (Alma, Balaclava with its immortal Charge of the Light Brigade, and Inkerman) took place from September to November 1854, months before Fenton's arrival. The remaining actions of any notable size centered around British and French efforts to seize Russian defensive works protecting the city of Sebastopol. Sebastopol was finally evacuated by the Russians more than two months after Fenton, having exhausted his supply of chemicals, departed for England.

From the detailed account Fenton left concerning his experiences during the war, it appears that he had few goals in mind while in the Crimea other than taking general scenes and photographing some of the better-known personalities. If a subject struck his fancy, he made an exposure. He wanted to photograph the besieged city of Sebastopol but could never get close enough. Consequently, the vast majority of Fenton's 360 scenes depicted posed groups of British and French soldiers in rear areas, officers with their aides, camp scenes, buildings, and the busy harbor at Balaclava. Perhaps his most famous view was an image entitled "The Valley of the Shadow of Death," taken in mid-April of 1855. Not to be confused with the site of the Charge of the Light

Brigade, this photograph showed a barren, nondescript dirt road strewn with cannonballs and would be considered dull by modern standards of war reportage. It is unfair, however, to evaluate subjectively Fenton's work from the perspective of more than a century hence, for he was a pioneer working with little or no precedent and was constantly plagued by adverse weather conditions and logistical problems, not to mention the dangers inherent in attempting to take views at the front during active hostilities.

But the total absence of views showing battlefield carnage, complete with dead soldiers—later to become prized subjects among Civil War photographers—cannot be overlooked. It has been suggested by Fenton's biographer that such scenes were not recorded in 1855, because the English were anxious to see their troops in good condition and because Victorian society would have shunned morbid photographs. Yet formal portraits of deceased persons were common during the mid-nineteenth century. Battlefield views showing clusters of dead soldiers—especially dead *enemy* soldiers—would have attracted Fenton's attention, and in my opinion he would have recorded such scenes had he been presented with the opportunity of doing so.

Fenton had no such opportunities, for certain conditions were necessary before any nineteenth-century photographer, with his assemblage of cumbersome equipment, could safely record a battle's immediate aftermath. Initially, there had to occur an action of noteworthy size in order to attract the photographer's attention. The action had to be a victory, with the friendly side remaining in undisputed possession of the field and out of the range of hostile fire during cleanup operations. Equally important, the photographer had to be present on the site with all his equipment before the ugliest of the scars were covered. Although Fenton did witness some heavy, albeit indecisive, fighting from a comparatively safe distance near the end of his stay, he did so without his equipment readily at hand (he was nearly out of chemicals anyway). Even if he had had his equipment with him, the opportunity of taking views safely never materialized. It is thus not surprising that corpse-strewn battlefields went unrecorded during the Crimean War.

Roger Fenton, though the best known of the Crimean War photographers, was not the only cameraman to follow the armies to the front. Other cameramen deserve recognition, such as a Romanian named Karl Baptist von Szathmari, who covered the campaign between the Russians and the Turks in the Balkans in 1854, and James Robertson, an Englishman best known for his documentation of deserted Russian forts and the ruins of Sebastopol after its evacuation in September 1855. The scenes they produced, or rather the scenes we have record of today, were similar in general content and approach to the work of Fenton.

The first war photographs ever seen by the general European public, the Crimean views attracted considerable attention, especially in Great Britain, when they were first issued. Although the views were printed and sold in extremely limited quantities and are today quite rare, they did receive media coverage and several were reproduced as woodcuts in the *Illustrated London News.* Most people who saw actual photographic prints did so at formal exhibitions. With the advent of peace in 1856, however, public interest in the views declined rapidly, and as a financial enterprise photographic coverage of the war proved unsuccessful.[6]

It cannot be determined how much exposure the American public had to the Crimean scenes. Most likely it was minimal, since there is no evidence that they were ever exhibited, or even offered for sale, in the United States. On the other hand, it is almost certain that some of the better-informed American photographers were at least aware of their existence. Quite probably Alexander Gardner, later to become one of the greatest of all Civil War photographers and the man who covered the battlefield at Antietam, had an opportunity to examine them firsthand before leaving his native Scotland in 1856 to emigrate to the United States. And thirty-one photographs of Sebastopol and its forts, taken (undoubtedly by Robertson) after the city was evacuated, were brought back to the United States by the American military commission sent to the Crimea in 1855 to observe European modes of warfare. The photographs were analyzed for information concerning gun emplacements and then submitted with the official report in 1858.[7] This is the first recorded instance in which photographs were utilized as a direct source of military intelligence by the United States Army. One of the members of the commission was a young captain named George B. McClellan, who would later command the Union forces at the battle of Antietam.

The next conflict to be covered by photography after the Crimean War was the Sepoy Mutiny in India, 1857–59. The cameraman most prominent in this venture was Felice Beato, a naturalized Englishman of Italian birth who took his series of artistically splendid architectural and landscape studies at the time of the British expedition to Lucknow in early 1858. Aside from one photograph of an execution scene and another showing scattered four-month-old skeletons of Indian mutineers, thought to have been dug up by dogs after they had been buried, there is little in Beato's series depicting the realities of war other than ruined buildings and posed groups of British soldiers.[8]

However, Beato's coverage of the Second Opium War in China two years later provides us with a more accurate indication as to what he would have photographed in India had he had the opportunity. On August 21, 1860, British forces attacked the North Taku Fort on the Pei-ho and successfully carried the ramparts. The photographer was on hand, ready with his equipment, and in complete safety recorded the scene of desolation soon after the capture. A valuable insight into Beato's reaction to the subject matter then afforded him is given in an eyewitness account written by an English surgeon named D. F. Rennie:

> I walked round the ramparts on the west side. They were thickly strewed with dead—in the north-west angle thirteen [Chinese] were lying in one group round a gun. Signor Beato was here in great excitement, characterizing the group as 'beautiful', and begging that it might not be interfered with until perpetuated by his photographic apparatus, which was done a few minutes afterwards.[9]

The scenes recorded by Beato at the North Taku Fort probably took a considerable time to reach England. They were never issued in large quantities and have remained obscure until recent years. Still, they are among the earliest photographs to have survived that show a freshly scarred battlefield complete with human dead. A number of battlefield stereophotographs, including at least one of dead soldiers awaiting burial at Melegnano, Italy, were recorded a year earlier during the Franco-Austrian War of 1859. But nearly all these views have, for all practical purposes, disappeared. Reference to them was made by Dr. Oliver Wendell Holmes, Sr., an avid American collector of stereo views, in an article that appeared in the *Atlantic Monthly* in July 1861. The photographs were obviously issued in extremely limited numbers—even Holmes did not own a copy of the Melegnano death study—and aside from Holmes's written description of the views, it is fairly certain that the American public never saw them firsthand. The likelihood exists that they were recorded by an amateur who distributed copies to only a handful of personal friends. Several cameramen are known to have covered the Franco-Austrian War, but scarcely any of their war photographs have survived.[10]

Although great progress had been made in the field of early war photography prior to the outbreak of the Civil War in 1861, the experience gained was generally scattered and often obscure. Without exception, the photographs were issued in limited quantities, precluding widespread exposure. If any one conflict can be said to have had a potentially influential effect on the initial course of photography during the American Civil War, it would have to be the Crimean War, with its predominantly posed group studies, camp scenes, and views behind the lines.

In the meantime, as European photographers traveled the globe in search of potential subjects, technological developments in the United States were rapidly setting the stage for widespread coverage of the Civil War. A brief review of these developments is essential to understand the commercial motivations that drew American cameramen to the front in unprecedented numbers.

Photography in the United States, as elsewhere, was by no means new at the time of the Civil War; the basic process was announced to the world in 1839. An entire generation of Americans had grown to adulthood without the vaguest recollection of a time when the photograph was not a common household item. But to most Americans who grew up during the 1840s and 1850s, including the bulk of those who fought during the Civil War, photography was primarily a portraiture medium.

The earliest processes most frequently encountered in the United States during the antebellum period were the daguerreotype (on silver-coated copper), the ambrotype (on glass), and, to a lesser extent, the tintype (on a thin sheet of iron). All these processes produced a direct positive image that was reversed, or backward, as in a mirror. And all were incapable of being mass-reproduced in their original photographic state, for they did not use a negative. These technological limitations did not pose a serious problem as far as studio portraiture was concerned, since people were already used to seeing themselves backward in the mirror. If a customer wanted several copies of his image, the cameraman would expose as many plates as the customer desired. Numerous exposures could be costly, so they were usually kept to a minimum.

On the other hand, the same technological limitations posed a serious handicap to recording outdoor scenes. Some early photographers were able to overcome the reversal effect by using devices placed in front of the lens, but most American scenic images that have survived from the 1840s and 1850s reveal that these techniques were not exploited on a wide scale. By far the greatest drawback to early scenic photography was the absence of a negative capable of mass reproduction. It simply did not pay for a cameraman to record thousands or even hundreds of copies of a specific scene in the hopes of marketing that image to an extensive audience. His time was more profitably spent recording single images on an individual-customer basis.

Perhaps the most revolutionary development in the history of early photography, aside from the original invention by a Frenchman, Louis Daguerre, was Frederick Scott Archer's development of the glass-plate negative in 1851. Archer, an Englishman, did not invent the photographic negative per se. Negatives on paper were known a decade before Archer's announcement, but their quality was comparatively poor and, more importantly, stringent patent rights severely limited their attractiveness to commercial photographers. Thus it was Archer's glass-plate process that was first made readily accessible to photographers the world over.

Although the paper prints derived from these negatives possessed none of the drawbacks of the direct-positive views, the glass negative took several years to catch on in the United States. American photographers had apparently grown used to taking the small, one-of-a-kind images, usually portraits and usually encased in delicate booklike frames, with ornate gilt mats and velvet inner cushions. But the relatively inexpensive paper prints derived from glass negatives were bound to catch on, as they eventually did.

During the late 1850s several companies, using Archer's process, began issuing three-dimensional stereoscopic photographs in quantity on the American market. With this development a stereo craze was born that would continue well into the twentieth century. For the first time, ordinary Americans could own photographs of sites far removed from their own environments. Here were the temples of Egypt, the ancient ruins in Rome, the castles of Spain, and the sacred cities of the Holy Land. Here too were native scenes of Niagara Falls, the Catskill Mountains, West Point, and the White House, places most Americans had known through their readings or through crude woodcuts but that comparatively few had ever seen depicted with the realism of the photograph.

Following closely upon the heels of the stereo craze that began building significant momentum in 1859 was the introduction of another glass-plate derivative, the *carte de visite* (visiting card). These small album cards made their appearance on the American market during the winter of 1859–60 and quickly grew in popularity. Although they lacked the three-dimensional attraction of the stereo views, they were of equally good quality and had the advantage of being the cheapest form of paper photograph then available to the public.

Both the stereo view and the album card made their debut on the eve of the Civil War. The significance of this coincidental development cannot be over-emphasized, for it would have an enormous impact on the extent to which the conflict was ultimately covered by photography. Artists such as Mathew Brady went to war knowing that they would have at their disposal not only a ready-made mass market enthusiastically awaiting their products but, of equally vital concern, that they would be able to supply that demand with images that could be reproduced in unlimited quantities at a price almost everyone could afford. It now appeared obvious to the more progressive American photographers that large investments in recording great events would reap substantial profits. The stage was set.

3

AMERICAN CAMERAMEN GO TO WAR

At four thirty in the morning of April 12, 1861, a signal was given to Southern artillerymen in Charleston Harbor to commence firing on the Federal sanctuary at Fort Sumter. With this one act of aggression the American Civil War was begun.

The word *war* was an abstract term to the vast majority of those who found themselves caught up in the swirl of excitement during the spring of 1861. Aside from those few in this country who had experienced personally the wars against the Mexicans and the Seminoles and sundry skirmishes on the frontier, Americans of the mid-nineteenth century had grown up on a visual conception of war depicted mainly through crude woodcuts, lithographs, and glamorous paintings. Of these, woodcuts were by far the most abundant and therefore constituted the most influential factor—especially the woodcuts that appeared in illustrated weeklies of the late 1850s, popular history books, and perhaps most influential of all, schoolbooks for children under the age of sixteen.

In the antebellum United States war was depicted by the visual arts as a glorious adventure. Elaborate paintings showed colonial militiamen struggling heroically against the British at Bunker Hill, lithographs depicted equally gallant episodes from the War of 1812, and woodcuts that portrayed fearless

Typical woodcut depiction of war during the antebellum period. "Colonel Harney at Cerro Gordo," from S. G. Goodrich, *A Pictorial History of America* **(1851).**

American officers leading their men against enemy hordes during the Mexican War abounded. The dead and wounded were invariably present, but somehow they always appeared intact—never mutilated, bloated, or rotting in the sun—and the aura of martyrdom usually triumphed, blending well into the excitement of living forms struggling for victory. In 1861, as volunteers responded to their respective governmental calls to resolve the national crisis by force, untold numbers did so with visions of school text woodcuts in their heads. The great adventure was about to unfold.

The first three months of the war were largely disappointing to the men who had enlisted to fight, for fighting was almost nonexistent between April and

July of 1861. Training was the order of the day and although the drill field did not provide the substance for dramatic war photographs, Northern cameramen were nevertheless quickly dispatched to the camps surrounding Washington, D. C., to produce stereo views and album cards (as well as larger photographs) of scenes reminiscent in content of those recorded by Fenton in the Crimea.

From beginning to end, the Civil War was covered mainly by Northern photographers, particularly in the realm of outdoor views. Southern cameramen had neither the supplies nor the financial backing necessary to initiate and sustain large-scale operations. Thus, Confederate photographic scenes are rarely encountered. Most Southern views and portraits that have survived were taken quite early in the war. Additionally, the eastern sections of the country received far greater coverage by field photographers throughout the war, especially during the first two years, than did the western theater. The reason for this emphasis on the East is probably related to the fact that Washington, D. C., and New York City were the home bases for most photographic operations covering the hostilities on any organized, extensive scale. Mathew Brady, for instance, had galleries in both cities.

As the spring of 1861 turned to summer, public demand for some sort of military resolution to the crisis intensified. In July 1861, Union general Irvin McDowell succumbed to the pressure and prematurely advanced against the Southern stronghold at Manassas, Virginia (see map on page 40). Neither army was fully prepared to fight, but on July 21 the first major action of the war took place at Bull Run, resulting in a disaster for the Northern cause.

The Bull Run campaign of 1861 plays an interesting role in the history of Civil War photography because it has commonly been accepted as fact that Mathew Brady recorded scenes on or about the field of action at the time of the battle. Accounts of Brady's participation in the campaign, all apparently having as their direct or indirect source Brady's own boastful words, lead one to believe that the undaunted photographer followed the Union army to the front lines.[11] And yet close examination of these accounts reveals no mention of any view that can be specifically associated with the Bull Run battlefield. In fact, not one *authentic* photograph has ever emerged that would support claims suggesting that any photographer took views on the battlefield in 1861. Although it is true that Brady himself stated that "our apparatus was a good deal damaged on the way back to Washington," a review of the events surrounding the Bull Run campaign, in conjunction with the conditions necessary for the photographic documentation of battlefields during the mid-nineteenth century (as applicable to Brady as they were to Fenton in the Crimea), indicates strongly that neither Brady nor any other photographer had an opportunity to record scenes depicting the havoc and confusion at Bull Run. Certainly no such scenes were ever made available to the public. And if negatives had been secured at Bull Run, photographic prints definitely would have appeared for sale in contemporary catalogs. Even a damaged plate, by virtue of its rarity and historical association, would have been enthusiastically received by the consumer market.

Only one actual photograph has surfaced during the past century that might support the contention that photographs of the Bull Run battlefield were taken in the summer of 1861. This view, attributed to Mathew Brady by the Library of Congress but never identified concretely as having been taken by Brady himself, came to light in 1954 and was entitled "Confederate Dead on Matthews Hill." The origin of the caption is vague and the image itself was obscure, if not largely unknown, prior to the discovery of a negative in the Brady-Handy collection only two decades ago.

For many years I have been suspicious of the caption "Confederate Dead on Matthews Hill," an obvious reference to the first battle of Bull Run. In my opinion it is doubtful that Brady would have had access to an enemy-held battlefield after the battle; his own account shows that he fled with the rest of the Union army. Certainly it defies logic to assume that Brady was recording scenes on the field during the actual fighting. Another suspicious element is that one of the four "bodies" visible in the scene, the one nearest the camera, was dressed in an overcoat, not the sort of apparel worn by soldiers at Bull Run in July 1861.

My doubts, however, could only be classified as speculative until more tangible evidence was uncovered. During the summer of 1974, these doubts were irrefutably confirmed. Sorting through some original stereo views on file at the Library of Congress I came across a companion view to the Matthews Hill photograph. The companion scene, completely unidentified as to subject or photographer, clearly showed the same four "bodies" at the identical camera location. Miraculously, all four appear very much alive, posed both kneeling and standing in the act of loading and firing their rifles.

Only two conclusions can be derived from studying the pair of photographs

"Confederate dead on Matthews Hill," photographer unknown, stereo, ca. 1861 (LC).

together. Either the photographer was on the line of battle with all his cumbersome equipment when a volley of enemy fire killed all four men (but did not touch or chase off the cameraman), or the two views were staged at some undetermined time and place by an unknown photographer. The first hypothesis is absurd, the second quite reasonable. Someone apparently told the soldiers to pretend they were fighting in the one view and then instructed them to pretend they were dead in the other. The scene's true location was probably on the outskirts of a training camp early in the war.

Regrettably, the original stereo view showing the four "bodies" very much alive cannot be located in the Library of Congress collections at this time. Thankfully, I thought to make a Xerox copy of the original when I first discovered it. Although the Xerox copy, presented here, does not reproduce the quality that could have been provided by a photographic copy, it does support adequately the existence of the companion to the more famous Matthews Hill scene.

With all fairness to Mathew Brady, who was frequently guilty of claiming undue credit, it seems that he did attempt to photograph the first great campaign of the war. Yet from an appraisal of the evidence at hand we can conclude only that his attempt was unsuccessful. Exposing the Matthews Hill photograph as a phony, though it played no influential role during the Civil War period and surfaced only two decades ago, nevertheless clears the way for a more accurate evaluation of later efforts in recording the war.

In light of Brady's failure at Bull Run, the first campaign of the Civil War to be covered successfully by photography took place near the end of 1861 and during the early months of 1862. The cameraman, a Brady employee named Timothy O'Sullivan, was dispatched to South Carolina to document Union efforts to secure blockade-related bases in the vicinity of Hilton Head, Beaufort, and Port Royal. Although the campaign began in November 1861 under the leadership of Brig. Gen. Thomas W. Sherman, the scenes recorded by O'Sullivan indicate that most if not all of his efforts were taken during the early months of 1862. Typical scenes from O'Sullivan's series, entitled "Illustrations of Sherman's Expedition to South Carolina," depict relatively static views of Union regiments lined up on parade at Beaufort, genre plantation scenes on Port Royal Island, deserted Confederate positions at Fort Walker, graves of Union soldiers at Hilton Head, and the nearby ruins of Fort Pulaski, Georgia, which surrendered to Northern forces on April 11, 1862. O'Sullivan covered the operations in comparative safety, recording images only after locales had been secured by friendly forces.[12]

At roughly the same time, Northern photographers were presented with their first opportunity of safely documenting areas in the vicinity of Manassas, Virginia, and the Bull Run battlefield. These locations, which had been occupied by the Confederate army through the fall and winter, were vacated in March 1862 for strategic reasons. Aware that Manassas and its environs had become household words in the North since the previous summer, Northern cameramen arrived on the scene in March to record the deserted Confederate barracks and fortifications as well as the battlefield itself. The two photographers most conspicuous in documenting the area were George N. Barnard and his assistant, James F. Gibson, both employees of Mathew Brady.

As winter changed to spring and the war approached its first full year of relatively indecisive action, Union general George B. McClellan, who replaced McDowell after Bull Run and spent the remainder of 1861 reorganizing and training his army, found himself under increasing pressure to extinguish the rebellion once and for all. Consequently, on April 4, 1862, McClellan launched his massive effort to capture the Confederate capital at Richmond, Virginia. The following three months of maneuvering, known as the Peninsula campaign, were largely nonproductive. But in terms of the evolution of war photography in the United States, those three months played a vital role in a maturation process that would culminate at Antietam several months later. And much of the credit for paving the way belongs to James F. Gibson.

From April 5 to May 3, 1862, little fighting occurred on the Peninsula as McClellan patiently prepared his forces for an all-out attack against the initial line of Confederate defenses at Yorktown. By the time the Union leader was ready to enact his plans, however, Southern positions were evacuated without a struggle. It was during this first week in May 1862 that Gibson, assisted by John Wood, began his work in the vicinity of Yorktown. The views produced by Gibson included scenes showing the enormous Union base area at Camp Winfield Scott, Union gun emplacements laboriously fortified but never brought into serious action, and various group portraits of Union officers and foreign military observers.

With the Confederate withdrawal northward toward Richmond, the Federal base of operations was moved several miles up the York and Pamunkey rivers to Cumberland Landing, near White House. Gibson, apparently staying close to headquarters, followed the move and resumed coverage of the campaign in mid-May.

On the last day of the month the two armies clashed at the battle of Fair Oaks (also known as Seven Pines). After two days of severe fighting, in which the Southern commander, Gen. Joseph E. Johnston, was wounded, Confederate forces again withdrew toward Richmond, leaving the field in the possession of the Union army. Inclement weather precluded the taking of photographs for several days after the dead had been buried, but Gibson was on hand with all his equipment at the earliest opportunity to record several of the more interesting points at Fair Oaks, including farmhouses, fresh graves, and Northern artillery batteries positioned behind recently dug gun emplacements. Despite the fact that little fighting occurred during the early days of June, when these photographs were taken, they were recorded in the midst of an active field campaign in which no one knew when or where the next blow would fall.

The blow fell on June 26, 1862, with a brutal Confederate counterattack led by the Army of Northern Virginia's new commander, Gen. Robert E. Lee. What followed was a series of engagements known collectively as the Seven Days' Battles. During this week-long period Union general McClellan moved his base of operations across the Peninsula to the James River, fighting defensively all the way in an effort to concentrate his army and supplies in the vicinity of Harrison's Landing.

Gibson did not take any undue chances throughout the seven days and stayed as close as possible to rear areas, but these areas did not remain in the rear for long during the constantly shifting tide of battle. On June 28 the cameraman found himself at Savage's Station, the location of McClellan's hastily established headquarters as well as the site of a large field hospital then receiving and caring for wounded from the battle of Gaines' Mill, fought the day before. Gibson recorded several photographs at Savage's Station, probably on the twenty-eighth, including one exceptionally poignant scene at the hospital showing dozens of wounded Union soldiers either lying or sitting on the ground awaiting medical treatment. A number of these men are seen wearing straw hats, indicating membership in the Sixteenth New York Infantry, which had been recruited in the northernmost counties of that state at the very outbreak of the war. The following day, June 29, Savage's Station was attacked. Union forces held on throughout the afternoon's fighting but retired early the next morning, leaving behind twenty-five hundred wounded. Among those doomed to be captured were the men photographed by Gibson.

A secure Union base area was subsequently established at Harrison's Landing after Confederate forces were checked in the campaign's last major action at nearby Malvern Hill on July 1, 1862. McClellan's drive toward Richmond had been a failure, and for the next month a period of general quiet ensued as the seat of war gravitated elsewhere.

Although Gibson was unable to cover any of the campaign's battlefields before the dead had been buried, he nevertheless produced some of the most immediate and effective battlefield views the country had seen until that time. There is little documentary evidence that the Peninsula series elicited any notable reaction from the Northern populace, but we can assume that Gibson's colleagues were impressed by what he was able to produce at the front. The lesson was obvious: a skilled photographer with initiative and courage enough to follow an army closely into the field—and stay with that army— would be afforded opportunities of recording timely, dramatic war photographs. Gibson proved that it could be done, and others would soon follow his lead.

Gibson remained active in the vicinity of the James River for an indefinite time during July, until he was either joined or replaced by Alexander Gardner, the manager of Mathew Brady's Washington gallery since 1858. Earlier in 1862 Gardner had spent much of his time copying maps and documents for the U.S. Topographical Engineers, presumably on a free-lance basis.

The names of other cameramen, most of whom are thought to have been employees of Brady, crop up sporadically and are credited with recording scenes on the Peninsula from June through August of 1862. Some of these men, such as George N. Barnard and John Wood, have been mentioned already. Others, such as David B. Woodbury, have not and deserve further study even though according to available evidence the number of views they produced did not approach the number produced by James Gibson. Brady himself apparently remained behind the scenes during this period, tending exclusively to the business side of his operations.

As Gibson, and later Gardner, documented the Union encampments in the vicinity of Harrison's Landing, Timothy O'Sullivan, lately returned from covering the Carolina campaign, prepared for his next major assignment, which was to follow Union general John Pope's Virginia campaign in July and August of 1862. Early July saw O'Sullivan at Manassas, recording casual studies of Union forces prior to active operations. During the next few weeks O'Sullivan moved southwestward with the army, producing a number of views depicting military bridges, railroad depots, and sundry scenes at Warrenton, Sulphur Springs, and Culpeper. His most outstanding achievement was a series of thirteen photographs taken on the Cedar Mountain battlefield several days after the action of August 9, not long after the Confederate withdrawal from the field. The dead of both sides had already been buried, but the bloated carcasses of horses provided the subject matter for at least one of O'Sullivan's views.

Another notable scene from this series shows an artillery battery crossing a stream, with the guns and horses stopped midstream when the exposure was made. The view was captioned by O'Sullivan as "Battery fording a tributary of the Rappahannock, on the day of the battle of Cedar Mountain." Unfortunately, the scene is nondescript in all other respects, and because O'Sullivan's coverage of the actual battle site took place a few days later, it is highly plausible that the battery crossing the stream was photographed at some distance from Cedar Mountain, perhaps several miles. As disappointing as the original caption is in its vagueness concerning unit and location, the view's interest as a visual record remains strong, with the knowledge that it was taken on the very day of the battle.

After Cedar Mountain, Pope's Virginia campaign gradually degenerated until finally, on August 29–30, Union forces were thoroughly routed at the second battle of Bull Run (Second Manassas). As had Brady the year before, O'Sullivan was forced to shelve his photographic operations as he, along with the shattered remnants of the Union army, sought the safety of Washington. Needless to say, no views of the Manassas battlefield were recorded in August 1862.

Despite occasional setbacks, photographic coverage of the war had still managed to make tremendous strides during the first eight months of 1862. And yet, though cameramen were rapidly increasing the immediacy of their war views, no one thus far had been presented with the opportunity of recording the stark horrors of a battlefield strewn with human dead. By the beginning of September, that opportunity would not be far off.

4

PHOTOGRAPHY AT ANTIETAM

With the Union army in confusion following the decisive Confederate victory at Second Manassas, Robert E. Lee quickly turned northward, launching his first great invasion of the war. On September 5, 1862, the lead elements of the Army of Northern Virginia crossed the Potomac River (near Leesburg, Virginia) into Maryland.

Lee's goals in the invasion were severalfold. He hoped to "liberate" Maryland, possibly move into Pennsylvania, threaten Washington, and at the same time provide war-torn Virginia with a much-needed breathing spell. A successful campaign of this type might also lead to European recognition of the Confederacy as well as a favorable peace settlement with the Federal government.

As Southern columns pushed northward into Maryland, General McClellan was hurriedly consolidating and reorganizing the various elements of his and defeated General Pope's Union forces near Washington. There was little time to spare, for close pursuit of the invaders was essential if the Confederate army was to be checked and the Union saved. Events moved rapidly; by September 6 the invading army had already reached the Maryland city of Frederick.

One of the most unusual Civil War photographs uncovered in recent years is a candid scene taken from the second-story window of a building on Market Street in Frederick by an unidentified but probably local cameraman. The view shows a column of armed Confederate infantrymen halted in front of J. Rosenstock's Dry Good and Clothing Store. Ever since its first widespread publication in the mid-1960s, this photograph has been presented as having been recorded sometime during the Confederate occupation of Frederick in 1862 (September 6–10).

After examining the photograph and interviewing its owner I can, however, regard only two items of information to be certain at this point—that the view was taken in Frederick and that the soldiers are Confederate. Southern forces passed through Frederick twice during the war, once in September 1862 and a second time two summers later, and it has not been definitely established which campaign the scene recorded. With continued research the authorship, date, and perhaps even the unit identification of this unique glimpse of the Confederate army engaged in active operations may one day be determined.[13]

While in Frederick, Lee, knowing that the Federal Army of the Potomac would react at a snail's pace, decided to split his command and head west in several prongs in order to capture the Northern stronghold at Harpers Ferry. From there Lee could continue northward, using South Mountain as a shield.

With uncharacteristic promptness, McClellan pursued his enemy and reached Frederick shortly after the city was vacated by the Army of Northern Virginia. On September 13, in a rare stroke of luck, Union soldiers found a copy of Lee's orders outlining the entire plan to divide the Confederate army and attack Harpers Ferry. McClellan pushed westward, hoping to strike the separated enemy forces before they could reunite. The next day, September 14, a series of bitter encounters took place at South Mountain as rearguard elements of the Army of Northern Virginia, realizing the precarious nature of their main command, sought to delay the unexpectedly rapid Union advance. The holding action at South Mountain, in conjunction with the reemergence of caution on the part of McClellan, gained enough time for the Confederates to capture Harpers Ferry and attempt to reunite the major portions of their army.

On September 15 the Confederates who had fought at South Mountain fell back through Boonsboro and took up defensive positions on the western bank of Antietam Creek in front of Sharpsburg. Here they awaited the arrival of the remainder of Lee's forces, which would continue to arrive piecemeal for the next two days.

Confederate soldiers in Frederick, photographer unknown, probably a plate, either September 1862 or July 1864 (Rosenstock).

On the other hand, McClellan was able to concentrate the bulk of his numerically superior army along the eastern bank of Antietam Creek within a day of the Southern retreat from South Mountain. Had he struck immediately, the Confederate forces then on the field could have been routed and perhaps destroyed. But McClellan, constantly paranoid about being outnumbered, chose to wait until he felt his battle plan was sufficiently refined. The delay was one of several opportunities lost by this Union commander.

The Battle of Antietam

A detailed account of the Antietam engagement's various phases, specifically as they relate to the photographic record, will be presented in later sections dealing with the individual photographs. The following overview is intended to familiarize the reader in a concise fashion with the battle's main events and results. Additionally, it will serve as introduction to a subsequent description of Alexander Gardner's movements across the field after the fighting.[14]

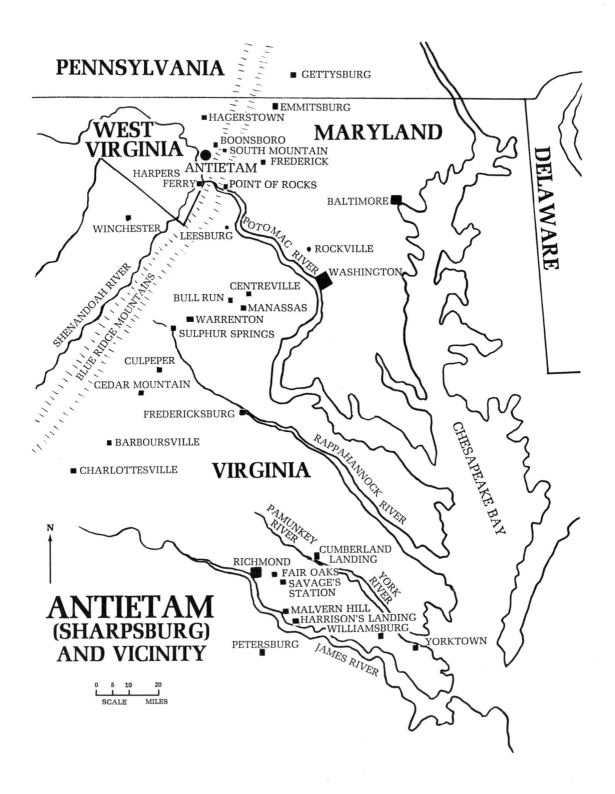

PENNSYLVANIA

■ GETTYSBURG

■ EMMITSBURG

● HAGERSTOWN

WEST
VIRGINIA

MARYLAND

DELAWARE

BOONSBORO
■ SOUTH MOUNTAIN
● FREDERICK

ANTIETAM

HARPERS
FERRY

● POINT OF ROCKS

■ BALTIMORE

WINCHESTER

LEESBURG

POTOMAC RIVER

● ROCKVILLE

WASHINGTON

SHENANDOAH RIVER

BLUE RIDGE MOUNTAINS

BULL RUN

CENTREVILLE

■ MANASSAS

■ WARRENTON

SULPHUR SPRINGS

CULPEPER

CEDAR MOUNTAIN

FREDERICKSBURG

CHESAPEAKE BAY

RAPPAHANNOCK RIVER

■ BARBOURSVILLE

■ CHARLOTTESVILLE

VIRGINIA

N

PAMUNKEY
RIVER

RICHMOND

CUMBERLAND
LANDING

FAIR OAKS
■ SAVAGE'S
STATION

YORK
RIVER

ANTIETAM
(SHARPSBURG)
AND VICINITY

MALVERN HILL
HARRISON'S LANDING
WILLIAMSBURG

PETERSBURG

YORKTOWN

JAMES RIVER

0   5 10   20
SCALE   MILES

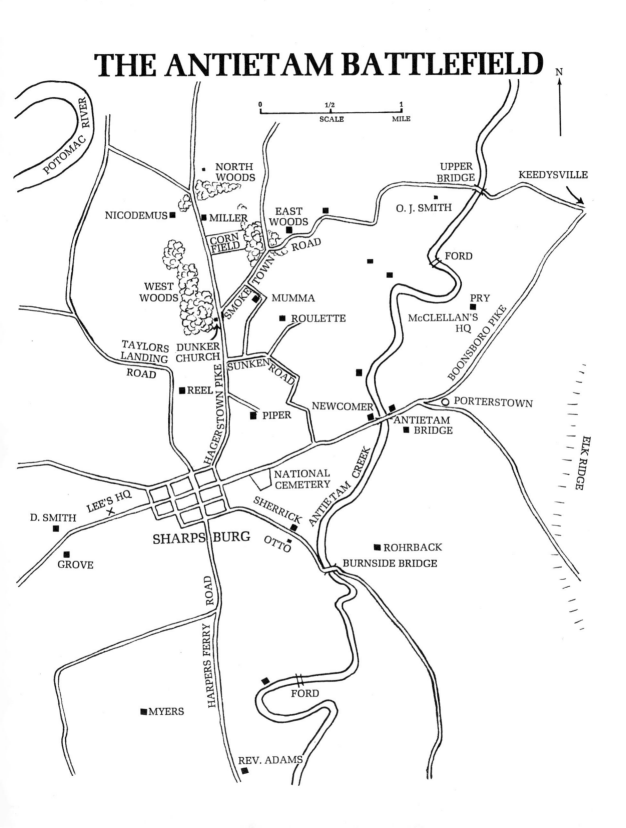

THE ANTIETAM BATTLEFIELD

POTOMAC RIVER

N

0   1/2   1
SCALE   MILE

NORTH WOODS

NICODEMUS

MILLER

EAST WOODS

O. J. SMITH

UPPER BRIDGE

KEEDYSVILLE

CORN FIELD

SMOKETOWN ROAD

WEST WOODS

FORD

PRY

MUMMA

McCLELLAN'S HQ

ROULETTE

BOONSBORO PIKE

TAYLORS LANDING ROAD

DUNKER CHURCH

SUNKEN ROAD

REEL

HAGERSTOWN PIKE

PIPER

NEWCOMER

PORTERSTOWN

ANTIETAM BRIDGE

ELK RIDGE

NATIONAL CEMETERY

ANTIETAM CREEK

LEE'S HQ

D. SMITH

SHERRICK

SHARPSBURG

OTTO

GROVE

ROHRBACK

BURNSIDE BRIDGE

HARPERS FERRY ROAD

MYERS

FORD

REV. ADAMS

ANTIETAM

By the early morning of September 17, 1862, those elements of Lee's Army of Northern Virginia then on the field were positioned west of Antietam Creek. The left flank rested north of the village of Sharpsburg at the West Woods. Facing generally northward, these troops continued across the open fields to the Samuel Mumma farm buildings. To the rear of the Confederate left flank was one of the battlefield's most distinctive features, the small, white brick Dunker Church located at the edge of the West Woods on the Hagerstown Pike.

Two Union infantry corps (the First, followed later by the Twelfth) had crossed Antietam Creek late on September 16. After some preliminary skirmishing with the Confederate left flank, Union forces were able to secure a foothold at both the North and East Woods. In this area McClellan's right flank would be established. Between the opposing lines lay a large field of corn on the farm of David R. Miller, today known as simply the Cornfield.

The remaining elements of the Army of the Potomac present on the field at daybreak rested in reserve along the east bank of the creek. Supporting the right was the Second Corps, located in the vicinity of McClellan's headquarters at the farm of Philip Pry. Opposite the stone bridge (hereafter referred to as Antietam Bridge) where the Boonsboro Pike crosses Antietam Creek lay the Union center, held by the Fifth Corps. To the south, and opposite a similarly constructed bridge (hereafter called Burnside Bridge) rested the left flank of the Army of the Potomac, held by the Ninth Corps.

Various Confederate units composing Lee's center and right flanks occupied the heights in front of and south of Sharpsburg, opposite but at varying distances from Antietam and Burnside Bridge. Due to the organizational complexities of Lee's order of battle at Antietam (elements were constantly diverted from their parent units to strengthen weak points along the line), references to the two basic corps of the Army of Northern Virginia—James Longstreet's command and Thomas J. "Stonewall" Jackson's command—can become confusing. The battle is therefore most readily understood, with a few exceptions, from the perspective of Union corps attacks and Confederate divisional responses.

The Army of Northern Virginia's strength at Antietam was approximately forty thousand. A number of these men did not arrive on the field from Harpers Ferry until after the battle had begun, but almost all saw action on September 17. McClellan's Army of the Potomac numbered roughly eighty-seven thousand at Antietam, of whom some sixty thousand were actually involved in

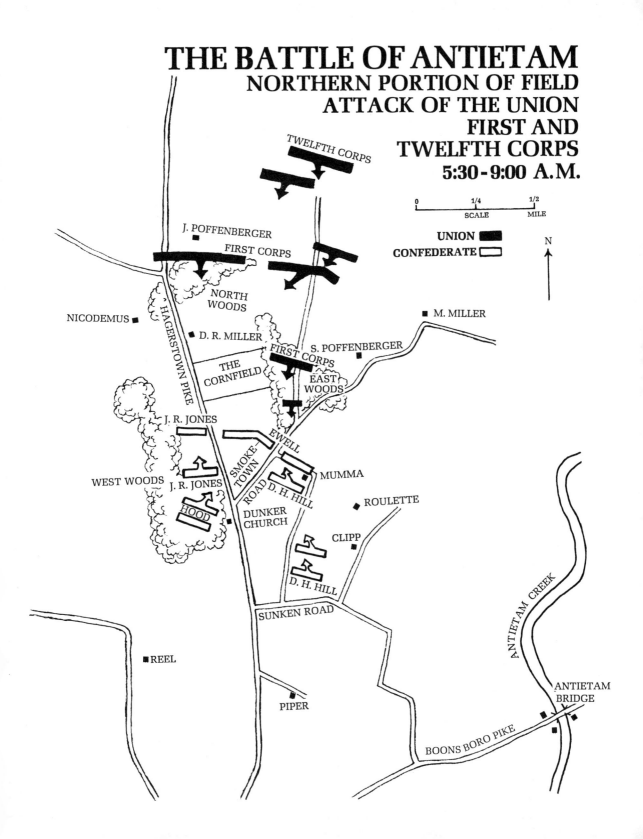

the battle. McClellan's inefficient use of his forces has been the subject of controversy ever since.

The fighting commenced on the northern portion of the battlefield at about dawn, September 17, as the Union First Corps under Gen. Joseph Hooker opened fire from the East Woods and emerged from the North Woods, charging through the Cornfield and along the Hagerstown Pike. Stiff resistance was immediately encountered as the Confederate divisions of generals Richard S. Ewell and John R. Jones met the attack and eventually launched their own savage counterattack.

Reserve units of the Union First Corps entered the fray, pushing the Confederates back. Badly mangled, Ewell's and Jones's men retired, but they were quickly replaced by Gen. John B. Hood's Confederate division, which charged out of the West Woods and into both the Cornfield and East Woods, throwing the Union First Corps back in confusion.

It was now seven thirty in the morning. As the First Corps struggled to rally its shattered ranks, the Union Twelfth Corps under Gen. Joseph K. F. Mansfield (soon to be mortally wounded) arrived on the scene, advancing onto the Miller farm and into the East Woods. Hood was forced to retire.

Three brigades of Gen. Daniel H. Hill's Confederate division took Hood's place. Moving from their reserve positions on the Mumma farm, Hill's men charged into the open fields on the Miller farm as well as into the East Woods to meet the onslaught of the Twelfth Corps. For more than an hour the fighting surged back and forth on the Miller farm until Hill's three brigades, driven to the point of exhaustion, fell back toward the safety of the West Woods and a nearby sunken road on the southern edge of the Mumma farm.

Most of the divisions of the Union Twelfth Corps were equally in need of rest and did not pursue, except for two brigades of Gen. George S. Greene's Northern division which, having escaped serious casualties in the initial encounter, advanced beyond the East Woods and secured a salient position on an open swell of ground opposite the Dunker Church and across the Hagerstown Pike from the West Woods.

For a short while a lull enveloped the field, but it did not remain quiet for long. Gen. John Sedgwick's division of Union general Edwin V. Sumner's Second Corps, held in reserve on the east bank of the Antietam during the early morning's fighting, was now closing in on the East Woods.

Shortly after nine o'clock in the morning, Sedgwick's battle lines passed

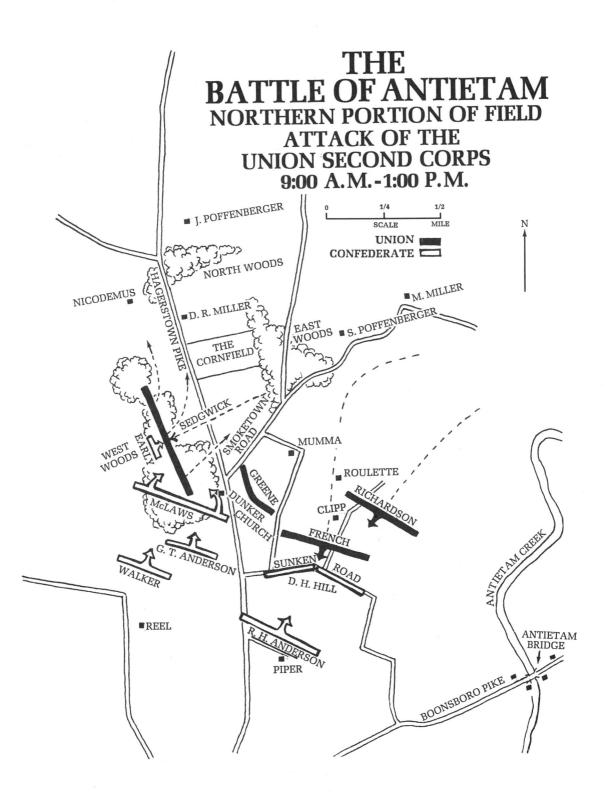

THE BATTLE OF ANTIETAM
NORTHERN PORTION OF FIELD
ATTACK OF THE
UNION SECOND CORPS
9:00 A.M.-1:00 P.M.

SCALE

0   1/4   1/2   MILE

UNION
CONFEDERATE

N

J. POFFENBERGER

NORTH WOODS

NICODEMUS

HAGERSTOWN PIKE

D. R. MILLER

M. MILLER

EAST WOODS

S. POFFENBERGER

THE CORNFIELD

SEDGWICK

SMOKETOWN ROAD

WEST WOODS

EARLY

MUMMA

ROULETTE

GREENE

RICHARDSON

McLAWS

DUNKER CHURCH

CLIPP

FRENCH

G. T. ANDERSON

WALKER

SUNKEN ROAD

D. H. HILL

ANTIETAM CREEK

REEL

R. H. ANDERSON

PIPER

ANTIETAM BRIDGE

BOONSBORO PIKE

through the East Woods and advanced across the no-man's-land on the Miller farm, toward the Hagerstown Pike and the Confederate-held West Woods. Aside from sporadic enemy artillery fire, little opposition was encountered.

What neither Sedgwick nor Sumner knew, however, was that strong Confederate reinforcements under generals Lafayette McLaws, G. T. Anderson, and John G. Walker were likewise moving toward the West Woods from the direction of Sharpsburg and were heading directly for Sedgwick's exposed left flank.

Entering the West Woods, Sedgwick's men were momentarily optimistic. The lack of resistance led them to believe that the enemy's momentum had been spent. Then from three sides—front, left, and left rear—the newly arrived Confederate units, together with Gen. Jubal A. Early's brigade of Ewell's division (held in reserve until now), struck the startled Union division with full force. Amazement quickly turned to panic as nearly one-half of the Federal soldiers fell within twenty minutes, the remainder retreating in varying aspects of disorder toward the shelter of the North and East Woods.

Flushed with victory, the Confederates pursued Sedgwick's decimated division beyond the West Woods but were forced to halt their advance because of protective fire from Union artillery batteries stationed along the eastern and northern edges of Miller's open fields, as well as infantry fire from Greene's two Twelfth Corps brigades located opposite the Dunker Church.

Not long after Sedgwick's disaster, Greene's men, supported by a section of Capt. Joseph M. Knap's battery, pushed forward into the West Woods at the Dunker Church. From shortly after ten o'clock until noon they held their advanced position, till compelled to retire by a Confederate counterattack that was in turn repulsed.

The original plan for Sedgwick's advance into the West Woods called for support on his immediate left. The task of providing this support was given to the remaining two divisions of the Union Second Corps, commanded by generals William H. French and Israel B. Richardson. Somehow French's division, followed later by Richardson's, became diverted, and as the rattle of musketry from the West Woods intensified, French turned southward, advancing over the William Roulette farm and toward Confederate positions at the sunken road (Bloody Lane).

There to bear the brunt of the Federal onslaught were D. H. Hill's two previously uncommitted brigades, later reinforced by Gen. Richard H. Anderson's division. From shortly after nine o'clock in the morning until one o'clock in the afternoon, nearly four hours, bitter fighting raged in the vicinity of Bloody Lane, with Union forces eventually capturing the trenchlike position—but not much else.

By one o'clock, Union general William Franklin's Sixth Corps had arrived on the field to strengthen the Federal positions. Aside from scattered artillery duels and infantry skirmishing during the afternoon, little notable action occurred north of Sharpsburg for the remainder of the battle. Although both sides suffered severely during the seven-hour morning engagement, the results were for the most part indecisive.

Meanwhile, on the southern portions of the field, fighting grew in intensity as the day wore on. McClellan's original battle plan had called for a Ninth Corps attack against Burnside Bridge in the morning. Once the bridge was captured, the corps would advance in full force against the Confederate right flank, thereby diverting enemy attention from the main push against the left flank in the vicinity of the West Woods.

The Ninth Corps, under the overall command of Gen. Ambrose E. Burnside (although technically led by one of Burnside's subordinates, Gen. Jacob D. Cox), made its first attempt to carry the bridge at ten o'clock in the morning. Two Confederate regiments of Gen. Robert Toombs's brigade, however, successfully shattered the initial assault from their strong position on the bluff overlooking the bridge. A second Union attack was likewise repulsed at about noon. Finally, at one o'clock, as fighting was drawing to a close on other portions of the field, a third charge carried the bridge as the defenders fell back to the main Confederate line along an open ridge running south of Sharpsburg.

The Confederate right flank, held by the division of Gen. David R. Jones, had been seriously weakened during the morning as troops were pulled out of line to reinforce the left flank. Had the Union Ninth Corps pressed forward immediately after capturing the bridge, it is unlikely that the Southern line could have held. But because of a two-hour delay in moving the corps over the bridge, Burnside was not ready to begin his advance on the western bank until three o'clock in the afternoon. The two-hour delay would soon prove costly.

Successful in their initial attack, the divisions of the Ninth Corps were able to penetrate the main Confederate line, throwing Jones's division into confusion. Good fortune was on the side of the South, however, for just when disaster seemed imminent, Confederate general Ambrose P. Hill's division arrived

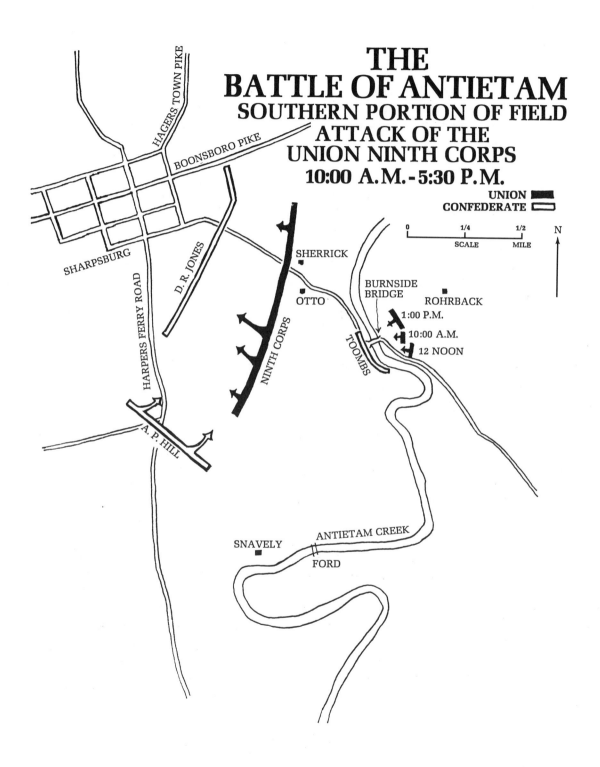

THE
BATTLE OF ANTIETAM
SOUTHERN PORTION OF FIELD
ATTACK OF THE
UNION NINTH CORPS
10:00 A.M. - 5:30 P.M.

UNION

CONFEDERATE

0   1/4   1/2

SCALE   MILE

N

HAGERS TOWN PIKE

BOONSBORO PIKE

SHARPSBURG

D. R. JONES

HARPERS FERRY ROAD

A. P. HILL

NINTH CORPS

SHERRICK

OTTO

BURNSIDE
BRIDGE

ROHRBACK

1:00 P.M.

10:00 A.M.

12 NOON

TOOMBS

SNAVELY

ANTIETAM CREEK

FORD

on the Union left flank after a seven-hour forced march from Harpers Ferry. The shock of Hill's flank attack turned the tide and sent the Ninth Corps reeling back toward the bridge. As evening settled over the field, the battle of Antietam drew to a close.

Both sides remained on the field throughout the next day, September 18, each army eying the other cautiously. McClellan, possessing a numerically superior force, including a significant number of units that had as yet seen no action on that field, oddly enough sat idle, allowing the Confederates a much-needed breathing spell in which to consider their next move.

To Lee it was obvious that the campaign, as originally conceived, was at an impasse. He had hoped that Maryland, a border state, would rally to the Southern cause. It did not. His Army of Northern Virginia had performed well and managed to hold its own thus far, extricating itself from more than one critical situation. But his army had been driven to the point of exhaustion and severe casualties, together with rampant straggling, had greatly reduced his ranks. He now found himself in a stagnant situation, face to face with a numerically stronger enemy in enemy territory. There was little to gain by continuing the struggle at this time and much to be lost if luck did not hold out.

Thus Lee made the decision on September 18 to terminate the Maryland campaign. During that night and into the early morning of September 19, the Army of Northern Virginia quietly fell back across the nearby Potomac River.

Belatedly, McClellan ordered an attack on the morning of September 19, only to learn shortly after daylight that he was no longer confronting an enemy force. Aside from a halfhearted pursuit made by elements of Gen. Fitz-John Porter's Fifth Corps, which resulted in some minor fighting at Blackford's Ford near Shepherdstown on September 19 and 20, active contact between the armies had been broken. For more than a month following the battle, the Army of the Potomac rested along the Potomac River from the vicinity of Sharpsburg southward to the reoccupied Harpers Ferry.

Because the invasion had been checked and the North saved, McClellan considered the battle a decisive victory. But many of his countrymen, including President Lincoln, had reservations regarding the extent of the victory. Expectations had run high in the North during the campaign. There was a widespread hope that this would be the last great encounter of the war and that the rebellion would be crushed once and for all—if only McClellan could destroy the Army of Northern Virginia rather than just check its advance.

ANTIETAM

As word circulated of one lost opportunity after another, usually resulting from McClellan's extreme caution and subsequent slowness in acting promptly and aggressively, frustration mounted throughout the North. Lincoln, observing that McClellan's inactivity after the battle would apparently continue indefinitely (McClellan claimed that he needed time to put his army back in fighting trim after the exhausting campaign), decided to visit the commander near Sharpsburg during the first week in October. His attempt at prodding McClellan to move rapidly against Lee proved futile and on November 7, 1862, McClellan was replaced as commander by General Burnside.

The war continued for two and a half more years. Although Antietam's military role in the conflict was largely indecisive, the political overtones assumed momentous proportions. Lee's failure to carry the war into the North convinced Great Britain and France that recognition of, and possible intervention on behalf of, the Confederate States of America would be unwise.

Additionally, Lincoln used the failure of the Confederate invasion as a backdrop for announcing his intention of declaring all slaves in areas then in rebellion to be forever free. The Emancipation Proclamation, issued on September 22, 1862, went into effect on January 1, 1863. With this declaration the war, which had begun in 1861 over the immediate issue of states' rights, henceforth assumed a broader purpose. No longer were the Southern states fighting simply for independence from what they considered to be a prejudiced and unjust government; they were now fighting directly for the survival of their time-honored way of life.

Although the battle of Antietam has left a mark on the course of American history, much of its far-reaching significance was unclear at the time. For days after the battle the previously obscure names of Sharpsburg and Antietam flooded the telegraph wires and newspapers. They were the topics of countless conversations, editorials, and heated arguments in communities large and small across the breadth of the country.

The initial excitement would soon level off as it became clear that the war was far from over, and, generally speaking, business returned to usual as the drama of the newspaper headlines decreased. Yet the curiosity stirred by this obviously historic event would remain high. What did the stone bridge crossed by Burnside's men look like? What did the village of Sharpsburg, and the often-referred-to sunken road, look like?

PHOTOGRAPHY AT ANTIETAM

From experience the Northern public could expect to see, within a matter of weeks, woodcuts in the illustrated weeklies and photographs depicting the battlefield's prominent features. What they most likely did not anticipate, however, was the kind of photographs presented to them by the prestigious Brady firm—photographs of horribly bloated corpses, clumps of human bodies strewn in grotesque positions, images so detailed that dried blood could be detected where it had once trickled out of an eye, an ear, and a mouth.

The Cameramen at Antietam

Exactly when Alexander Gardner and his assistant, James F. Gibson, the men through whose efforts these startling scenes were secured, reached Antietam is unclear. Because no Maryland campaign scenes were recorded by the cameramen prior to the battle, it appears certain that they did not accompany McClellan's army to the field.

The campaign was a relatively brief one, lasting only a little more than two weeks from the time Washington first learned of the invasion until the final skirmish at Blackford's Ford. What with the disorder and uncertainty that must have existed in Brady's Washington gallery as well as in the city itself following the disaster at Second Manassas, it seems reasonable that Gardner and Gibson did not venture forth to journey into Maryland until it was clear that McClellan was closing in on the Confederate army and that the outlook was at least potentially optimistic.

With little question, the cameramen would have followed the Army of the Potomac's most direct route from Washington to Antietam Creek, via Frederick, passing over the South Mountain battlefield sometime on or after September 15. Since the photographers did not stop to record any scenes on the South Mountain field, they must have reached the mountain pass at a time when it appeared obvious that more significant events had either transpired or were then unfolding farther west.

The earliest date appearing on a photograph caption in Gardner's Antietam series places the cameramen at McClellan's headquarters on the day of the battle, September 17. Although I have reservations concerning the accuracy of this caption (reservations that will be discussed in detail with the presentation of the photograph itself, view I-2), it is fairly certain that Gardner was on hand prior to the withdrawal of the Confederate army; in other words, by September 18 and possibly on the very day of the battle.

Regardless of when Gardner and Gibson arrived, the dates on which the cameramen recorded the bulk of their Antietam series are generally decipherable since Gardner had the foresight (at least at Antietam) to provide such information in a sufficient number of original captions.

The cameramen began their work in earnest on September 19, within hours after it was confirmed that the Confederates had withdrawn from the field. Until that time no other American battlefield had been photographed as soon after the battle as was Antietam. Gardner exploited the opportunity to the fullest.

He commenced work on the northern portion of the field. According to dated captions and other evidence, his views of dead soldiers opposite the Dunker Church were recorded on September 19. Views of dead soldiers along the Hagerstown Pike, near the Miller barn, and in Bloody Lane, judging by the proximity of these places to the Dunker Church, were most likely taken on the same date. Other views were recorded in the general vicinity, but because Gardner's captions do not account for his whereabouts on September 20, it is plausible that several of the northern field scenes were produced on the latter date.

On September 21, Gardner moved southward to concentrate his efforts on Burnside Bridge. September 22 found him at Antietam Bridge and for a brief period at McClellan's newly established headquarters somewhere in the vicinity of the village of Sharpsburg. The scenes of the village itself may have been recorded then, although they could have been recorded the day before, when the cameramen traveled from the northern field toward Burnside Bridge.

There are two distinct groups within the Antietam series—those views taken on the actual battlefield shortly after the fighting, or between September 19 and 22; and a second group, comprising exclusively outdoor portraits recorded during Lincoln's visit on October 3 and 4. Because none of the Antietam views can be documented as having been taken during the eleven-day period between September 22 and October 3, the possibility exists that Gardner returned to Washington after completing his work on the battlefield, only to learn of Lincoln's impending visit. This would have necessitated a second trip to record the historic meeting between the president and McClellan. Gibson was not credited with having taken any views in October, making it uncertain whether he was still operating at Gardner's side.

In all, some ninety-five different photographic negatives were exposed at Antietam in September and October of 1862. Of these, seventy were taken within five days of the battle: fifty-five stereo negatives (also used for printing album cards) by Gardner, seven stereo negatives by Gibson (all of either Burnside or Antietam Bridge), and eight large eight-by-ten-inch plates, all recorded by Gardner.

The remaining twenty-five exposures were made by Gardner during the first week in October—twelve stereo negatives and thirteen eight-by-ten-inch plates. With the possible exception of several views taken at the Elk Ridge signal station, none of Gardner's October photographs can be classified as battlefield scenes, since they were taken at various postbattle headquarters located off the main field and closer to the Potomac River.

Considering Gibson's coverage of the Peninsula campaign, which made him one of the most experienced Civil War photographers to that time, it is surprising that he took so few views at Antietam. His responsibilities during the Maryland operation must have centered primarily on the necessary tasks of sensitizing and developing plates. Gardner's selection of Gibson as an assistant was calculated, however. Indeed, Gardner, whose previous experience in photographing battlefields was limited and probably did not extend beyond the camp scenes he recorded along the James River in July and August, must have considered himself fortunate to have at his disposal the advice and skills of a man such as Gibson.[15]

Sometime during the third week in October, the public was given its first glimpse of the Antietam series. The reaction, as mentioned, was one of extreme interest. But, ironically, the names of the men directly responsible for recording these scenes—Alexander Gardner and James F. Gibson—do not appear in contemporary comments. Instead one reads only repeated praise of Mathew Brady for his skill and enterprise.

Both Gardner and Gibson copyrighted their appropriate views in their own names (undoubtedly at their own insistence), and this information appeared in fine print along the lower front edge of all original album cards and stereo views issued by the Brady firm in 1862. But few people took the trouble of reading the fine print, and all attention instead was drawn to the words "Brady's Album Gallery," prominently displayed on each identifying label. More significantly, Brady's promotional efforts were designed to give the impression that Brady alone was responsible for producing the scenes.

Brady's lack of concern regarding specific credits was not an uncommon practice at the time. Most large firms then in the business of producing photographic scenes for the mass market rarely mentioned the names of individual cameramen on the mounts or in their catalogs. A firm such as E. & H. T. Anthony of New York published and distributed wholesale thousands of stereo scenes from all over the world. Later in the war the Anthonys would handle the publication of most of Brady's stereo titles, but, interestingly enough, Brady would insist that each label note that the negative was taken by Brady & Co.

It cannot be denied that Mathew Brady, perhaps more than any other individual, was the prime mover of initial efforts to establish a corps of photographers who would systematically cover the war on a grand scale. Without his organizational and leadership abilities, along with his financial backing, it is doubtful that the war would have been covered as extensively as it was—especially during the crucial formative years of 1861 and 1862. Because of Brady's failing eyesight, however, it seems that his occasional appearances at the front during the war were more supervisory than anything else. There is even some doubt as to whether Brady personally recorded any Civil War photographs at all.[16]

But Brady, though universally lauded for the Antietam series, was not present with Gardner and Gibson on the Antietam battlefield, and it must have irritated Gardner to see Brady receive credit for the most sensational series of war photographs yet presented to the American public. Gardner's stringent insistence on seeing that each cameraman be properly identified and his negatives copyrighted most likely had much to do with his subsequent decision to leave Brady's firm. His break with Mathew Brady would be permanent.

Exactly when Alexander Gardner left Brady has not been determined, but it was sometime after November 1862 and before May 1863. During the latter month Gardner formally announced the opening of his own gallery in Washington. He took with him some of Brady's most experienced cameramen (including Gibson and O'Sullivan), together with all the original Antietam negatives, all the Cedar Mountain negatives, most of the Peninsula negatives, and many more. From 1863 through the end of the war, these scenes would continue to be sold, but under Gardner's label, not Brady's. The names of the specific cameramen were duly noted on Gardner's labels as well as in his catalogs.

PART TWO

THE ANTIETAM PHOTOGRAPHS

5

THE PRESENTATION

Few Americans of the mid-nineteenth century did more to promote the pleasures of collecting stereo photographs than Dr. Oliver Wendell Holmes, Sr., the noted Boston physician, poet, and writer. For Holmes the stereo view was a unique source of both entertainment and education.

In 1859 Dr. Holmes's first extensive article dealing with stereo views was published in the *Atlantic Monthly*. Two years later a second article appeared in the same journal describing a large number of memorable views he had seen, including battlefield stereos taken during the Franco-Austrian War of 1859.[17]

With the advent of war in the United States, Dr. Holmes, then aged fifty-one, found himself bidding farewell to his own son and namesake, Oliver Wendell Holmes, Jr., who joined the Twentieth Massachusetts Volunteers as a lieutenant. In March 1862, young Holmes, at the age of twenty, was promoted to the rank of captain and served with his unit throughout the Peninsula campaign.

September 1862 saw the Twentieth Massachusetts taking part in the effort to check the Confederate invasion of Maryland. With considerable apprehension, Dr. Holmes followed the newspaper reports of the ensuing campaign, knowing that a great battle was imminent and that his son's unit would probably be involved. Dr. Holmes later recalled what it was like in Boston on September 17,

THE PRESENTATION

1862: "The air had been heavy all day with rumors of battle, and thousands and tens of thousands had walked the streets with throbbing hearts, in dread anticipation of the tidings any hour might bring."

That evening Dr. Holmes and his family went to bed in a state of anxiety, thoughts of the young captain uppermost in their minds. Then, "In the dead of the night . . . my household was startled from its slumbers by the loud summons of a telegraphic messenger. We rose hastily, and presently the messenger was admitted. I took the envelope from his hand, opened it, and read: —'Hagerstown 17th, To Oliver Wendell Holmes—Capt. Holmes wounded shot through the neck thought not mortal at Keedysville.'" The telegram was signed by a William G. Leduc.

A series of images flashed through Dr. Holmes's mind as he struggled to interpret from his medical experience the exact nature of his son's wound. He reread the brief message over and over again, searching for clues in each word. The shaken father would never forget his precise thoughts at that time: "*Through* the neck,—no bullet left in wound. Windpipe, food-pipe, carotid, jugular, half a dozen smaller, but still formidable, vessels, a great braid of nerves, each as big as a lamp-wick, spinal cord—ought to kill at once, if at all. *Thought not* mortal, or *not thought* mortal,—which was it? The first; that is better than the second would be.—'Keedysville, a post-office, Washington Co., Maryland.' Leduc? Leduc? Don't remember that name.—The boy is waiting for his money. A dollar and thirteen cents. Has nobody got thirteen cents? Don't keep that boy waiting,—how do we know what messages he has got to carry?"[18]

What followed for Dr. Holmes was a long and frustrating journey by train and wagon to the Antietam battlefield in search of Captain Holmes. He finally found his son; the wound, as it turned out, was not serious. Oliver Wendell Holmes, Jr., returned to Boston with his father to recuperate, eventually rejoined his unit, survived the war, and in later years became famous as an associate justice of the U.S. Supreme Court.

OVERLEAF

LEFT: **Oliver Wendell Holmes, Jr., photographer unknown, album card, ca. 1861 (MOLLUS-Mass.);** RIGHT: **Dr. Oliver Wendell Holmes, Sr., photographed by Black and Batchelder of Boston, album card, ca. 1862 (author's collection).**

OLIVER WENDELL HOLMES, JR.

DR. OLIVER WENDELL HOLMES, SR.

ANTIETAM

Regrettably, thousands of traumatic experiences similar to the situation in which Dr. Holmes found himself in the wake of the battle of Antietam did not end as happily. Students of history tend to treat great battles largely in terms of generals' names, tactical deployments, causes, results, and the ever-present statistics. But in human terms the clinical, impersonal facts are meaningless unless one stops to reflect upon the pain and suffering they represent. Antietam's casualty figure of twenty-six thousand is more than just a sterile number, for it represents the personal tragedies of twenty-six thousand individual soldiers, and in broader terms the figure represents the twenty-six thousand individual households and families whose lives were thrown into emotional confusion and, in thousands of cases, altered irrevocably by the events of September 17, 1862. In untold instances those hit hardest, in terms of emotional agony, by the bullet piercing a skull, the piece of shrapnel tearing through vital organs, were the people still at home—the wives, daughters, sons, brothers, sisters, fathers, and, perhaps most vulnerable of all, the mothers.

Unless the reader is permitted to become intimately acquainted with the personal lives of at least some of these soldiers and their families, the battlefield photographs of nameless corpses fallen at Antietam will remain cold and remote curiosities. Thus, included in this presentation of the Antietam battlefield photographs are vignettes about common soldiers who fought and in most cases fell, dead or wounded, in or near the scenes recorded by Gardner and Gibson. Photographic portraits of all individuals chosen are presented. In fact, the subjects were selected primarily on the basis of the availability of such portraits. Unfortunately, locating images of common soldiers who were casualties at Antietam—especially Confederates—proved more difficult than I had anticipated. Limited availability therefore necessitated the inclusion of several portraits that are of admittedly poor quality. But it was deemed more essential to tell the stories of these men than to ensure consistently high quality throughout the various portraits.

Because the personal lives of most of the men depicted have never before been researched, or even discussed in any detail in prior published works, their stories have remained hidden for the past century in local newspaper notices, government military records, pension records, and census reports. Often from only scraps of remaining evidence I pieced together the capsule biographies of these individuals. Who were they? Did they grow up on farms, or were they from villages and cities? Did they attend school as children? Who were their mothers, fathers, brothers, and sisters? Were they married? Were their families well-off financially, or were they poor? What were their occupations? More elusive details could be determined only indirectly, based on what life was like in their particular regions of the country.[19]

With but a few exceptions, most of those individuals studied might be classified as typical Civil War soldiers in that they came from a variety of backgrounds that were commonly encountered in the ranks of their respective armies. Regional differences between Northern and Southern soldiers were not as pronounced as one might expect, whereas there were numerous similarities among the men.

As typical Civil War soldiers, all those depicted were white, all were Christian, and all spoke the same language. As Americans they shared a common national heritage. Historical figures such as George Washington, Benjamin Franklin, and Thomas Jefferson were revered by Northerners and Southerners alike. The same clothing and hairstyles were equally widespread. In fact, except for the differences in military uniforms, it is literally impossible to distinguish between the portraits of Union soldiers and their Confederate counterparts. In terms of age, most were born during the decade from 1834 to 1844, placing them in their late teens and twenties at the time of Antietam. The vast majority were mere children when the sectional differences that would ultimately seal the fate of many took tangible form.

It was indeed sad to delve into the family lives of these soldiers, knowing in advance the tragedy, pain, and hardships that would befall them at Antietam. And yet, only by unraveling the far-reaching effects of these tragedies can one begin to appreciate the enormity of the battlefield photographs.

The Antietam Photographs

Of the ninety-five images recorded by Gardner and Gibson at Antietam, sixty-three are presented in this study. Those views not included were generally eight-by-ten duplicates of subjects already represented in stereo (or vice versa), group portraits from the October series that were of a repetitious nature, and similarly repetitious views of the Burnside and Antietam bridges.

The cameramen's enchantment with the two bridges is indicated by the fact that more than twenty negatives (nearly a third of the entire September series) were expended on them from various angles. Twelve of the best and most representative examples have been selected for inclusion.

ANTIETAM

Many of the more famous Antietam views, such as the scenes taken across from the Dunker Church, the views of Bloody Lane, and vistas of the village and bridges are quite easily located on the battlefield today. Other scenes, including the death studies along the Hagerstown Pike, have been located with less precision in the past—sometimes with obvious inaccuracy. And still other Antietam scenes, including several seemingly nondescript death studies, have never before been identified as to their subject's location.

Over a period of nearly two years (1974–76) I sought to become intimately acquainted with the terrain at Antietam to determine the precise location of all the battlefield scenes. In most instances my efforts met with considerable success, and a number of heretofore unidentified photographs will be located precisely for the first time on the following pages. Wherever the original camera position was determinable, a modern photograph was taken of the identical scene. Recorded for the most part between February and April 1976, these modern versions will appear throughout the text with their respective 1862 photographs.

Unfortunately, the locations for a handful of original views remain elusive even after a most intensive field investigation. Regardless of the degree of success, however, the results of my findings will be discussed more fully with the individual photographs.

For the purpose of this presentation the Antietam photographs have been broken down into six basic groups that approximate both a geographic progression across the field and the chronological sequence of events during the battle. The complexities of the battle itself made it difficult at times to decide in which group a specific view should be placed. Particularly troublesome were the views recorded on the northernmost portions of the field. The morning's fighting occurred in several phases, each either covering or overlapping much of the same ground as the others. In such cases the dominant subject of each photograph was studied to determine where it could be presented most appropriately, even though it may have been recorded only a few yards from a scene in another group.

The six basic groups are as follows: I—the east bank of Antietam Creek, including General McClellan's headquarters, the Elk Ridge signal station, and Antietam Bridge; II—the Miller farm, an identification used here to delineate the ground over which the earliest phase of the battle occurred, an area including the Hagerstown Pike, the open ground south of the Cornfield, and the neighboring Mumma farm; III—the West Woods, here used to identify that phase of the morning's battle highlighted by Union general Sedgwick's, and later General Greene's, attempts to carry the woods, including views taken opposite the Dunker Church and, again, the ground south of the Cornfield; IV—Bloody Lane, including the Roulette farm and the hospital of Union general French's division, located on the O. J. Smith farm a mile and a quarter in the rear; V—Burnside Bridge, including the southern portion of the battlefield; and VI—miscellaneous, including the village of Sharpsburg, group portraits, and Lincoln's October visit.

Each group is accompanied by a detailed map showing all identifiable camera positions within that group, as well as the locations of units specifically mentioned in the caption narrative. The names of soldiers discussed in the vignette studies will also be found on the maps accompanying the unit with which each served at Antietam.

Each battlefield photograph is identified by the Roman numeral of its group, followed by a second number that places the photograph within that group. All photographs are introduced by formal titles that include a brief description of each scene (these descriptions are my own—original titles, where mentioned, appear in quotes), the name of the cameraman, the photograph's original form of publication (including stereo numbers, which do not reflect the order in which views were taken), the date on which the photograph was recorded, and the source of the photograph reproduced in this book. A key to the source abbreviations follows.

Picture Sources
Cook Collection, Valentine Museum; **Fredericksburg National Military Park; Georgia Department of Archives and History; Goodrich:** S. G. Goodrich, *A Pictorial History of America* (Hartford: House & Brown, 1851); **Green:** Robert M. Green, *History of the One Hundred and Twenty-fourth Regiment Pennsylvania Volunteers* (Philadelphia: Ware Bros. Co., printers, 1907); **LC:** Library of Congress; **McGuire:** Mr. John L. McGuire; **Miller:** Francis T. Miller, ed., *The Photographic History of the Civil War* (New York: Review of Reviews Co., 1911); **MOLLUS-Mass.:** Military Order of the Loyal Legion, Massachusetts Commandery, U. S. Army Military History Research Collection; **Monroe County Historical Commission Archives; Museum of the Confederacy; Regtl Comm.:** The Regimental Committee, *History of the One Hundred and Twenty-fifth Regiment Pennsylvania Volunteers* (Philadelphia: J. B. Lippincott Co., 1906); **Rosenstock:** Mr. Benjamin B. Rosenstock; **Thomas:** Henry W. Thomas, *History of the Doles-Cook Brigade Army of Northern Virginia, C. S. A.* (Atlanta: Franklin Printing and Publishing Company, 1903); **Westbrook:** Robert S. Westbrook, *History of the 49th Pennsylvania Volunteers* (Altoona, Pa.: Altoona Times, 1898). All modern photographs were taken by the author.

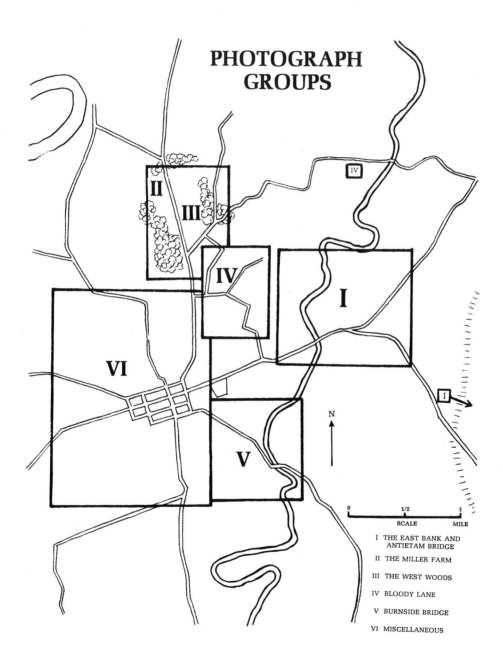

PHOTOGRAPH GROUPS

II

III

IV

I

IV

VI

V

N

SCALE

0   1/2   1
                      MILE

I   THE EAST BANK AND
    ANTIETAM BRIDGE

II   THE MILLER FARM

III THE WEST WOODS

IV   BLOODY LANE

V   BURNSIDE BRIDGE

VI   MISCELLANEOUS

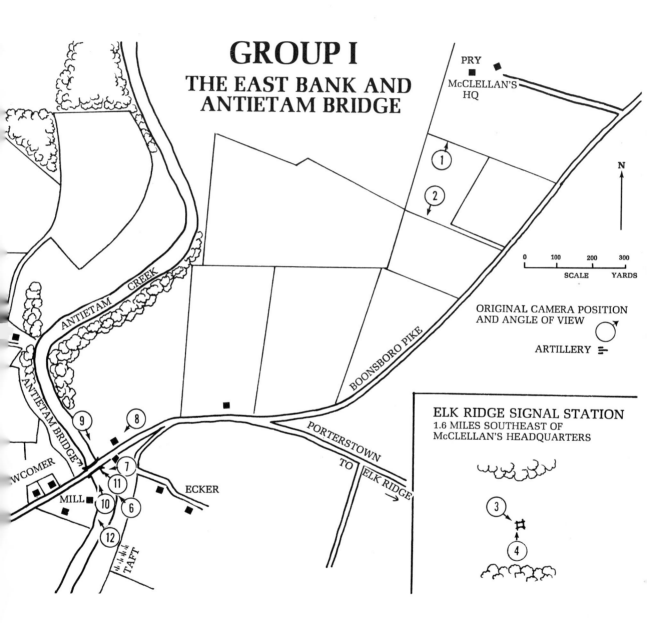

GROUP I
THE EAST BANK AND ANTIETAM BRIDGE

PRY

McCLELLAN'S HQ

N

ANTIETAM CREEK

BOONSBORO PIKE

0   100   200   300
SCALE   YARDS

ORIGINAL CAMERA POSITION AND ANGLE OF VIEW

ARTILLERY

ELK RIDGE SIGNAL STATION
1.6 MILES SOUTHEAST OF McCLELLAN'S HEADQUARTERS

PORTERSTOWN

TO ELK RIDGE

ANTIETAM BRIDGE

WCOMER

MILL

ECKER

TAFT

6

GROUP I: THE EAST BANK AND ANTIETAM BRIDGE

I–1 McClellan's headquarters at the Pry house, Gardner, stereo #576, September 17 or 18, 1862 (LC).

On September 15, 1862, the Confederate forces that had held the Union army at bay the day before at South Mountain retired westward across Antietam Creek and took up defensive positions in front of Sharpsburg. Throughout the same afternoon and on into the next day, the closely pursuing Army of the Potomac established positions along the opposite bank of the creek. On a hill overlooking this awesome scene of massive deployment stood the brick farmhouse of Philip Pry, the subject of photograph I-1.

Since moving into the house in July 1844, life had been good to Philip Pry. The 125-acre farm was a prosperous one and during the early days of September 1862, Pry, then aged forty-four, together with his wife, Elizabeth, thirty-two, and his four young sons, Samuel, fourteen; Alfred, twelve; Jacob, five; and Charles, three, could anticipate nothing that would interfere with preparations for the fall harvest.

Then came the armies, pouring through the gaps at South Mountain with their long, seemingly endless columns of infantry, artillery, cavalry, and wagon trains laden with supplies and tons of ammunition. Within twenty-four hours of the arrival of the first elements of the Army of the Potomac, a group of

I–1

I–1 modern

mounted officers galloped up the tree-lined dirt lane leading from the Boonsboro Pike to the Pry farmhouse. A young staff officer in the group, believed to have been Capt. George A. Custer, informed the farmer that General McClellan had chosen to locate his field headquarters at the brick house.

For the next four days the Pry farm was the scene of much activity as couriers dashed to and fro with urgent messages, conferences were held, and plans developed. During the battle, McClellan spent most of his time in the vicinity of the farmhouse, observing distant troop movements through field glasses from a number of vantage points in the surrounding fields as well as from a trap door on the roof of the house itself.

Two Union generals who were wounded during the battle, Hooker and Richardson, received medical treatment at the Pry home, Richardson dying from his wound in a second-floor bedroom on November 3, 1862. Before his death, however, Richardson was visited by Abraham Lincoln, who made a special trip to the farm in October while conferring with McClellan.

On the morning of the battle, the Pry family was moved (at McClellan's insistence) to Keedysville, where they were boarded with friends. Returning to their home after McClellan moved his headquarters farther westward on September 20, the Prys found a scene approaching desolation. Their extensive crops of wheat, corn, and apples, together with their stock of cattle, sheep, and hogs had been all but totally consumed by the Union army. Their fields were trampled, their fences heavily damaged.

Not until after the war would any financial compensation be granted by the Federal government, but by then the family, never able to recuperate from the staggering losses of 1862, had come into hard times. In 1873 Philip Pry sold his property and moved to Tennessee. There he and his wife would die. By request their bodies were sent back to Keedysville to be buried near their former homestead.

Gardner's photograph of the Pry house is one of the earliest to have been taken at Antietam. Interestingly enough, the photographer's original caption made no mention of General McClellan but instead referred to the building as "General Hooker's Headquarters." The camera position was located on an open hill across from the house. Although the image was not dated, it is fairly certain that it was recorded within a short while of photograph I-2. The latter view, taken from a camera position only 150 yards away but looking in another direction, was claimed by Gardner to have been recorded on the day of the battle. My reservations regarding the dating of that view—and hence both views—are discussed in the next caption.

As the modern version of Gardner's photograph of McClellan's headquarters shows, the Pry house still stands today, and although the structure was damaged by fire several months after the modern version was recorded, it still appears basically as it did in 1862. The barn in the foreground of the modern view is a later addition, though the older barn at the extreme right is probably the original. The Pry buildings are now owned by the National Park Service.

I–2

I–2 modern

I–2 Union reserve positions near McClellan's headquarters, Gardner, stereo #671, September 17 or 18, 1862 (LC).

Few photographs in the Antietam series have attracted as much interest over the past century as has this scene, originally entitled "View of Battle-field of Antietam, on day of battle, Sept. 17, 1862."

Until recent years it was not known precisely where the scene was located. In the absence of this information, and relying solely on Gardner's brief description, historians have commonly accepted that the photograph depicted actual fighting somewhere on the battlefield. But in 1963 it was determined conclusively that the camera was located on the hill in front of McClellan's headquarters and that the view showed Union reserves located behind the lines on the eastern side of Antietam Creek.[20]

The smoke in the right distance, previously thought to indicate rifle fire, turned out to be smoke from campfires; upon close examination, the artillery battery in the left distance stands inactive, its guns still attached to their limber chests. The man in the foreground, probably posed, is gazing through his binoculars toward the front-line positions near Bloody Lane, a mile distant and on the opposite side of Antietam Creek.

Whether or not Gardner was deliberately vague in his caption, hoping to make it seem as if he had recorded an actual battle photograph, cannot be established. On the other hand, my previous research on Gardner captions suggests that he was not above occasionally stretching the truth in order to increase the historical nature of his views.[21]

For the most part, Gardner's captions tally well with a logical interpretation of events as they occurred at Antietam. Most of his caption references regarding when and where he took views are believable. But in this instance the caption, and more specifically the date, warrants closer investigation.

It already has been established that the view was taken in a rear area, from a camera position located only 150 yards from the photograph of McClellan's headquarters. The shadows in both I-1 and I-2, particularly as they silhouette the man with the binoculars in the one, and darken the southeastern face of the Pry house in the other, indicate that both were recorded in the afternoon. Disregarding the one dated caption, there is nothing in either view that would confirm the specific afternoon as being that of September 17. On the contrary, the completely inactive artillery unit located to the rear of the infantry indicates the photograph was *not* taken on the day the battle was fought, for according to available evidence, on the afternoon of September 17 all reserve artillery units in the vicinity of McClellan's headquarters were posted on the ridge beyond and to the right of the infantry reserves.

On September 17 Gen. George W. Morell's division of the Fifth Corps was located where the infantry campfires appear in the photograph. But the dormant artillery unit cannot be accounted for on the afternoon of September 17. The following day, however, Gen. Andrew A. Humphreys's Fifth Corps division arrived on the field and replaced Morell's at the identical site. Since there was no battle on September 18, there would have been no pressing need for the use of Humphreys's artillery units on the ridge to the right of the infantry, as there was for Morell's batteries the day before.

Therefore, it seems more probable that the artillery unit depicted belonged to Humphreys's division, which arrived on September 18, rather than to Morell's or to anyone else's who was on the field the day of the battle.

Of equal importance is an analysis of the two photographs in relation to the remainder of the views taken at Antietam. These are the only two photographs in the entire series of ninety-five views that appear to have been recorded before September 19, the day on which the Union army gained undisputed possession of the battlefield. If Gardner's caption identifying the one photograph as having been taken on September 17 is accurate, then Gardner had to have been present and recording scenes at Antietam on the very day of the battle—an exciting supposition from any standpoint, considering the historical vibrations that would have been associated with any and all photographs recorded on "day of battle." Yet the cameraman exposed only two plates that day, none the following day, and began his series of ninety-three additional scenes only after the main event had passed its climax.

Based on the evidence at hand and knowing that Gardner did, on occasion, stretch the truth, it seems more logical that he arrived on the field late on the afternoon of September 18 during a period of general inactivity and recorded his first two views at that time, resuming his work in earnest the next day. The latter scenario at least provides a logical continuity to Gardner's coverage of the field.

Although it is my belief that both photographs were recorded on September 18 rather than September 17, I do not wish to leave the impression that the question has been settled. The evidence is weighty, but not conclusive. Accordingly, I have dated these two views as having been recorded on either September 17 or 18.

The reserve area photographed by Gardner has changed little over the past century. Yet because the entire field of vision, including the hill from which both this and the preceding view were recorded, remains in private hands, the land is continuously threatened by the prospect of future housing developments. A grove of pine trees that today covers the eastern portion of the hill in front of McClellan's headquarters forced me to record the modern view of the reserve area several yards to the right of the original camera position, thus explaining why the field in the foreground differs in its slope from the ground in the original view.

ANTIETAM

I–3 a and b   Union signal station at Elk Ridge, overlooking the Antietam battlefield, Gardner (a) plate, September or October 1862 (MOLLUS-Mass.), (b) stereo #633, September or October 1862 (LC).

I–4   The Elk Ridge signal station, Gardner, plate, September or October 1862 (LC).

I–5   Signal Corps detachment on Elk Ridge, Gardner, plate, probably October 1862 (LC).

Early on the morning of September 16, 1862, as General McClellan cautiously prepared his forces for the upcoming battle, a Union signal corps detachment was directed to establish a station on the crest of Elk Ridge (also known as Elk Mountain or, locally, Red Hill). From here enemy troop locations and movements could be observed and reported directly to McClellan's headquarters at the Pry house, less than two miles away.

Modern view of the Antietam battlefield from the site of the Elk Ridge signal station.

GROUP I: THE EAST BANK AND ANTIETAM BRIDGE

Because no distant photographs were recorded from this position in 1862, a modern view has been included to give the reader an idea of this station's unparalleled importance at the time of the battle. Visible in the distant center of the modern view, two and a half miles to the west, is the village of Sharpsburg, its rooftops glimmering in the sun. The dark grove of trees to the immediate right of the village marks the location of the Antietam National Cemetery.

According to official reports, the log tower present in Gardner's photographs was not constructed until after the battle of September 17, when a gap was cleared on top of the mountain to facilitate future observations. During the actual fighting, the detachment was at times forced to make its observations from the top of a tree, the flagman being posted in the branches below.[22]

It is not known whether Gardner visited the signal station in September or in October, since none of the Elk Ridge scenes was dated in the original captions. In 1866, when Gardner's *Sketch Book* was published, the first view shown here (3a) was labeled September 1862. But a nineteenth-century print of the group portrait (5), today in the collections of the Library of Congress, bears the handwritten date of October 1862.

Clothing variations among some of the identical soldiers who appear in both views may indicate that Gardner visited the station at two separate times, perhaps in a frustrated attempt to record a distant panorama of the battlefield. If such an attempt was made, it probably failed because of either atmospheric conditions or the position of the sun.

During my research on these scenes, I was fortunate to come across a nineteenth-century print of view 3a bearing a notation, written by a Civil War veteran, identifying several of the men who appear in all four Elk Ridge photographs.[23] Gardner's captions provided the name of another. Interestingly enough, none of these men was stationed on Elk Ridge during the battle, all being posted there sometime after September 20. The signal tower was manned, presumably, by the same group until the Union army moved south in late October.

Views 3a and 3b show the station from an identical camera position. The flagmen in both views are believed to be facing westward, into the afternoon sun and toward the battlefield. The man seated on top of the tower to the left in 3a is the leader of the detachment, 1st Lt. Edward C. Pierce, who was transferred to the Signal Corps from the Third Maine Infantry in December 1861. Pierce, aged twenty-four in 1862, was originally from Nashua, New Hamp-

I–3a

I–3b

I–4

I–5

shire, and worked before the war as an ornamental painter. During the battle
of Antietam, he helped man a signal station close to the front lines and near
the North Woods. Fewer than ten months after this photograph was recorded,
Pierce would serve with distinction at Gettysburg as a signal officer on Little
Round Top. He married after the war and died in Boston in 1896.

Seated directly under Pierce in view 3a is 2d Lt. Frederick W. Owen of
Brooklyn, New York. In December 1861, Owen was detached from the Thirty-
eighth New York Infantry to receive training as a signal officer. During the battle of Antietam, Owen served under fire at an advanced signal station near the
front lines in the vicinity of the Roulette farm. On September 19, 1862, he was
directed to follow Union general Porter's Fifth Corps to Blackford's Ford,
where, for the next twenty-four hours, he helped direct the fire of an artillery
battery. Owen rejoined the Thirty-eighth New York in March 1863 and eventually rose to the rank of lieutenant colonel.

The flagman in view 3a has not been identified, but the man standing directly beneath him is Pvt. Harrison W. Gardiner of Augusta, Maine. Like

GROUP I: THE EAST BANK AND ANTIETAM BRIDGE

Lieutenant Pierce, Gardiner was originally a member of the Third Maine, and the two would again serve together at Little Round Top on July 2, 1863. To the right of Gardiner stands another former member of the Third Maine, Pvt. Robert J. Morgan of Bath, Maine, who was transferred to the Signal Corps in March 1862.

Alexander Gardner's stereo version of this same scene, view 3b, shows Lieutenant Pierce to the far left, his blouse now removed. In the center sits Lieutenant Owen, whereas the flagman to the right may be Private Gardiner, judging from his clothing.

In the next photograph, view 4, the cameraman has shifted his position to a point opposite the southern face of the tower. Standing to the left is Private Morgan. The flagman, now wearing his blouse, is Private Gardiner. The officer posed peering through the telescope, apparently gazing in the direction of Sharpsburg, is Lieutenant Pierce, and to the right sits the third officer of the detachment, 2d Lt. Aaron B. Jerome. Originally of the First New Jersey Infantry, Jerome joined the Signal Corps in March 1862, but he did not reach Antietam from his previous station at Point of Rocks, Maryland, in time for the fighting on September 17, 1862. Jerome served as a signal officer, including duty on Little Round Top at Gettysburg, until September 1864, when he resigned from the army. He died after the war in San Francisco.

The final Elk Ridge view shown here (5) is a group portrait that may have been taken on a different day. Seated against the tree to the left is Private Morgan. Lieutenant Owen is posed seated with his left hand on his thigh in front of and to the left of the white signal flag; the man seated next to him on the right, a telescope on his lap, is Lieutenant Jerome. (Note that Jerome's clothing in this scene appears to be entirely different from that worn in view 4.) Standing behind Jerome to the right is Private Gardiner. The next standing figure, holding the darker signal flag, is identical to the flagman in view 3, though his name is unknown. And finally, the last seated officer on the right is Lieutenant Pierce. (The black men in this scene are servants.)

The summit of Elk Ridge is readily accessible today by automobile. The land is divided into privately owned lots, and several houses, some in the process of construction at the time of this writing, are located in the approximate vicinity of the signal station site. From clearings, the modern visitor is provided with a breathtaking panorama of the Antietam battlefield similar to that observed by the Union signalmen photographed by Gardner more than a century ago.

I–6 **Antietam Bridge, view looking northwest, Gibson, stereo #608, September 22, 1862 (LC).**

I–7 **Antietam Bridge, view looking west, Gardner, stereo #583, September 22, 1862 (LC).**

I–8 **Antietam Bridge, view looking southwest, Gibson, stereo #607, September 22, 1862 (LC).**

Between dawn and eight o'clock on the morning of September 15, 1862, fourteen Confederate infantry brigades, totaling more than ten thousand men under the commands of generals Longstreet and D. H. Hill, retired westward along the Boonsboro Pike and crossed Antietam Creek at the bridge shown in these photographs.

As the units reached the open ridge just beyond (visible in the backgrounds of views 6 and 7), they were directed off the road and into adjoining fields to form a line of battle facing eastward (toward the camera positions). Here, in a line a mile long, the veterans of the battle of South Mountain awaited the approach of the Union army as well as the remainder of their own men, then in the vicinity of Harpers Ferry.

Harpers Ferry had surrendered to the Confederate forces that same morning (September 15), and it was hoped that McClellan's pursuit could be delayed long enough at Antietam Creek for Lee to reunite his army at Sharpsburg.

Approximately two hours after the initial Confederate line was established, the leading units of the Union army came into sight, approaching the bridge from the direction of Boonsboro and along the same road used by the Southerners a short while before. The first Union regiment to reach the bridge was the Fifth New Hampshire Infantry, with its skirmishers thrown out in advance.

One of the junior officers of that regiment, Lt. Ira T. Bronson of Bath, New Hampshire, would later recall how an enemy sniper, hidden behind a bush on the east bank, fired in his direction as he neared the creek. The first shot missed, but two more rounds followed quickly, each striking the lieutenant's clothing. Realizing the danger Bronson was in, members of his company began firing at the bush, whereupon the sniper made a hasty retreat for the bridge. Miraculously, the lone Confederate, still under fire, reached the bridge unharmed; in a gesture of defiance, he turned and swung his hat at the enemy infantrymen before dashing to the safety of the opposite bank.[24]

I–6

I–6 modern

Later on September 15, the responsibility of holding the bridge and preventing its possible destruction by the Confederates was given to the United States regulars of Gen. George Sykes's division of the Fifth Corps. On the morning of September 16, after the Confederate battle line had fallen back closer to Sharpsburg, several companies of the Fourth United States Infantry were thrown across Antietam Bridge and deployed as skirmishers to the right of the pike along the bank, and to the left under the cover of Joshua Newcomer's large barn (visible to the left in view 7).

At about noon on the day of the battle, Union cavalry under Gen. Alfred Pleasonton made a demonstration against the Confederate center, which was then located where the National Cemetery now lies. The cavalrymen, accompanied by several batteries of horse artillery, crossed the bridge at a gallop and took positions in the vicinity of the ridge beyond. Throughout the afternoon of September 17, these units, together with some of Sykes's regular infantry, engaged Confederate forces at a distance, thereby diverting a small portion of the enemy's attention from other points on the field.

Aside from this relatively minor demonstration, however, little fighting took place at the Confederate center. Had McClellan chosen to attack that position with the bulk of his available Fifth Corps units held in reserve on the eastern side of the creek, Antietam Bridge certainly would have been used by the assaulting forces. But most of the Fifth Corps units saw no action on September 17; consequently, Antietam Bridge, though potentially important as a tactical structure, played a diminutive role during the battle.

Five days later, Gardner and Gibson completed their September series of battlefield photographs by recording a group of views at Antietam Bridge. Two of those shown here (6 and 7) were taken from a steep bluff to the southeast. Gibson's version (6) was taken looking toward the northern portions of the battlefield. Barely visible on the center horizon is the West Woods, with the East Woods detectable on the far right horizon. Just below the East Woods appears a farm undoubtedly serving as a hospital when this scene was recorded. These buildings may be found on official maps, but it is not certain who was living there in 1862. The house and several outbuildings still stand today under private ownership.

Gardner's photograph of the bridge (7) shows the farm of Joshua Newcomer, located opposite the bridge on the western side of Antietam Creek. Behind the barn is the ridge upon which the Confederates first established their line on the

GROUP I: THE EAST BANK AND ANTIETAM BRIDGE

I–7

I–7 modern

I–8

I–8 modern

morning of September 15 and which was occupied by Pleasonton's men during the afternoon of September 17.

The third photograph, view 8, was recorded by Gibson from the northern side of the Boonsboro Pike. The stone building in the left distance (no longer standing) may have been a turnpike tollhouse, whereas the log dwelling in the foreground (note the adjoining thatch-roofed outbuilding) has been improved over the years but still retains its basic character. Beyond the bridge is the Newcomer barn, which, though it stands today (and is privately owned), is currently in need of much repair; it is difficult to make out in the modern version.

I–9

I–9 modern

GROUP I: THE EAST BANK AND ANTIETAM BRIDGE

I–9 Antietam Bridge, view looking southeast, Gardner, plate, September 22, 1862 (MOLLUS-Mass.).

I–10 Antietam Bridge, view looking north, Gardner, plate, September 22, 1862 (MOLLUS-Mass.).

I–11 Antietam Bridge, view looking northwest, Gardner, stereo #581, September 22, 1862 (LC).

Although Antietam Bridge played a minor role during the battle, there can be little doubt, judging from the quantity of negatives expended on it, that the bridge was considered by Alexander Gardner to be a good subject. Yet the fact that all the Antietam Bridge views were taken on September 22, 1862, the last day on which views were recorded at Antietam prior to Lincoln's October visit, may suggest that Gardner was preparing to return to Washington on September 22, and, as at Burnside Bridge the day before, he found himself becoming increasingly liberal in the expenditure of glass plates.

In view 9, Gardner has positioned his camera at the edge of a large cornfield that covered most of the eastern bank of the Antietam just north of the Boonsboro Pike. The high bluff in the background is where he and Gibson stood when they recorded views 6 and 7. Densely wooded today, the bluff provided a clear field of vision in 1862. For a time during the battle, Capt. Elijah D. Taft's Fifth Battery of New York Light Artillery was positioned in another cornfield barely visible on the crest in the photograph. (Gardner recorded an identical stereo version of this scene that was listed in his 1863 catalog as view #609.)

Only one scene showing Antietam Bridge was recorded from the west bank of the creek. The eight-by-ten-inch version is shown here in view 10, taken looking toward the flat ground north of the Boonsboro Pike. (An identical stereo version was listed in Gardner's catalog as view #578.)

Visible to the far right in this view are the remnants of a dam that straddled the creek as it flowed past a mill owned by the Newcomer family (see I-12). On September 16, 1862, two companies of the Fifth New Hampshire Infantry were detailed to destroy the dam, presumably in an effort to lower the water level at fords farther upstream. The New Hampshire soldiers were unsuccessful for lack of proper tools, but, judging from this photograph, the task was eventually completed by others, perhaps by the engineer battalion then assigned to the

I–10

Army of the Potomac.[25] The original camera position for view 10 is currently inaccessible, preventing taking a modern version.

The final view of the bridge (11) was originally entitled "Picnic Party at Antietam Bridge, September 22, 1862." The two ladies who apparently arrived at the scene in the carriage were either accompanied or joined at the bridge by two men. An examination of the scene under magnification reveals that each woman is holding a piece of hardtack and that the woman on the left has taken two bites from hers. The man in uniform is bending over in the process of stirring the contents of a can in the other woman's hand with what appears to be either a bayonet or a long knife. The odd, almost lighthearted nature of this photograph, recorded only five days after the battle, stands in marked contrast to the bulk of Gardner's Antietam series.

As is obvious from the modern versions of the Antietam Bridge photographs, the original structure, built in the early 1800s, is no longer standing. It was destroyed by a flood in 1891.

I–11

I–11 modern

I–12 Newcomer's mill, Gardner, stereo #582, September 22, 1862 (LC).

Built in 1782 by Christopher Orndorff, the mill to the right in this view (also to the left in I-7) had served the farming community surrounding Sharpsburg for sixty years prior to the battle. It was finally torn down in 1904, after standing for 122 years.

The old Orndorff house, likewise dating back to the eighteenth century, may be seen in the left background. The Orndorffs were highly respected members of the Sharpsburg community, and, according to family records, a number of notable figures were from time to time entertained at the homestead. Among those listed in the family records were George Washington and Gen. Horatio Gates.

At the time of the battle of Antietam, the Orndorff farm and mill were owned and operated by the family of Joshua Newcomer. The 1860 census records list Joshua as a farmer, whereas his son William was described as being in charge of the mill. A close examination of Gardner I-7 reveals that two houses stood side by side on the Newcomer farm to the right of the Boonsboro Pike. The original dwelling, closest to the creek and visible in the left background in view 12 (as well as in view I-7), has since been razed. Only the later house remains on the site today. It may have been that Joshua, aged fifty-two at the time of the battle, lived in the original house with his wife, Mary, fifty, whereas the newer house was perhaps built to accommodate his son William, then twenty-four, and the latter's family.

During the battle, the Newcomer property was occupied by United States regular infantry of the Union Fifth Corps. As was the case with most farms in the Sharpsburg area, the Newcomer farm was probably serving as a hospital when photographed.

I–12

I–12 modern

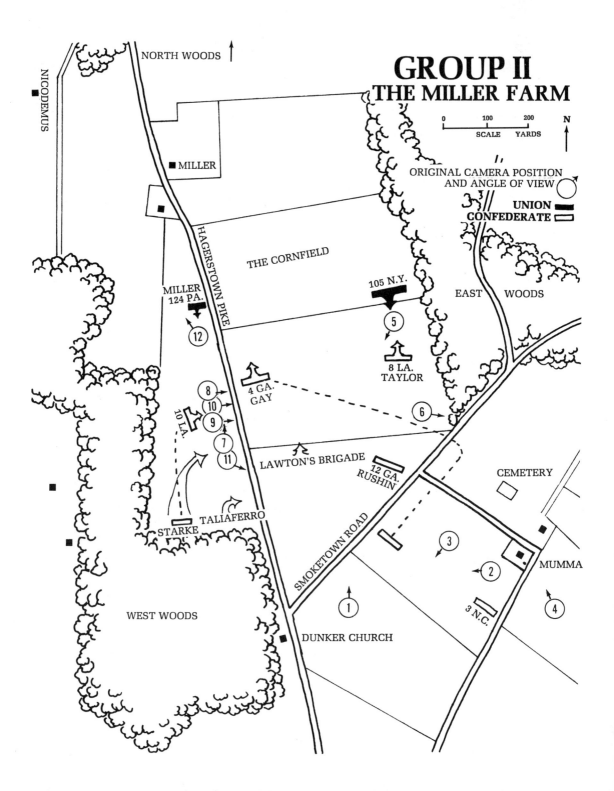

GROUP II
THE MILLER FARM

NORTH WOODS

NICODEMUS

MILLER

0   100   200
SCALE   YARDS

N

ORIGINAL CAMERA POSITION
AND ANGLE OF VIEW

UNION
CONFEDERATE

THE CORNFIELD

105 N.Y.

EAST   WOODS

MILLER
124 PA.

HAGERSTOWN PIKE

12

8 LA.
TAYLOR

5

8

4 GA.
GAY

10

9

10 LA.

6

7

11

LAWTON'S BRIGADE

12 GA.
RUSHIN.

CEMETERY

TALIAFERRO

STARKE

3

2

MUMMA

SMOKETOWN ROAD

1

3 N.C.

4

WEST WOODS

DUNKER CHURCH

7

GROUP II: THE MILLER FARM

II–1 Knap's Battery on the battlefield, Gardner, stereo #577, September 19, 1862 (LC).

The main subject of this superb Antietam photograph is Independent Battery E, Pennsylvania Light Artillery, commanded during the battle by Capt. Joseph M. Knap. Although the battery's participation in the actual fighting at Antietam is more appropriately discussed in the following chapter dealing with the struggle for the West Woods, the photograph's significance as a visual document goes beyond the subject of the battery.

Gardner's original caption for the view identified it simply as Knap's Battery on the Antietam battlefield. In the absence of additional information, subsequent captions over the years have never attempted to elaborate upon Gardner's identification. But the photograph is rich in detail and shows an unusually expansive background—unlike many views in Gardner's Antietam series. What portion of the battlefield was depicted in this photograph?

To answer that question, it was first necessary to establish where Knap's Battery was located immediately after the battle. Once a general area was established, the specific location could then be sought through a field investigation.

II–1

II–1 modern

GROUP II: THE MILLER FARM

Knap's Battery was with the Twelfth Corps and fought on September 17 along the Smoketown Road, between the East and West Woods. At one time on September 17, a section of the battery was sent in advance to the Dunker Church to support General Greene's salient position at the West Woods. During the inactivity of September 18, the entire battery was positioned near the East Woods. On the morning of the following day, shortly after it was discovered that the Confederate army had retreated, General McClellan issued orders for the Twelfth Corps to proceed to Harpers Ferry. Knap's Battery was put in motion and left the battlefield sometime on the late morning or afternoon of September 19.

Because Gardner did not begin his work on the battlefield proper until the morning of September 19, the photograph was most likely recorded on that day and shortly before Knap's departure from the vicinity of the East and West Woods. I therefore focused the initial efforts of my field investigation in that area, attempting to match the lay of the land in the photograph with the peculiarities of the terrain as it exists today. Contemporary battlefield maps showing wood lines were essential to the success of this investigation, for vast portions of timber once composing the East, West, and North Woods are no longer standing.

The image itself provided additional evidence. Judging from the dead horse in the left foreground, the view was taken on the battlefield proper. The woods in the distant background were most likely one of the three that dominated the scenery on the northern portion of the field, where Knap's men were positioned.

Under high magnification a quality modern print made from the original glass negative revealed several features, including a distinctive tree on the left horizon, three of its branches reaching skyward like a pitchfork; a pair of parallel rail fences running, apparently along a road, behind the men and guns of the battery; and a large cornfield in the distance.

The distinctive tree looked quite similar to one I had already identified from two other photographs (II-7 and II-12) as having been located in the western portion of the North Woods. Additionally, Knap's various positions in the vicinity of the Smoketown Road made it logical that the rail fences in the photograph bordered that road. And finally, the location of the cornfield, in relation to the North Woods and the road, suggested that it was probably the famous Cornfield on the Miller farm.

On the basis of this evidence I was able to determine a potential camera position—one that was subsequently confirmed with examination of that site today. The view was taken from a point just south of the Smoketown Road, looking toward the North Woods. The North Woods are gone, but a portion of the East Woods, visible to the far right in the modern view, still stands. More importantly, the lay of the land today matches in all particulars the terrain depicted photographically. And the location is one that correlates well with a knowledge of Knap's various positions at Antietam.

What previously had been regarded as simply a photograph of a battery located somewhere on or in the vicinity of the battlefield turned out to be a unique panoramic documentation of the open fields on the Miller farm, just two days after the battle. No other photograph taken on the northern portion of the battlefield portrays as well the broad expanse of terrain between the East, West, and North Woods—an area that was the scene of approximately five hours of almost continuous slaughter on the morning of September 17, 1862. Most of the land depicted in the background of this view, including the entire area of the Cornfield, is currently in private hands.

At dawn on the day of the battle, Gen. A. R. Lawton's Georgia brigade, of Ewell's division, stretched across the open fields visible in the photograph (beyond Knap's Battery), facing both north and northeastward toward the distant Cornfield and woods. Connecting Lawton's right flank with the Smoketown Road and Gen Isaac R. Trimble's brigade of Alabama, Georgia, and North Carolina troops was Trimble's Twelfth Georgia Regiment, which faced slightly to the right, toward the East Woods. Behind the camera position stood four batteries of Confederate artillery, their guns aimed over the heads of the infantry and toward the distant woods.

Shortly prior to dawn, or at about five thirty on the morning of September 17, scattered rifle fire from opposing skirmishers commenced and grew steadily in intensity. As the sky began to lighten, revealing through the morning mist the indistinct outlines of the surrounding terrain, the lead elements of Union general Hooker's First Corps emerged from the North Woods. Confederate artillerymen opened on Hooker's men as soon as they were distinguishable while the main lines of Southern infantry waited silently in the open fields for the enemy to advance within range of their rifles. Knap's Battery did not become engaged until two hours later, when the Twelfth Corps arrived in support of the First.

JOSEPH M. KNAP

ANTIETAM

Joseph M. Knap, who appears mounted on horseback to the extreme right in Gardner's photograph and who is the subject of a more formal portrait taken later in the war, was born in Brownville, near Watertown, Jefferson County, New York, in 1837. His father was involved in manufacturing. During the 1850s, when Joseph was in his teens, the family moved to Pittsburgh, where his father and uncle jointly operated an ironworks.

As he grew older, young Knap became involved in the business and was employed as a manager when the war broke out. During the summer of 1861, he joined Company L of the Twenty-eighth Pennsylvania Infantry as a lieutenant. The following October he was promoted to captain and was placed in command of the newly formed Battery E, which was composed largely of excess soldiers from the overstrengthened Twenty-eighth, together with new recruits.

Prior to Antietam, Knap served as the battery commander in the Shenandoah Valley and fought later at the battle of Cedar Mountain on August 9, 1862. At Antietam the captain, then aged twenty-four, lost eight of his men—killed, wounded, or captured.

Captain Knap resigned from active service soon after the battle of Chancellorsville in May 1863 to accept an important position in a government cannon foundry at Pittsburgh. The next year he served briefly as a major with a militia artillery unit (at which time the formal portrait was taken), but he saw no further action during the war. He married in 1864, became a family man with three children, and lived until 1920.

Even after the resignation of its original commander, Battery E continued to call itself Knap's Battery, obviously because of great esteem for the young officer. The unit served through the end of the Civil War, saw action at Gettysburg, Chattanooga, Missionary Ridge, Resaca, New Hope Church, Kennesaw Mountain, Peach Tree Creek, and Atlanta, and accompanied Sherman on his march to the sea. The unit was formally disbanded two months after Appomattox, more than two and a half years after Antietam.

THOMAS JEFFERSON RUSHIN, photographer unknown, melainotype (tintype), ca. 1858 (Ga. Dept. of Archives and History).

EVALINE MISSOURI RUSHIN, photographer unknown, ambrotype, ca. 1861 (Ga. Dept. of Archives and History).

In 1837, the same year Joseph M. Knap was born in Brownville, New York, a boy was born to Elizabeth Rushin, aged eighteen, and her husband, Joel, twenty, of Marion County, Georgia. The Rushins named their son Thomas Jefferson, after the author of the Declaration of Independence. It was their second child, the first, George Washington Rushin, having been born two years before.

By 1850, when young Thomas was reaching the awkward age of puberty and his older brother was fifteen, there were six additional children in the family, including Evaline Missouri Rushin, then aged nine. According to census records, the father, Joel, was well-off financially and owned twenty-one slaves. The Rushins lived on a plantation at Buena Vista in western Georgia, near Columbus, not far from the Alabama state line. The area was moderately hilly and the soil fertile, with cotton production being extensive.

It was in this rural environment that the Rushin children grew to adolescence. The storm clouds of sectional strife gathered periodically in far-off Washington and at the Georgia state capitol in Milledgeville, but as the crises came and went, life continued as usual on the plantation. For the Rushin children during the 1840s and early 1850s, there were school lessons to be learned, chores to be performed, and for Thomas, George, and their younger brothers, such activities to look forward to as hunting, fishing, and swimming. Evaline and her sisters spent many hours observing and learning the domestic arts necessary to become cultured young ladies.

By 1861 several of the older children had grown to adulthood. Thomas, then aged twenty-four, and his older brother George, twenty-six, had taken off on their own to become farmers, and Evaline, twenty, had married a local boy named James Lowe. Joel Rushin, then forty-five, became active in state politics and began serving in the Georgia senate as early as 1859.

The Rushins were a secure family and maintained close ties with one another. George, Thomas, and Evaline, though grown, stayed in Marion

THOMAS JEFFERSON RUSHIN

County and probably visited their forty-four-year-old mother often, especially during periods when their father was away in Milledgeville. Joel himself communicated faithfully with his wife by mail.

During the winter of 1860–61, sectional differences accelerated. In November 1860, Lincoln was elected president of the United States, and the following month South Carolina seceded from the Union, with Georgia following in January 1861. In April 1861, after Fort Sumter was fired upon, the call to arms was universal. In Marion County, as in most others throughout the country, citizens were astir with excitement. For the Rushin family the issue was Southern independence from an unjust Federal government. Lincoln had called for troops to put down the armed rebellion, and the South responded accordingly.

Two days before Fort Sumter, Thomas Rushin's older brother George enlisted in Company A, Third Georgia Cavalry. The day after Fort Sumter surrendered, Evaline Rushin Lowe's husband, James, joined the "Buena Vista Guards," Company I of the Second Georgia Volunteer Infantry. On June 15, 1861, Thomas Rushin enlisted in the "Marion Guards," Company K, Twelfth Georgia Volunteers. Few doubted that their cause would prove triumphant within a brief time.

But as the months dragged on and the new year came and went, the newspaper columns began to fill with reports of one terrible battle after another. The casualty lists swelled beyond belief. For those who had friends and relatives at the front, the conflict that had begun a year earlier in an almost festive atmosphere of brass bands, patriotic speeches, and colorful uniforms was slowly evolving into a horrible, uncontrollable nightmare with no end in sight.

The year 1862 was filled with great anxiety for Joel and Elizabeth Rushin. Their son George was serving in the western theater under Gen. Braxton Bragg, whereas Thomas and yet a third son, John, twenty-two, were in Virginia with Evaline's husband, James. For Evaline, the emotional strain must have been overpowering. With the safety of her three brothers and husband constantly on her mind, we can well imagine the dread with which she received each letter from the front.

We can also guess the images of home and family that flooded twenty-five-year-old Sgt. Thomas Rushin's mind as he waited nervously for the sun to rise on the morning of September 17, 1862. With his comrades of the Twelfth Georgia Infantry, Rushin was positioned in an open field adjoining the

GROUP II: THE MILLER FARM

Smoketown Road, north of Sharpsburg. In front of him, not more than two hundred yards away, were the East Woods, occupied by enemy infantry the previous evening. Everyone sensed that on this day one of the greatest battles of the war would be fought and that thousands would be killed and maimed by day's end. But for now there was nothing to do but wait.

At dawn the waiting ended. Scattered skirmish fire had intensified, and soon the enemy was seen advancing in force. Southern gunners opened on the exposed Northern infantrymen with shot and shell, whereupon Union batteries returned fire from the heights beyond Antietam Creek to the east, then from positions to the north. The deadly missiles shrieked and droned overhead, exploding in midair to send pieces of shrapnel tearing into the ranks of the infantry below.

Trimble's Confederate brigade, with the Twelfth Georgia on its left, opened fire on the East Woods in response to enemy volleys erupting from the treeline. Farther to the left in the open fields, on the Miller farm, Union infantry were rapidly closing in on Lawton's Georgia brigade, and the fighting soon became general from the East to the West Woods. The rattle of infantry fire blended with the thunder of artillery to produce a maddening noise as dense clouds of sulfurous smoke accumulated in the woods and over the fields.

Through the haze, members of the Twelfth Georgia could see an enemy regiment (the 105th New York) approaching in the open, along the edge of the woods. Capt. James G. Rogers, commander of the Twelfth, called to his men to concentrate their fire on the exposed regiment, which was done with telling effect. Still the Union infantry came, and for nearly an hour the Twelfth fought stubbornly to hold its position. But their casualties were mounting and ammunition was running critically low. At about 6:45 A.M., the Twelfth Georgia, along with the remainder of Trimble's brigade, was pulled back from their line near the Smoketown Road and replaced by Gen. Harry T. Hays's Louisiana brigade, which had been moved up in support of Lawton's men.

The Twelfth Georgia, like most Confederate units, was understrength to begin with and suffered heavily during the hour it was engaged at Antietam. Between daybreak and six forty-five in the morning, sixty-two men, or roughly a third of its total strength, were killed or wounded. Among the lifeless, torn bodies left sprawled in the open field where they had fought were those of its commander, Captain Rogers, and the sergeant from Company K, Thomas Jefferson Rushin.

Rushin's body was eventually buried by enemy details after the battle. Understandably, the weary Union soldiers did not care about identifying the individual graves of Confederate dead, and today, perhaps somewhere in the Confederate cemetery at Hagerstown, Maryland, lies the body of the young man from Buena Vista, Georgia, under a headstone marked simply "unknown."

It probably took more than a week for word to reach Joel and Elizabeth Rushin that their second eldest son had been killed in action at an obscure place in Maryland called Sharpsburg. It is not difficult to picture the gloom that descended abruptly upon the rural homestead, upon Thomas's parents, his sister Evaline, and the younger children in the family as well as upon friends and neighbors.

To add to this gloom, the family learned a short while later that Thomas's older brother George had become a casualty of the war in the west and was at that time lying in critical condition at a hospital in Knoxville, Tennessee. On November 1, 1862, George Washington Rushin, at age twenty-seven, the oldest son of Joel and Elizabeth Rushin, died.

The remaining members of the family who served in the war, John Rushin and Evaline's husband, James, were both wounded at different battles, but both survived the war to begin life anew in the ruins of the devastated South.

II–2 Dead Confederate soldier, Gardner, stereo #554, probably September 19, 1862 (LC).

II–3 Confederate dead gathered for burial, Gardner, stereo #557, probably September 19, 1862 (LC).

Although it cannot be proven conclusively, it is my opinion that these Gardner photographs of Confederate dead were recorded within a hundred yards of each other, on the property of Samuel Mumma and in the field adjacent to and southeast of the Smoketown Road.

At first I made no connection between the two views. But after examining the original glass negative for the scene of the lone soldier (2), I noticed at the extreme upper edge a long row of bodies in the distance. The shadings of the

II–2

II–3

II–3 modern

uniforms in the second scene (3) seemed to match the pattern of lights and darks present in the row of bodies appearing in the background of the first, namely, from right to left, a gray form with a stark white exposed area, split into two sections, followed by darker uniforms, then lighter uniforms, then darker, and so on.

This connection appears logical when one considers Gardner's work pattern at Antietam and on other battlefields. Civil War photographers usually took their views in groups. Where one view was taken, often another and frequently several additional scenes were recorded nearby. This work pattern was directly related to the fact that the photographers had to sensitize, expose, and develop their plates on the spot. Portable darkroom wagons were essential. Each time the photographer moved to a different area, the cumbersome and fragile equipment had to be packed up and moved as well. Thus it usually did not pay to set up the darkroom equipment for just one exposure.

It is unfortunate from a historical standpoint that Gardner did not include more of the background in his view of the lone soldier. The original captions for both views are too vague to be of any value, other than the mention in one that the lone soldier was found on a "hill-side." For some unknown reason, probably ignorance, the latter scene was included with the Cedar Mountain photographs in Francis Miller's classic ten-volume *Photographic History of the Civil War* (1911).[26] Contemporary evidence, however—specifically Gardner's original catalog—makes it clear that the view was recorded at Antietam, not Cedar Mountain.

For more than a year and a half I explored the twelve square miles of battlefield at Antietam in search of a land configuration matching that in view 3. We are looking uphill toward a barren crest. The absence of distant woods eliminates most angles of view on the northern portion of the field, and the lack of distant ridges or mountains likewise eliminates most views looking eastward toward Antietam Creek. I was able to uncover only one probable camera position that matched the scene recorded in 1862.

Because the trees and bushes that traversed the scene at the time of the battle are no longer present, the intermediary ridge does not show as clearly in the modern photograph as it does in the original. A sketch of this foliage in the modern view better indicates that slope.

As I have depicted on the accompanying group map, Gardner's camera was, I believe, positioned facing southwestward, looking uphill toward one of the highest points on the Antietam battlefield. The distant trees visible to the far right in the original view probably indicate the southern edge of the West Woods.

On the morning of September 17, 1862, this field served as a staging area for successive Confederate infantry brigades, including Gen. Roswell S. Ripley's, Gen. Alfred H. Colquitt's, and Gen. Samuel Garland's. Although these units, comprising soldiers from Georgia, Alabama, and North Carolina, were rarely under direct infantry fire at this position, they were exposed to almost continuous artillery fire from Union batteries located on the far side of Antietam Creek. Judging from official Confederate reports, losses from this fire, especially in Ripley's brigade, were severe.

There are approximately twenty-five bodies in view 3. If the camera position for this view is what I believe it to have been, most of these soldiers were probably from North Carolina, Alabama, and Georgia. But the anonymity present in this long line of corpses has a numbing effect on the mind. We see groups, but we must think in terms of individuals. By focusing attention on the individual soldier in view 2, Gardner has shown us that he was acutely sensitive to the personal tragedy that surrounded the men on the battlefield. Unless the viewer reflects, however, it is easy for Gardner's message to become lost. Do we see simply a dead soldier and then pass on to the next photograph? Or do we see in this photograph someone's son or brother? Do we see the expression on a mother's face in some far-off home as she reads the first sentence of a letter she prayed would never come? Such things are as much a part of these photographs as the images before our eyes.

II–4 Ruins of the Mumma house, Gardner, stereo #574, September 19 or 20, 1862 (LC).

On the afternoon of September 15, 1862, when it appeared certain that a major battle would soon take place in the countryside adjacent to Sharpsburg, the Confederates urged farmers to leave the area for their own safety.

Samuel Mumma, the sixty-year-old owner of the property pictured in this photograph, decided to heed the advice, since the Southern forces had already established their lines close to the farm buildings and cannonading was then in progress. With little hesitation, he and his wife, Elizabeth, forty-six, and their eight children, ages eleven to twenty-six, sought the shelter of a large church four miles distant. The next evening, September 16, Mumma's two oldest sons returned to the farm to gather some clothing but found that the house had been ransacked and everything of value stolen.

When the battle began on the morning of September 17, two Confederate brigades were located in the vicinity of the Mumma farm buildings. The three right-flank regiments of Trimble's brigade were on the front line, stationed in a farm lane extending northwestward from the house to the Smoketown Road and facing the East Woods, visible in the right background of Gardner's photograph.

In reserve, two hundred yards behind Trimble, was Ripley's brigade, positioned in the open field believed to be the scene of the preceding two photographs. This brigade's left flank, bordering the Smoketown Road, was held by the Fourth Georgia Infantry. On the right flank, and directly facing the Mumma farmhouse, was the Third North Carolina Infantry.

Once the battle began and Union infantry fire from the East Woods intensified, General Ripley became concerned that the brick farmhouse and adjacent barn would be occupied by enemy sharpshooters who could fire at members of his staff and regimental officers. The general called for a squad of soldiers to burn the buildings to the ground. The task was accomplished by a half-dozen volunteers from the Third North Carolina.

The fire raged throughout the morning and sent an enormous column of black smoke high into the air. So prominent was the blaze that it was mentioned frequently in battle reports, especially those of Union general Greene's division of the Twelfth Corps, which passed by this ground at about nine o'clock the same morning.

II–4

GROUP II: THE MILLER FARM

Samuel Mumma's farm was a total loss. In addition to the destruction of his house and barn, together with several outbuildings, he lost all his crops and personal belongings. The value of his losses exceeded ten thousand dollars. The Mumma family stayed at the home of Joseph Sherrick (see view V-7) that winter and began building a new house and barn on the original site the following spring.

Samuel Mumma suffered greater financial loss from the battle than any other farmer in the area. Ironically, he was unable to secure any compensation from the Federal government, which reimbursed local residents only for damage caused by its own forces. Because the enemy had destroyed the Mumma farm, the Federal government did not consider itself responsible. Somehow, Samuel Mumma was able to start from scratch and survive.

The house and barn, rebuilt in 1863, may be seen in the modern version of Gardner's photograph. The roofless white brick springhouse, seen to the right in the 1862 view, was the only salvageable structure on the farm after the battle, and currently it still stands. Of additional interest in the 1862 view is Gardner's darkroom wagon, visible to the left beyond the fence. Today the Mumma farm is under the jurisdiction of the National Park Service.

II–4 modern

II–5 Confederate dead on the Miller farm, view looking toward the West Woods, Gardner, stereo #569, September 19, 1862 (LC).

Like many views recorded by Alexander Gardner shortly after the battle, this scene was originally identified in vague terms. In fact, Gardner's caption described it simply as "View on Battle-field of Antietam." Although the photograph was otherwise unidentified, I was able to determine the view's precise location by first examining the image itself, which revealed several features of potential significance. There is a definite mound, or swell, in the earth dominating the foreground. Protruding from this mound on the left is a distinctive, angular slab of limestone outcropping. Traversing the horizon is an extensive wooded area.

A knowledge of the Antietam battlefield as it appeared in 1862, together with a familiarity of areas known to have been covered by Gardner, indicated that the distant woods were most likely one of three that dominated the field at the time of the battle—the North Woods, West Woods, and East Woods. The two large trees seen in the distance to the right of the standing soldier and just above those seated on the mound looked strikingly similar to a pair of trees I previously had concluded from another photograph (III-7) were located in the West Woods.

My subsequent field investigation for this view thus focused on locating a rock on a mound at a point where a large body of woods, possibly the West Woods, would have appeared in the distant background in 1862.

As is supported by the modern version of this photograph, a finite camera position was located in which all these features were matched to the present terrain as well as to already identified Gardner photographs. Gardner recorded this scene from a point some fifty yards south of the original boundary of the famous Cornfield, looking southwestward toward the West Woods. The earthen mound, with its distinctive limestone outcropping, still exists in relatively unchanged form. Expected variations in soil level, though slight, have uncovered a portion of the outcropping, making it come to more of a point as it buries itself into the ground, but the presence of the rock itself, positioned on a mound of earth, is more than mere coincidence. Nowhere else on the battlefield is there such a distinctive combination of terrain features.

In the modern version of this scene there is a second outcropping on the mound several yards behind and to the right of the one in the foreground. This

II–5

II–5 modern

second outcropping is hidden in Gardner's photograph by the foliage growing in 1862 and is further obscured by the numerous loose rocks seen scattered about the top of the mound. These rocks, perhaps thrown there by David Miller, the man who farmed this land at the time of the Civil War, make the rise appear slightly higher or fuller in 1862 than it does today.

From this point and camera angle, I determined that the woods in the distance were indeed the West Woods. This fact was confirmed by the two large trees referred to earlier, for according to the camera angle represented here, the pair of trees was located at a point in the West Woods where the woods turned sharply westward from the Hagerstown Pike—precisely the same point where the two large trees appear in the independently confirmed view III-7.

The dead tree to the extreme right in view 5 and the tree on the mound are also both distinguishable, after lengthy examination, in the background of the Knap's Battery photograph (II-1), but only under extreme magnification. Even then both features are obscure, for they are partially camouflaged by other foliage.

My research on these photographs entailed the use of high-quality, eight-by-ten-inch glossy prints, often produced directly from the original negatives. The glass-plate negatives themselves are important documents and were inspected for details that did not show up on the prints. Generally speaking, however, I have refrained from referring to obscure features that are not readily visible. The relationship between views II-1 and II-5 is mentioned here only to inform the reader that supportive evidence does exist, although for the purpose of this study it was sufficient to base my identification of view 5 primarily on the rock, the mound, and the two trees in the distant woods.

Few areas on the Antietam battlefield saw as much concentrated and continuous fighting during the battle as did that portrayed in Gardner's photograph of the mound. It was here, early in the morning of September 17, that the first lines of Union infantry to emerge from the southern edge of the Cornfield came under the direct fire of Confederate infantry located in the open fields beyond.

Initially, the 105th New York Volunteers of Gen. Abram Duryea's brigade, Gen. James B. Ricketts's division of the Union First Corps, passed over the area in the immediate foreground of this view. Within a half hour, the 105th

GROUP II: THE MILLER FARM

New York was forced back by Trimble's Confederates, along with the remainder of Duryea's brigade.

Next to arrive at this point was the Thirteenth Massachusetts of Gen. George L. Hartsuff's brigade, also of Ricketts's division. Hartsuff's line soon received the brunt of a Confederate counterattack from Hays's Louisiana brigade, which, having relieved Trimble's brigade on Lawton's right flank, swept across the open ground, pushing the Union line back into the Cornfield. For a time the area in the vicinity of the mound was swarming with Confederate infantrymen of Hays's five Louisiana regiments, who were in turn forced back by a relentless Union counterattack that left dead and wounded strewn about the ground.

Judging from their uniforms, the dead soldiers seen gathered at the base of the mound in Gardner's photograph are all Confederates. The live Union soldiers gazing at the bodies were probably asked to pose by Gardner. Initially, bodies of both Confederate and Union soldiers were buried on the battlefield where they fell, in either individual or mass graves. Generally, the army in possession of the field paid greater attention to identifying its own dead. Thus, most Confederate soldiers who fell at Antietam were buried in mass graves without any individual identification. For example, the gravemarker would read, "80 rebels buried here." Many families traveled to the battlefield hoping to reclaim the identifiable bodies of loved ones, which were then reburied in hometown cemeteries. After the war, the remaining Union dead were gathered and reinterred in the Antietam National Cemetery. Confederate dead were eventually reburied in the Rose Hill Cemetery in Hagerstown.

Because many Southern units suffered heavy casualties near the earthen mound, it is impossible to determine the specific unit or units to which the men in this photograph belonged. Still, the possibility clearly exists that some of them were members of Hays's Louisiana brigade, and perhaps one or more of them had been acquainted with the subject of the following biographical sketch.

THOMAS TAYLOR, photographer unknown, ambrotype, 1861 (Cook coll., Valentine Museum).

Thomas Taylor was twenty years old in 1861, when he enlisted in the Phoenix Guard, Company K, Eighth Louisiana Infantry. His army papers described him as single, a farmer, five feet nine inches tall, with light complexion and hair and blue eyes.

There are only scattered bits of information concerning his childhood and family. He was born in Assumption Parish, Louisiana, apparently sometime in 1841. Because Assumption was still his residence at the time of his enlistment, it can be presumed that he grew up there as well.

His father, Miles Taylor, was a practicing attorney with an office in New Orleans, fifty miles east of Assumption. How much time Miles Taylor spent with his family in the country is not known, but we can guess that he was frequently away on business. The New Orleans directory for 1850 listed him with the law firm of Janin and Taylor, 17 Royal Street. In 1858 he was listed by himself with an office at 6 Exchange Place.

Since Thomas gave his occupation as a farmer, either he had left home by 1861 and was employed by a local farmer or he was living and working at the family homestead in Assumption. Papers in Thomas's military file show that he had at least one sister and a younger brother, but I was unable to locate the Taylor family in the Louisiana census records and know nothing of Thomas's mother or the names of other children.

I have recently learned that Thomas Taylor's father, Miles Taylor, was elected in 1854 to serve in the U.S. Congress as a Representative from Louisiana. He served in Washington from March 4, 1855, until February 5, 1861, on which date he delivered a speech informing the House of Representatives that Louisiana had seceded from the Union and that he was returning to his home to cast his lot with his state.

Although Miles Taylor would have spent most of his time in Washington between 1855 and 1861, he did not consider himself a resident of that city and was not listed in the Washington census records for 1860. Whether his family accompanied him to Washington when he was there or remained in Louisiana is not known. But regardless of Miles Taylor's various professional commit-

THOMAS TAYLOR

ments on the eve of the war, it appears fairly certain that his son, Thomas, spent most if not all of his formative years in the parish where he was born.

Assumption Parish, drained by Bayou Lafourche, consisted of land that was low, marshy, and subject to flooding. But the soil was rich and well suited for agriculture. Sugar and cotton plantations abounded and, at the time of the war, slaves composed more than half the parish's total population. Assumption's northern boundary was located only two and a half miles from the Mississippi River.

As a young boy growing up in Assumption during the 1840s and 1850s, Thomas undoubtedly spent many hours hunting game and exploring the swamps near his home. As one who called himself a farmer at age twenty, he probably began his education in raising crops and livestock when he was quite a bit younger.

How frequently Thomas Taylor accompanied his father to New Orleans is not known, but it seems likely that among his childhood memories would have been scenes of riverboats docked at various levees, of the distinctive railings on the buildings in New Orleans, the crowds, and the hustle and bustle of a large city going about its business. There would also have been memories of his father's office, the desks cluttered with paperwork and shelves packed with law books.

When the war came, Thomas saw many of his close friends and others throughout the state rushing to join units then being formed for the defense of the South. Sometime during the two months following the arrival of the news that Sumter had been shelled, he made the decision to enlist as well. On June 19, 1861, he left his home in Assumption and traveled to nearby Donaldsonville, where he joined the "Phoenix Guard." From there he was shipped farther north to Camp Moore, a large training area at Tangipahoa, Louisiana. Here he received his first taste of army life.

The photographic portrait of Thomas Taylor was taken shortly after his enlistment and reflects his state of mind at that time. There is no hesitation or fear in his countenance—only determination and pride. One wonders exactly what was going through his mind at the moment long ago when this portrait was taken. Perhaps he was thinking of how impressed his father, family, and friends would be when they saw him in uniform. (Most soldiers had portraits such as this taken in hometown studios before leaving for the front. Photographers were also known to frequent large training areas to record similar studies.)

By the end of 1861, Taylor had been promoted to the rank of sergeant. He served with his unit throughout the spring and summer campaigns of 1862. Three weeks prior to Antietam, he was stricken by an acute case of diarrhea, but he recovered enough to accompany the regiment into Maryland.

At sunrise on the morning of September 17, Taylor was in the ranks of the Eighth Louisiana when General Hays was ordered to move the brigade from its reserve position at the West Woods to the open field on the Miller farm, in support of Lawton's brigade, located just north of the Smoketown Road. Here the brigade would await orders to advance toward the distant Cornfield. The fighting had already commenced.

Although the waiting may have seemed an eternity to the members of the Eighth Louisiana, it did not last long. At approximately 6:45 A.M. the regiment, along with the brigade, began its advance. Hays's men covered the ground from the edge of the East Woods to a point opposite the center of the Cornfield. Lawton's brigade extended their line toward the Hagerstown Pike on the left. As the two brigades approached the Cornfield, they could see, dimly visible through the smoke, an equally long line of enemy infantry straight ahead.

Enemy rifle fire intensified. The crack of individual weapons was soon lost in the deafening roar, but one could perceive the effect as soldiers to the immediate right and left dropped with increasing rapidity.

The slaughter was appalling as Hays's brigade finally reached the Cornfield, forcing the enemy to retire. In the process, the brigade passed the mound of earth with the tree on top. It is doubtful that many noticed the mound that morning, and for those who did, including perhaps Thomas Taylor, the memory could have been no more than a fleeting one. Some may have noticed it because it provided cover, others because it temporarily broke up their line. But there were more important things on the minds of Hays's Louisianans as the men loaded and fired their rifles as fast as they could, with the enemy only yards away.

Union forces fell back into and beyond the Cornfield, then fresh Northern troops made a devastating counterattack. Ammunition was running low and casualties had been staggering, but the Louisianans held on until they could hold no longer. The order was passed through the ranks for Hays's brigade and the Eighth Louisiana to fall back. Other Confederate brigades were waiting to go in, and it was urgent to clear the field of fire as fast as possible.

Thus ended the brief participation of Hays's Louisiana brigade at Antietam. It had been engaged in direct contact with enemy infantry for all of fifteen or twenty minutes, but it lost during that period more than one-half its men, either killed or wounded.

For Thomas Taylor those minutes in the open ground just south of the Cornfield signaled the beginning of a painful ordeal that would not end with the battle. He was among the casualties of the Eighth Louisiana left behind out of necessity when the brigade fell back. He most likely lay where his unit suffered its greatest casualties, somewhere in the vicinity of the earthen mound. His leg was bleeding from an ugly wound at the knee joint.

Thousands of wounded men who fell between the lines at Antietam would not receive help until the next day. The intervening hours, while the men lay in the heat of the sun, were filled with physical and mental torture. There was the excruciating pain of wounds to endure, a continuous pain that intensified as the hours passed. Then there was the maddening, unquenchable thirst that invariably accompanies any great shock to the body. Cries for help and pleas for water went unheeded. There were too many wounded. Few stretcher-bearers dared to venture into the no-man's-land between the lines. Completely helpless, the wounded were also in great danger of being hit again. Many were.

Sometime after the battle, Thomas Taylor was picked up by enemy stretcher-bearers and brought to a field hospital in the rear. He was listed as dangerously wounded. On September 28, 1862, he was transported as a prisoner to a hospital in Frederick, Maryland, and from there was later transferred to Saratoga, New York. Eventually, eight months later, he was shipped to City Point, Virginia, where on May 23, 1863, he was exchanged and admitted to a Confederate hospital in Petersburg, Virginia. At Petersburg, Taylor was examined and given a sixty-day furlough. But he was crippled and would never again be able to rejoin his unit.

New Orleans and the adjacent countryside were by then under Union control, and Thomas Taylor feared returning home. He tried to secure a position with the Confederate Quartermaster Department in Montgomery, Alabama. Included in his military file is a letter of reference written on September 22, 1863—more than a year after Antietam—describing the young man's situation in these terms: "He is the son of Miles Taylor of Louisiana and his full name is Thomas Taylor. He is now, and I expect will be for some time to come on crutches and has been staying with me for the last two months. His father is a prisoner I suppose in New Orleans. His younger brother is in the Army west of the Mississippi, and he has no idea where his sister is."[27]

Another letter in the file, written on October 14, 1863, mentions that Taylor "is going on crutches and from present appearances will not be able to dispense with them for a long time to come."[28]

The last paper in his file bears the dateline Montgomery, Alabama, May 15, 1865. It was Taylor's oath of allegiance to the United States of America. At this point all trace of Thomas Taylor's story comes to an end. Many decades after the war, a woman named Mary May of New Orleans donated some of Taylor's personal effects to the Museum of the Confederacy in Richmond, Virginia, where they are preserved today. Included is the jacket he is believed to have worn at Antietam.

II–6 Dead horse of a Confederate colonel, near the East Woods, Gardner, stereo #558, on or about September 20, 1862 (LC).

This unusual and previously unpublished Antietam photograph was originally captioned "Dead: Horse of Confederate Colonel; both killed at Battle of Antietam." Had Gardner known the name of the colonel and indicated that name in the caption, the task of pinpointing the scene's location would have been accomplished with little effort. But in the absence of the colonel's name, the task required considerably more research.

Fortunately, Gardner was not the only individual to take notice of this horse. Its serene, lifelike pose startled many who, until close inspection, could not believe that the horse was actually dead. Among those who mentioned the horse in their writings were Gen. Alpheus S. Williams of the Union Twelfth Corps, who observed it on September 19 while riding over the area where his men had fought two days before; and Dr. Oliver Wendell Holmes, who saw it on September 21 while searching for his son. Their descriptions are detailed enough to leave no doubt that the horse they saw was the one in the photograph. In fact, Holmes would later see Gardner's photograph and mention that it was the same horse.[29]

From references to other sights visited by the two men, it is clear they saw the horse on the field of the morning's battle, indicating that the trees dominating the background of the photograph were most likely a part of the East, West, or North Woods. The image also shows that the woods are on a higher level at this point than the field in which the camera was placed. Furthermore, the woods increase in density toward the left and become exceedingly sparse to the right, indicating that whatever woods it was, it was photographed near one of its corners. Such clues served to reduce the number of potential camera positions significantly.

My subsequent field investigation was also guided by the knowledge that a Confederate colonel had been killed at the location. Fifteen Southern colonels fell at Antietam, including seven lieutenant colonels, so through a process of elimination I was able to determine where all units that lost their colonels fought. Conversely, areas occupied by various Confederate units whose colonels survived the battle unscathed were not considered likely possibilities.

All this information eventually led me to the one point where I believe the photograph must have been taken. This point, located in Miller's open field

II–6

II–6 modern

north of the Smoketown Road, matched all criteria perfectly, and no other site on the battlefield even came close. As indicated on the map, Gardner's camera would have been facing eastward, looking toward the East Woods. Not only is this an area in which Gardner is known to have worked, but it is also an area in which a number of Confederate colonels fell.

Among those regiments that lost colonels was the Sixth Louisiana of Hays's brigade. Sometime during either the advance toward or retreat from the Cornfield, the commander of the Sixth, Col. Henry B. Strong, was killed. His body was later recovered by his men, probably during a period of truce that occurred the next day, September 18, and was buried in a hollow just south of the nearby Dunker Church. Although it is basically speculation that the horse photographed by Gardner belonged to Colonel Strong, there exists some circumstantial evidence to support this contention.

It had been passed by word of mouth that the horse belonged to a Confederate colonel who had been killed. Dr. Holmes himself stated that the horse was "said to have belonged to a Rebel colonel, who was killed near the same place." (None of the accounts mention where the colonel was buried.) Whoever the colonel was, his death was common knowledge to the Union forces who had fought in this area.

I subsequently sought to uncover, from accounts written by Union soldiers who fought near the Cornfield and East Woods, as many references as I could that indicated an awareness on the part of Union soldiers that an enemy colonel or colonels had fallen.

The references I found made mention of only one individual. The most detailed account, written by a member of the 125th Pennsylvania Volunteers, stated that one of the gloves of a dead Confederate colonel, H. B. Strong of the Sixth Louisiana, was picked up "near the edge of the east woods, south of the cornfield" and waved triumphantly in the air by the adjutant of the regiment.[30] Thus, there exists at least the possibility that the horse, believed to have been photographed in the same area, also belonged to Strong.

Gardner's photograph of the horse may have been recorded anytime between September 19 and 21. And yet, because no human dead are present in the scene, it can be assumed that burial operations had already made significant headway by the time this photograph was recorded. Gardner's last views in the vicinity of the East Woods (see views VI-5 and VI-6) were taken on the morning of September 21, shortly before he moved southward to Burnside Bridge. His whereabouts on September 20 cannot be accounted for, but from the large number of scenes he recorded on the northern portion of the Antietam battlefield, it seems logical that he was working in the northern areas on that day. I have therefore dated the photograph of the dead horse as having been taken on or about September 20, 1862.

Currently, all the land depicted in this scene is privately owned. Most of the East Woods are long since gone, and telephone poles in the right background of the modern version mark the location of the Smoketown Road.

ANTIETAM

II–7 through 11

Gardner recorded in the following five photographs the same group of bodies. It took roughly ten minutes for Civil War photographers to sensitize, expose, and develop each negative. Adding to that the time spent studying and selecting the best camera positions, we can estimate that Gardner probably expended upward of an hour producing this series of five views. Indeed, more plates were exposed on this specific group of dead soldiers than on any other at Antietam, suggesting that these dead were among the first, if not *the* first dead photographed by Gardner at Antietam.

The amount of time spent with this one group is perhaps indicative of Gardner's fascination and even excitement at being confronted for the first time in his career with the opportunity of recording human wreckage on a freshly scarred battlefield.

In any case, there is no doubt that these scenes, otherwise undated, were taken during Gardner's first day on the battlefield proper, September 19, 1862.

II–7 Confederate dead along the Hagerstown Pike, Gardner, stereo #560, September 19, 1862 (LC).

Of the five scenes in this series, the first presented here was the most important in establishing the scene's location as well as the unit identity of most of the dead portrayed.

The original caption for this view, "View in the Field, on the west side of Hagerstown road, after the Battle of Antietam," provided description enough, in conjunction with a knowledge of where the woods and fields were located along the pike in 1862, to ascertain Gardner's most likely camera position. That position was subsequently confirmed by a modern field investigation.

This view was taken from a point along the Hagerstown Pike, five hundred yards north of the Dunker Church. It was recorded along the western side of the pike, looking toward the North Woods which traverse the horizon, becoming less distinct to the right because of imperfections in the original negative. (Unfortunately, an opaque substance was at one time applied to the skyline on the original negative, apparently to increase the contrast between the woods and the sky. In the process, portions of the tree line were obliterated.) The dirt lane seen to the left is not the Hagerstown Pike but one of Miller's farm lanes.

II–7

II–7 modern

The Hagerstown Pike is located to the immediate right of the post-and-rail fence, beyond which lies a parallel fence bordering the eastern side of the pike.

With the possible exception of the lone body seen lying in the field to the far left, all the dead photographed in this group were Confederates, a fact supported by Gardner's original captions as well as by an examination of the soldiers' uniforms. The main group of dead, photographed as they fell, stretches along the length of the rail fence, indicating that their line of battle at the time they were killed ran parallel to the fence in a north–south direction.

The land adjacent to the Hagerstown Pike in this area was the scene of much bitter fighting from the opening of the battle through the attack and repulse of Sedgwick's division of the Union Second Corps later in the morning. But during the entire battle only one Confederate brigade actually formed its line behind the rail fence at this specific site and sustained heavy casualties while positioned in this particular north–south configuration. That unit was Gen. William E. Starke's Louisiana brigade, comprising the First, Second, Ninth, Tenth, and Fifteenth regiments of Louisiana Infantry, together with the attached First Louisiana Battalion.

Even so, it is not certain that all the dead in these five photographs were Starke's men, especially when one considers that other Confederate units suffered casualties while passing over this ground at different times during the morning of September 17. But I feel safe in stating, given the relationship between the location of the bodies and the rail fence, together with additional information provided in the next caption, that most were members of Starke's Louisiana brigade, killed during the period when that brigade was locked in a deadly firefight with the Sixth Wisconsin Volunteers of Gen. John Gibbon's brigade, Gen. Abner Doubleday's division of the First Corps, located at the time only fifty yards away on the eastern side of the pike.

Gibbon's men were among the first Union soldiers to be thrown into the battle on the morning of September 17. They began their advance along the Hagerstown Pike shortly after dawn and encountered the first line of Confederate infantry in the fields adjoining the pike. This Confederate line, facing northward, extended from the fence along the pike, westward across the field in the foreground of view 7. It was composed of two brigades of "Stonewall" Jackson's old division (commanded by Gen. John R. Jones), supported less than 250 yards to the rear by the remaining two brigades of the division, Starke's and Gen. W. B. Taliaferro's.

The advanced Confederate brigades held their position for nearly forty-five minutes but were forced to fall back upon the approach of Union reinforcements coming to the aid of Gibbon. By this time, the main thrust of the Union pressure was being applied from the eastern side of the pike.

Starke's and Taliaferro's brigades, waiting in reserve at the northern edge of the West Woods (where the woods doglegged westward from the pike) were ordered forward as soon as retiring friendly units had passed safely to the rear and into the West Woods. When Starke's men, with Taliaferro's brigade on their right, emerged from the woods at approximately 6:45 A.M., they found that the heaviest concentration of enemy fire was coming from their right. To confront the enemy head-on, they wheeled to the right and lined up behind the rail fence on the pike's western border.

The modern version of this view shows that over the past century a number of changes have occurred in this area, including the destruction of the North Woods, along with the removal of the parallel rail fences along the pike. Although this area saw some of the heaviest fighting on the bloodiest single day in American history, all the land seen in the modern version, except for thin strips on which monuments are located, is today privately owned.

II–8

II–8 Dead of Starke's Louisiana brigade along the Hagerstown Pike, Gardner, stereo #567 (LC).

As mentioned in the discussion on the preceding view, most of the Confederate dead photographed by Gardner at this point along the western edge of the Hagerstown Pike were probably members of Starke's Louisiana brigade. I was therefore not surprised when I uncovered the original Gardner caption for this scene, "View on Battle-field: Group of Louisiana Regiment, as they fell, at Battle of Antietam. The contest at this point had been very severe."

There were only two brigades of Louisiana infantry at the battle of Antietam, Hays's and Starke's. Hays's brigade, including Sgt. Thomas Taylor's regiment, the Eighth, fought and suffered all its casualties in the fields adjoining the edge of the East Woods. None of Hays's men fell along the Hagerstown Pike. Starke's brigade not only fought along the pike but also suffered most of its casualties in the area depicted by this and the other four photographs in the group. Thus, it can be only Starke's men to whom Gardner's caption referred.

The dead in this view, particularly the man with his arm in the air and the figure with the raised knee to his immediate left, are both clearly distinguishable under magnification in the background of view 7. Both bodies lie next to the section of fence where the top rail is missing and the second rail is resting partially on the ground (twelve rail sections from the right in view II-7).

Since view 8 was the only one of the five photographs in this group to be identified by a state designation in Gardner's captions, there must have been something in this specific scene that alerted Gardner to the fact that the men were from Louisiana. Close inspection of view 8 reveals that the dead soldier with his arm in the air is wearing a knapsack. It was not an uncommon practice during the Civil War for soldiers to stencil their regimental designations on their knapsacks, and it seems most likely that Gardner inspected these bodies before or after photographing them and came across the identification of this man's unit on his knapsack.

View 8, as was the case in most of the following companion scenes, was taken looking eastward, directly toward the Hagerstown Pike. Visible across the pike in this photograph is a civilian carriage probably belonging to one of the tourists in the throngs who flocked to the battlefield as soon as it was safe enough to witness the site of the fighting. Many relics were picked up as souvenirs by these early curiosity seekers, a number of these souvenirs, including canteens, bullets, and artillery shells, being today scattered around the country in public and private collections.

The turnpike from Sharpsburg to Hagerstown, covering a distance of some thirteen miles, was constructed about the year 1856, only six years prior to the battle of Antietam. It is therefore quite probable that the rail fencing erected along the pike, visible in all five of Gardner's photographs, was constructed at about the same time. This fencing, mentioned in numerous accounts of the battle, stood six rails high (the bottom rail is often obscured by foliage) and was of such sturdy construction that it was not easily dismantled. The top rail was said to have stood five feet off the ground.

For the most part, rail fences on the Antietam battlefield were constructed by farmers who frequently laid one rail on top of another in a zigzag fashion. Such stretches, wherever they proved to be obstacles to lines of infantry, were torn apart easily by skirmishers. But the formidable fencing at the Hagerstown Pike survived the battle intact, aside from a few scattered sections. Even at the time of Sedgwick's advance against the West Woods, after more than three previous hours of fighting along the pike, Union soldiers reported that their men were forced to climb over the fence, whereas their officers on horseback sought scattered breaks through which their horses could pass.[31]

Located directly across the Hagerstown Pike during the battle, where the carriage stands in this photograph, stood the Union regiment that caused many of the casualties in Starke's brigade, the Sixth Wisconsin. The brigade to which this unit belonged, Gibbon's, was composed entirely of Midwestern regiments and soon came to be known in both armies as the Iron Brigade. During its encounter with Starke's Louisiana brigade along the pike, the Sixth Wisconsin was accompanied on its right flank by the Second United States Sharpshooters of Col. Walter Phelps's brigade.

No modern versions have been included for view 8 and two of the additional companion scenes recorded by Gardner along the Hagerstown Pike in 1862, as the fence rails are long since gone and postbattle farm buildings on the opposite side of the pike currently obstruct the entire field of vision looking eastward from this site.

II-9 Confederate dead along the Hagerstown Pike, Gardner, stereo #559, September 19, 1862 (LC).

II-10 Confederate dead along the Hagerstown Pike, Gardner, stereo #566, September 19, 1862 (LC).

II-11 Confederate dead along the Hagerstown Pike, Gardner, stereo #556, September 19, 1862 (McGuire).

Although the rail fence behind which Starke's men fought provided an effective barrier against any potential enemy charge, the rails themselves afforded little protection from the devastating Union rifle fire, as bullets tore into the rails and through the gaps between rails. The Union troops suffered heavy casualties as well, but they soon received the direct support of Capt. Joseph Campbell's Battery B, Fourth United States Artillery, then located farther up the pike in the direction of the Miller farm buildings.

Starke's Confederates, on the left of the line along the pike, now found themselves in a critical position, for in their haste to change direction from north to east they had exposed their left flank. The Union gunners of Battery B wasted little time taking advantage of the situation. The resulting artillery fire, consisting of grape and canister, enfiladed the Confederate line while Union infantry across the pike continued to hold their own.

Casualties mounted. (The Louisiana brigade commander, Gen. William E. Starke, was himself fatally wounded early in the fighting.) After roughly fifteen minutes at the rail fence, the Louisiana brigade was forced to relinquish its position, and along with Taliaferro's men the brigade retired to the protection of the West Woods.

It was during those fifteen minutes between 6:45 and 7:00 A.M. on the morning of September 17, 1862, that most of the dead in Gardner's group of five photographs fell. Two of the three views shown here, 9 and 10, were taken looking toward the East Woods, visible in the distance and just under the top rail in view 9. The dead men in the latter photograph may also be seen in view II-7, immediately beyond the three bodies in the foreground. Likewise, the bodies in view 10 are distinguishable in view II-7 as well, but they are located farther in the background.

View 11 is the only one of the group that cannot be found in view II-7. Yet it was taken at the same place, for the fence appears to be an extension of the

II—9

II–10

II–11

II–11 modern

fencing in the other scenes. Additionally, Gardner's original caption for view 11 was entitled "Confederate Soldiers, as they fell inside the fence, on the Hagerstown road, at the Battle of Antietam," clearly linking it with the other four scenes.

In the extreme right-hand portion of this photograph the fence along the far side of the pike dips abruptly as if beginning a descent. After studying the terrain in this area today, it is my determination that view 11 was recorded only several feet from the camera position for view II-7, but looking very nearly in the opposite direction or, more precisely, due southeast as compared with the northward direction of view II-7.

Depicted in these five photographs are clusters of bloated, decomposing corpses only two days after they had been killed. Who were these men? What were their names? How old were they? Where were they from? Were they married, or single? The questions are legion. Although it would be impossible in this instance to determine the personal identity of any individual body, I nevertheless had access to the complete Antietam casualty list for at least one of the regiments of Starke's brigade, the Tenth Louisiana. The chances are great that many of the dead on that list are bodies in Gardner's five photographs.[32]

The Tenth Louisiana suffered heavily at the rail fence on the morning of September 17. According to the list of names, twenty-two members of that regiment were killed at Antietam. The ages of those twenty-two ranged from Pvt. Peter Collins of Company D, from Saint Landry Parish, a laborer in civilian life, who was twenty at the time of the battle, to Sgt. John Thompson of Company H, from New Orleans, formerly a sailor, who was forty-four. Sergeant Thompson was the only one on the list of killed who was married.

Louisiana was a melting pot at the time of the Civil War, and units from that state typically contained a high percentage of men born in foreign countries. More than half the members of the Tenth who were killed at Antietam, such as the following, were born outside the United States: Pvt. David Holmes, aged twenty-seven, of Company A, a painter, born in Ireland; Sgt. Joseph Joyce, thirty-three, Company D, a shoemaker, born in England; Pvt. Henry Friday, twenty-nine, Company D, a baker, born in Germany; Pvt. Juan Tacon, twenty-nine, Company G, a laborer, born in Mexico; Sgt. Alexander Feuga, twenty-one, Company I, a cook, born in France, and Pvt. Christopho Salomicho, forty-one,

137

Company I, a sailor, born in Greece. Many of these men were living and working in New Orleans at the time of the war's outbreak.

Despite the variety of occupations reflected in this list of names, roughly half the members of the Tenth Louisiana killed at Antietam were either farmers or laborers, including the majority of those who were born in Louisiana. Among the latter were Cpl. John Sloan, twenty-seven, of Company E and Pvt. J. H. Jackson, thirty-five, of Company K, both farmers from rural Saint Landry Parish, located some thirty-five miles west of Baton Rouge. Another native-born soldier was Cpl. Joseph Augé, twenty-four, of Company K, a farmer from Lake Charles, located in the prairie country of southwestern Louisiana, thirty miles from the Texas state line.

The personal tragedy surrounding the death of each of these men was of little concern to the Union soldiers who buried them in mass graves sometime within forty-eight hours after Gardner left this stretch of the Hagerstown Pike. And yet each of these mangled, bloated corpses, stiffened by rigor mortis in a variety of often grotesque positions, represents the termination of roughly twenty to forty years of human experience. For Christopho Salomicho this experience began in far-off Greece during the 1820s. For John Sloan it began on a small Louisiana farm during the year 1835. These men all shared their one last experience along a turnpike fence at a place few, if any, had ever heard of before September 1862.

JOHN T. GAY, photographer unknown, probably an ambrotype, ca. 1860 (Thomas).

After driving back the two Confederate brigades of Starke and Taliaferro, Gibbon's troops, accompanied by Phelps's brigade, were in turn forced from the fields east of the Hagerstown Pike by a Southern counterattack from the direction of the West Woods. The Confederate troops involved in this attack were members of Gen. John B. Hood's division, which swept northeastward into the Cornfield and East Woods.

Gibbon's men retired westward across the Hagerstown Pike, whereas Phelps's brigade fell back toward the buildings on the Miller farm. In the meantime, fresh troops of the Union First Corps, elements of Gen. George G. Meade's division of Pennsylvania Reserves, were thrown into the Cornfield in an effort to stop Hood, whose passage north of and beyond that field was subsequently blocked.

By the time Hood's men were forced to retire, Gen. Roswell S. Ripley's Confederate brigade of Georgia and North Carolina troops was ready to take Hood's place in defending the open corridor between the East and West Woods. Positioned on the left flank of Ripley's brigade was the Fourth Georgia Infantry, including among its members that morning a twenty-nine-year-old soldier named John T. Gay of Company B.

Little is known of Gay's life before the war. He was born in Georgia during or about 1833, and in 1860 he was one of five clerks employed by J. A. Reide, a La Grange, Georgia, merchant. The 1860 census for La Grange lists Gay by his nickname "Jack" rather than by the formal name, John T., which appears in all military records.

Judging from his profession, John Gay probably received an adequate education in his youth. Whether he was born and raised in the village of La Grange, Troup County, Georgia, is not known, but since he was the only person named Gay residing in La Grange—in fact, in all of Troup County in 1860—it is likely that his closest relatives were then living in another part of the state, perhaps in an adjoining county.

Located in western central Georgia and bordering Alabama, Troup County consisted primarily of rolling farm country with rich soil that was ideal for growing cotton, corn, and pines. La Grange was a small village at the time of the war, with a population of fewer than a thousand. As the seat of rural Troup

JOHN T. GAY

GROUP II: THE MILLER FARM

County, however, it was the focal point of most local activities and boasted a courthouse, a jail, two academies, a railroad station, several stores, and a number of stately homes located along broad, tree-lined streets. A weekly newspaper, the *Citizens' Reporter,* informed village inhabitants, as well as those living on nearby farms and plantations, of local and national events.

It was not long after the first news of Fort Sumter reached La Grange that John Gay, at age twenty-eight, decided to volunteer his services to the state of Georgia. On April 26, 1861, Gay, probably accompanied by a number of enthusiastic friends, walked into the Troup County courthouse and enlisted as a private in the "La Grange Light Guards," soon to become Company B, Fourth Georgia Volunteer Infantry.

During the year that followed, Private Gay would learn that army life was not the glamorous adventure he had probably envisioned in April 1861. He would spend many long hours marching and drilling, performing boring work details, digging latrines, waiting for the battles that never seemed to materialize. There was guard duty at all hours of the night and day in both good weather and bad.

The hospital records of the Fourth Georgia indicate that Gay was highly susceptible to sickness, especially during the winter of 1861–62. He suffered on different occasions from chills and fever, gastritis, and tonsillitis.

But by the time of the Maryland campaign Gay was a combat veteran. On June 27, 1862, in the midst of the Seven Days' Battles, he was promoted to third lieutenant, a rank distinctive to the Confederate army, and thus served as a junior officer of Company B at Antietam.

Ripley's brigade spent most of the first two hours of fighting on the morning of September 17 in reserve on the Mumma farm. At approximately 7:30 A.M., Hood's two brigades were forced to retire toward the West Woods (one of Hood's regiments, the First Texas, having sustained 82.3 percent casualties—the greatest percentage loss incurred by any unit from either side during the entire war). Ripley's line was ordered forward.

As the four regiments of Ripley's brigade advanced, they could see through the smoke the strong line of enemy infantry in the Cornfield to their front. Then, unexpectedly, a second line of enemy infantry (Gen. Marsena R. Patrick's brigade of the First Corps) appeared as if out of nowhere on the left, from across the Hagerstown Pike, heading directly for Ripley's exposed left-flank unit, the Fourth Georgia. The situation was desperate, for at that same time the first elements of the Union Twelfth Corps were arriving on the field to aid the First

Corps. It was imperative that the four Confederate regiments hold on for as long as possible.

For the members of the Fourth Georgia on the firing line during the period that followed, the crescendo of small arms and artillery fire was deafening. The men's eyes could perceive only vague shadows of the enemy through the thickening white smoke. Soldiers were falling on all sides; sometimes their mouths were seen to open, indicating a scream that could not always be heard. Fear for one's own safety—thoughts that had dominated the mind while waiting to go in—had disappeared. Almost mechanically, weapons were loaded, fired, loaded, and fired.

Gay stood on the line with his men. Then suddenly a powerful blow to the body. No pain at first, but involuntarily he fell sprawling to the ground. Within moments his entire system was in shock.

Thus it was that John Gay received his first wound during the war. Exactly where on the field he fell is not known, but it was undoubtedly at an advanced position on the Miller farm, for his torn, bleeding body was eventually recovered by Union stretcher-bearers. As did many wounded soldiers at Antietam, Gay quite probably found himself stranded between the lines for twenty-four hours or more before help was able to reach him. He had been hit in the chest, causing a potentially critical wound accompanied by excruciating pain once the shock wore off.

After receiving initial treatment at a crowded Union field hospital, Gay, on September 28, began the ordeal of being transferred from one hospital to another. First he was shipped to U.S. General Hospital No. 4 at Frederick, Maryland, then, on October 2, was transferred to another hospital at Chester, Pennsylvania. From there he was moved to Philadelphia and eventually was exchanged, in December 1862. (Prior to 1864, the exchange of prisoners was a common practice). On December 19 Gay was admitted to a Confederate general hospital in Petersburg, Virginia. Despite all this painful movement, his condition steadily improved. Finally, on the day before Christmas, 1862, he was given a furlough of forty days and allowed to return to La Grange, Georgia, to complete his recuperation.

Unlike countless others who were casualties at Antietam, John Gay recovered enough from his wound to rejoin his unit, in Virginia. His name had been mentioned favorably in Gen. D. H. Hill's official report of the battle, and on January 6, 1863, he was promoted to the rank of first lieutenant.

GROUP II: THE MILLER FARM

On July 12, 1864, nearly a year and ten months after Antietam, Gay received a second wound, at Fort Stevens, outside Washington, D.C., and was treated at a hospital in Richmond. After another furlough home, he again rejoined the Fourth Georgia and served with his unit until the battle of Fort Stedman, Petersburg, Virginia, on March 25, 1865, where he received still a third wound, this time in the leg. Two weeks later, while Gay was being treated at a hospital in Richmond, Lee surrendered at Appomattox.

For all practical purposes, the war had ended, and thousands could now return to their homes and families in both North and South, including those few survivors of the original La Grange Light Guards—the men who had enlisted with such enthusiasm four years earlier.

For John Gay, however, the struggle continued. Doctors tried to save his leg by performing a resection, but his body had lost its resilience. Complications developed and on April 28, 1865, John Gay's fight for life came to an end. He died nineteen days after Appomattox.

ANTIETAM

II–12 Union burial detail on the Miller farm, Gardner, stereo #561, September 19, 1862 (LC).

As was the case with a number of Gardner's Antietam photographs, the precise location of this scene has remained unknown for more than a century.

Like most of the Antietam scenes, this view was made on a stereo negative. Such negatives produced a double image through two separate lenses, the right lens invariably showing a little more to the right than the left lens and vice versa. When double prints were made from the negative and mounted on standard-sized stereo cards, space limitations as a rule necessitated that the photographer crop the edges of both prints. This cropping also extended to the production of album cards. Thus, only when both halves of the original stereo negative still exist are we able to study the entire field of vision captured by the camera.

Fortunately, in many cases both halves of the original stereo negatives recorded at Antietam and on other Civil War battlefields have survived. But in an equal number of instances only one half has remained and, regrettably, hundreds and perhaps thousands of these fragile plates, recorded during the war years by scores of cameramen, have not survived the ravages of time. In such instances the contemporary prints made from original negatives, though usually cropped, are all that remain available for study today.

The Antietam photograph presented here has been published in only a handful of prior works, and the print used was generally made from the left half of the original stereo negative, showing, again, more to the left but less to the right. Significantly, it was the right-hand edge that held the key to the precise location of this otherwise nondescript scene.

The presence of a rather large burial detail in the foreground, together with the group of bodies, alerted me to the fact that wherever this scene was, it was located on the battlefield proper and not in a rear area. Furthermore, my experience indicated that it was probably recorded in or near an area where Gardner is known to have taken other scenes.

But only upon inspection of the right half of the original negative, which is today preserved by the Library of Congress, did I notice something in this view that I had never seen before—a barn along the right-hand edge.

There were only a few barns on the battlefield proper in 1862. My research consisted of narrowing the site possibilities, based on the lay of the land at

II–12

II–12 modern

Antietam in conjunction with the barn inadvertently captured by the right-hand lens of Gardner's camera. I was also aided by another clue in the photograph that pointed to Gardner's most likely camera position. In the distant tree line just beyond the barn is a distinctive tree with three of its branches grouped together like a pitchfork. There is a gap in the woods to the left of this tree, a gap that reminded me of a similar one I had noticed previously in view II-7, taken looking toward the North Woods. Referring to that photograph (which had to be used cautiously, due to the opaque material that had obliterated portions of the distant tree line) I found, again, to the right of the gap, a large tree with three of its branches reaching into the air.

If the tree and gap were indeed identical in the two views, it meant that the barn must have been the one located on the Miller farm, adjoining the Hagerstown Pike on its western side.

This connection, although potentially significant, could be considered only hypothetical until a modern field investigation of all 1862 barn sites on the battlefield was conducted. Only then, through the process of elimination, would I be able to confirm that the barn in Gardner's photograph was in fact the Miller barn. This confirmation was subsequently achieved.

Gardner's camera position for this scene was in an open field on the Miller farm, approximately sixty yards west of the Hagerstown Pike and some three hundred yards north of the camera position for view II-7. In light of both the subject matter and the view's proximity to the other scenes recorded at or near the Hagerstown Pike, there can be little doubt that view 12 was likewise recorded on September 19, 1862.

It is probably because of the presence of the burial detail that Gardner produced only one negative of this group of bodies. Glass-plate negatives of the Civil War period were not sensitive enough to stop motion, and all movement produced a noticeable blur on the finished plate. The burial detail was willing to halt its activities for one exposure, but they probably would not have tolerated successive interruptions. Thus, after one exposure, Gardner apparently moved elsewhere in search of additional subject matter.

Although Gardner's caption did not mention whether the dead in this view were Union or Confederate, the location of the scene, together with an examination of the uniforms on the three bodies to the left that are not covered by blankets, indicates that they were Northerners. Many Federal units suffered casualties on this ground, including regiments from Gibbon's and Patrick's brigades of the First Corps, three companies of the 124th Pennsylvania Volunteers of the Twelfth Corps, and, later, scattered elements of Sedgwick's division of the Second Corps.

Today, all the land visible in Gardner's original photograph is privately owned. The Miller barn that stood in 1862 is no longer standing, having been replaced at an unknown date by a similarly shaped second barn, visible at the same location in the modern photograph. To the left in this modern version appears another barn constructed after the war. The latter barn stands on property owned at the time of the battle by a farmer named Nicodemus. His original farm buildings might have been visible in Gardner's photograph were it not for the intervening foliage and the general haziness of the background.

As mentioned before, the North Woods, which dominate the distance in Gardner's photograph, are no longer there; nor are the two other great bodies of timber, the East and West Woods, that dominated the scenery on the northern part of the Antietam battlefield in 1862.

ANTIETAM

GEORGE D. MILLER, photographer and type unknown, 1861 (Green).

The lead elements of the Twelfth Corps began deploying on the northern edge of the battlefield between 7:15 and 7:30 A.M. They had reached the scene of action none too soon, for the First Corps was rapidly approaching the point of exhaustion.

The Twelfth Corps had crossed Antietam Creek the night before to support the First, but when the fighting erupted at dawn on September 17, the Twelfth Corps was located about a mile behind the First. Why it took the Twelfth nearly two hours to reach the scene of action and deploy on the field can only be surmised.

The commander of the Twelfth, Gen. Joseph K. F. Mansfield, had been with the corps for only two days prior to the battle, and many of his lead regiments were composed entirely of raw recruits who had enlisted only a month before. Although it is possible that Mansfield moved slowly because he did not realize the urgency with which his troops were needed, a more believable explanation is that the delay was caused by a combination of inexperience and ineffective leadership. Unfortunately, Mansfield was mortally wounded shortly after reaching the scene of action and left no official explanation of his corps' tardiness at Antietam.

One of the first regiments of the Twelfth Corps to deploy on the battlefield was the 124th Pennsylvania Volunteers of Gen. Samuel W. Crawford's brigade, Alpheus S. Williams's division. The 124th was one of the new regiments, having been organized just six weeks prior to the action. Among its members present for duty on the morning of September 17, 1862, was a twenty-three-year-old private named George D. Miller.

Miller was born on a farm in Upper Providence, Delaware County, Pennsylvania, on February 3, 1839. Because his parents, Lewis and Ann Miller, were Quakers, as a young boy George would have been taught the precepts of pacifism. At the time of the Mexican War, George was only seven years old and he must have overheard war-related discussions between his parents, perhaps at the dinner table, and among members of the local Quaker congregation.

But along with their abhorrence of war, most Quakers were also sensitive to the issue of slavery expanding into the new territories to the west. There can be no doubt that George Miller's upbringing included numerous lectures in

GEORGE D. MILLER

school, at the meetinghouse, and at home concerning the evils of the South's "peculiar institution."

The area in which George was raised, located only ten miles east of Philadelphia, consisted of moderately rolling farmland. The soil was fertile and most farmers concentrated their efforts on producing wheat, corn, and potatoes. In 1860 the total population of Upper Providence Township numbered 884, of whom 100 were listed as Free Colored. Adjoining the township on the south was the borough of Media, the seat of Delaware County.

When the war broke out in April 1861, George Miller, then twenty-two, was living at home, helping his father on the farm. Probably due in part to his upbringing and perhaps also because of his parents' wishes, George chose not to involve himself in the conflict. But the temptation to do so must have been great, especially during the exciting days and weeks that followed the surrender of Fort Sumter.

Remaining on the farm throughout the next year, George tended to the business of plowing fields, planting crops, and caring for livestock. Sometime before the end of 1861 (probably on a trip into Media to purchase supplies) George visited a local photographer and had his portrait taken (the one shown here).

By the summer of 1862, the war that everyone had thought would be over in a few months was still growing in scope and intensity. McClellan's failure on the Peninsula had produced nothing but frightfully long casualty lists. The Rebel army had proven itself to be strong and capably led. McClellan was crying for more reinforcements.

To the Lincoln administration, as well as to the country as a whole, it was clear that even greater sacrifices would be required if the Union were to be saved. On July 2, 1862, Lincoln issued a call for 300,000 more troops to serve for a period of three years. Then on August 4, 1862, another call was issued for an additional 300,000 men to serve for a period of nine months.

In order to raise these volunteers and meet individual state quotas, mass meetings were held in villages, towns, and cities throughout the North during the months of July and August. Patriotic speeches were the order of the day. Volunteers were needed now; no longer could able-bodied men of military age stand idly by with the country on the brink of grave peril. The message, repeated over and over, did not fall on deaf ears. Men who had previously hesitated to become involved, for whatever personal reasons, responded by the thousands to the often eloquent and sometimes hysterical speeches delivered at these meetings.

On August 4, 1862, George Miller enlisted in the army at Media. Five days later, at Harrisburg, he was mustered into Company D of the newly formed nine-months' regiment, the 124th Pennsylvania Volunteers. The records show that he was five feet seven and one-half inches tall, weighed 138 pounds, had brown eyes and dark hair.

On August 12, 1862, the regiment left Harrisburg for the camps around Washington. Here they could expect to spend the next couple of months or so in intensive training, for it required many long hours of drilling at company and regimental level to become an effective fighting force. Strict discipline, the precise meaning of various orders, and all the peculiarities of army life had to be learned, which could not be done overnight. Men had to be conditioned to the physical strain of long marches. Target practice and bayonet drills were also essential, for although many of these recruits, especially those from rural areas, were already familiar with firearms, many, including large numbers who had grown up in cities such as Pittsburgh and Philadelphia, were not.

But the events of the war were taking on a sense of greater urgency by the last week in August and the first week in September. The Union Army had met with disaster at Second Manassas, and now for the first time the Confederate Army of Northern Virginia was invading the North.

It must have been with considerable apprehension that the commander of the 124th Pennsylvania received orders at the end of the first week in September to break camp and proceed with dispatch to Rockville, Maryland. Here the regiment would be attached to the veteran Army of the Potomac, then hurriedly preparing for the campaign that they hoped would repel the invaders. With only a little more than three weeks of training, the 124th found itself being moved directly to the front and toward what was promising to be one of the war's most desperate confrontations.

Many of the new recruits were still adjusting to being away from home and family for the first time in their lives. The excitement of the mass meetings, the electrifying speeches were now behind them. For many recruits, the full weight of their decision to enlist was just now sinking in. The patriotic words that had filled them with such excitement several weeks earlier were losing their glow. The novelty of seeing themselves in uniform was wearing off. The sense of power they felt when first issued military rifles and bayonets was fading.

ANTIETAM

According to his own account, George Miller's personal fears focused more on being wounded than killed. The thing he dreaded most was the amputation of one of his arms or legs. The thought of being held down while the surgeon's knife cut into his flesh, slicing deeper and deeper until the saw was called into play, haunted him constantly.

The 124th was not engaged at South Mountain but passed over the freshly scarred battlefield on the grueling forced march to Antietam. As the unit passed by a busy field hospital, Miller saw a sight that played havoc with his worst fears. There near the roadway was a cartload of amputated human limbs, "mostly legs that had been taken off above the knee."[33] It seemed unreal to see them in such quantity, unattached to anything. There were the toes, the ankles, the hairs about the shins and calves, the knee caps, and then nothing but a bloody stump and a circle of bone.

Two days later, at seven thirty on the morning of September 17, 1862, the 124th Pennsylvania was at the North Woods. The time had finally come for these raw recruits to experience for themselves what it was like to be in a battle.

Everyone was tense as the order was given to remove all knapsacks and blankets at the woods. These articles could be recovered later, but for now it was deemed best to be as free as possible from excess weight. Wounded men were staggering from the front lines, from the direction of the smoke and gunfire. It was too late to worry anymore.

The 124th dressed its line and waited. Off to the left, other Twelfth Corps units were already engaged. Still the 124th waited. Finally, a little after 8:00 A.M., the order was given to advance. Seven of the regiment's ten companies moved out along the eastern side of the Hagerstown Pike and into the Cornfield while the remaining three companies, including George Miller's Company D, advanced past the Miller barn on the pike's western side.

As the members of Company D moved forward, up the hollow from the barn, they could see ahead of them a lone group of skinny trees directly in their path (the trees in the foreground of view 12). Off to their right was a dense body of woods (the West Woods), from which they were receiving their first rifle fire from an enemy force. To the left, across the fence-lined turnpike, the main body of the regiment was becoming engaged in the Cornfield.

The right-flank companies continued forward. Men began to fall from gunshot wounds. Hardly had Company D become engaged when George Miller felt a sharp blow to his body. He looked down and saw a hole in the front of his frock coat, at the left side of the abdomen near the bottom of the rib cage. Almost instinctively his hand reached around to his back. He could feel the second tear in his clothing, and his hand was full of blood. The bullet had passed completely through his body.

A friend, Charles Eckfeldt, was nearby. Miller called out to him for help. Eckfeldt rushed over and helped Miller off with his belt. Eckfeldt's rifle had been struck by a bullet, rendering it unserviceable, so Miller gave him his. With a parting gesture, Eckfeldt returned to the line of battle as Miller started for the rear, undoubtedly with the aid of other comrades.

Soon in almost unbearable pain, George Miller awaited death at a field hospital for the rest of that day as well as each day for the next month. In fact, the agony was so intense that he welcomed death as the only possible relief from his suffering. The bullet had severed his colon and foul-smelling excrement oozed through the wound for roughly ten days. Word of his situation reached his family in Upper Providence, but there was little they could do besides worry and pray for him. Sometime during late October or early November, Miller took a turn for the better. Eventually he was able to return home and lead some semblance of a normal life. On October 17, 1865, he married a girl named Ann at a Quaker meetinghouse in West Chester, Pennsylvania, became a merchant in lumber and coal, and the father of three children, a boy named Henry and two girls, Mary and Anna.

George Miller died on June 21, 1919, at the age of eighty. Although he survived by some fifty-six years his wounding at Antietam, the medical records in his pension file indicate that he suffered almost continuous severe pain from his wound for most if not all of his remaining years.

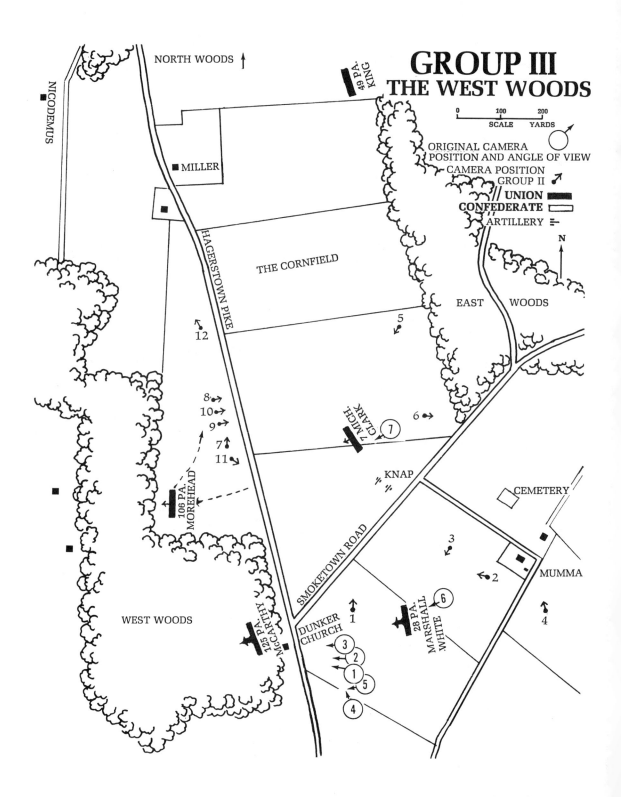

GROUP III
THE WEST WOODS

NORTH WOODS ↑

NICODEMUS ■

■ MILLER

49 PA. KING

0   100   200
SCALE   YARDS

ORIGINAL CAMERA
POSITION AND ANGLE OF VIEW
CAMERA POSITION
GROUP II
UNION
CONFEDERATE
ARTILLERY

N

HAGERSTOWN PIKE

THE CORNFIELD

EAST WOODS

12

8
10
9
7
11

5

7 MICH. CLARK

7

6

KNAP

106 PA. MOREHEAD

CEMETERY

3

2

MUMMA

WEST WOODS

SMOKETOWN ROAD

125 PA. McCARTHY

DUNKER CHURCH

1

28 PA. MARSHALL WHITE

6

4

3

2

1

5

4

8

GROUP III: THE WEST WOODS

JOHN S. McCARTHY, photographer unknown, probably a tintype or ambrotype, August 1862 (Regtl. Comm.).

The Twelfth Corps, having replaced the shattered First Corps on the northern portion of the battlefield, fought bitterly for an hour and a half to break the Confederate lines in the vicinity of the Hagerstown Pike, the Cornfield, and the East Woods.

Facing the Twelfth during this period were three Confederate brigades, Ripley's, Colquitt's, and Garland's, all of D. H. Hill's division. Although badly outnumbered, Hill's men were for a time successful in checking the Union advance. But the odds were against them and eventually, after suffering great losses, all three brigades were forced to retire south of the West Woods.

Many units of the Twelfth Corps had also sustained heavy casualties and did not pursue. There were some exceptions, however. Two brigades of Gen. George S. Greene's division advanced beyond the Smoketown Road to the fields on the Mumma farm, where they halted to regroup and await a fresh supply of ammunition. Another Federal unit, the 125th Pennsylvania Volunteers of Crawford's brigade, Williams's division, actually penetrated the West Woods at the Dunker Church, a daring move considering that the regiment was one of the new nine-months' units and that it was acting alone.

JOHN S. McCARTHY

GROUP III: THE WEST WOODS

In the ranks of the 125th that morning was a twenty-three-year-old private named John S. McCarthy, who, along with the rest of his comrades, had been in uniform for only a month prior to Antietam. McCarthy's records listed him as a farmer, single, five feet eight inches tall, with brown hair, blue eyes, and a fair complexion. His photographic portrait, shown here, was taken shortly after his enlistment in August 1862. It would be a memento for the folks back home and perhaps something he could proudly show his grandchildren in later years, provided he survived.

John S. McCarthy was born on a farm in Airy Dale, Huntingdon County, Pennsylvania, on August 5, 1839. Airy Dale'was a small agricultural community located eight miles east of the county seat at the borough of Huntingdon. The county consisted of various types of terrain, including mountains and scenic, fertile valleys. Iron and coal mining was extensive, while farmers, for the most part, concentrated their efforts on raising dairy cattle and crops of wheat, rye, and corn.

John's parents, John R. and Eleanor L. McCarthy, were married in 1837 and eventually had nine children, the youngest of whom, William, was born in 1853. John, the second oldest child, shared much of the responsibility on the family farm, since his father was frequently in poor health and suffered from a spinal disease.

All the McCarthy children attended school when they were young, and apparently John excelled in his studies. A letter written long after the war by Joseph Hamilton, a neighbor who had grown up with the McCarthy children, recalled that John "was an active, industrious young man" who worked on his father's farm during the summers and taught school during the winters, "giving his wages to the support of the family."[34]

In 1862 the McCarthy farm consisted of 134 acres. The family owned one horse, three cows, and a buggy. It was probably because of the needs of the farm, together with his father's poor health, that John hesitated to enlist during the first year of the war. Then came the mass appeal for more troops during the summer of 1862. War meetings were held at nearby Huntingdon, and McCarthy undoubtedly attended. Given his concern for his parents' welfare, it is also safe to guess that he spent many hours discussing with them the prospect of his leaving the farm to join the army. On August 13, 1862, he enlisted at Huntingdon in Company H, 125th Pennsylvania Volunteers.

Bidding farewell to his mother, father, brothers, and sisters, John McCarthy was sent to Harrisburg with thirty-seven other recruits. Crowds gathered at the Huntingdon railroad depot to send them off while a band played "Auld Lang Syne" and various patriotic tunes. Within a week, the regiment was shipped out from Harrisburg to Washington.

When the Maryland campaign commenced a short while later, the 125th Pennsylvania and two other new Pennsylvania regiments (including George D. Miller's unit, the 124th) were attached to Crawford's combat-seasoned brigade of Williams's division of the Twelfth Corps.

It was Crawford's brigade that led the Twelfth Corps advance onto the field at Antietam. During the ensuing confusion, the 125th became separated from the remainder of the brigade, and as the Confederates were falling back, the regiment found itself in an open field near the western edge of the East Woods, at the Smoketown Road. The men were ordered to lie face down for protection. One of the soldiers would later recall looking up and seeing little puffs of dust being kicked up as bullets struck the ground about them. In the distance, through the battle smoke, could be seen the West Woods and the small white Dunker Church six hundred yards away. No Union troops were visible to either the immediate right or left of the regiment. They were by themselves in an advanced position.

A short while later, an unknown officer galloped up to the commander of the 125th, Col. Jacob Higgins, and ordered him to advance his men into the distant woods. Higgins called the regiment to its feet and shouted the command "Forward!" With bayonets fixed, the line moved out rapidly across the open fields. By this time, however, enemy resistance was slight and after several minutes the men reached the edge of the West Woods. Here the 125th halted. Company G was thrown into the woods as skirmishers; Company B was sent to reconnoiter the Dunker Church. They found the building full of Confederate wounded. Subsequently, the entire regiment was ordered into the woods to await reinforcements.

A brief lull now settled over the battlefield. It was approximately 9:00 A.M. and Sedgwick's division of the Second Corps, having passed through the East Woods, was then advancing across the Miller farm toward the West Woods. The Thirty-fourth New York Regiment of that division soon passed by the Dunker Church and lined up to the left and rear of the 125th Pennsylvania.

The next twenty minutes would see one of the greatest slaughters of the war as Sedgwick's men, together with the 125th Pennsylvania, were caught in a savage Confederate counterattack that threw the Union lines into confusion and drove them out of the woods, back across the fields to the east and north.

The 125th suffered its greatest casualties during those twenty minutes, and it was undoubtedly at that time that John S. McCarthy was struck by an enemy bullet. He never felt any pain, for the bullet passed through his head, killing him instantly.

The West Woods remained in Confederate hands from the day of the battle until the early morning hours of September 19. During that period many of the bodies of Union dead were rifled for equipment, money, and trophies. Personal items that might have been used later as identification, including letters from home, diaries, and inscribed bibles, made excellent souvenirs and were often removed.

At about three o'clock on the afternoon of September 19, two days after the battle, the 125th Pennsylvania commenced its march from Antietam to Maryland Heights, opposite Harpers Ferry. Here the men began the sad task of writing letters to the families of those comrades who had been killed and wounded. One of those letters was addressed to Mr. and Mrs. John R. McCarthy of Airy Dale, Huntingdon County, Pennsylvania.

John S. McCarthy's body is not listed among the known dead buried in the Antietam National Cemetery. Although it is possible that his remains were eventually returned to Huntingdon County by his family, the odds are greater, considering that his body probably fell into enemy hands, that he today lies buried under an anonymous tombstone at Antietam.

III–1 Confederate dead, view looking toward the Dunker Church, Gardner, stereo #552, September 19, 1862 (McGuire).

III–2 Confederate dead, view looking toward the Dunker Church, Gardner, stereo #562, September 19, 1862 (MOLLUS-Mass.).

III–3 The Dunker Church, Gardner, stereo #573, September 19, 1862 (MOLLUS-Mass.).

The three views shown here were all made in the open ground east of, and across the Hagerstown Pike from, the Dunker Church. The church itself stands prominently in the background, with the West Woods looming just beyond.

It was to the right of the church that the 125th Pennsylvania Volunteers entered the woods, to be joined a short while later by the Thirty-fourth New York. The West Woods no longer exist, but today monuments (not visible in the modern version) locate the positions where those two units suffered their greatest casualties.

The dead Confederates in the foreground of views 1 and 2 are identical, Gardner having shifted his camera only a few feet between the two exposures. Gardner must have considered that this scene afforded subject matter of outstanding potential, and great care was taken to achieve the most effective possible composition.

These two views are among the best known of Gardner's Antietam photographs. The version shown here for view 2 has nevertheless remained obscure until now. This photograph, made from the right half of the stereo negative, is important because it shows the dead horse to the far right, the significance of which will be discussed later in the section dealing with view III-4. Damage to this half of the original negative has partially obliterated some of the dead soldiers.

The open rise of ground on which these Confederate soldiers fell was then part of the farm of Samuel Mumma. From the beginning of the battle until the area was occupied by two brigades of George Greene's Union division, the rise served as a Confederate artillery position. Stationed during the battle where the abandoned limber chest stands in the photograph was Capt. W. W. Parker's (Virginia) Battery of Col. S. D. Lee's Artillery Battalion, and it is possible that the limber chest, as well as some of the eight dead men visible here, belonged to that battery.

III–1

III–2

III–3

On the other hand, the official records show that Lee's entire battalion of six batteries suffered a combined loss of only eleven killed. Because these eleven fell over a much larger area than that covered by the photograph, the chances are equally great that several of the eight bodies visible here were Confederate infantrymen killed during one of three Southern counterattacks following the repulse of Sedgwick's division from the West Woods.

In view 3, Gardner focused all his attention on the small white church, one of the most distinctive landmarks on the Antietam battlefield. The land on which the building stood was originally owned by Samuel Mumma, who in 1851 deeded it to the German Baptist Brethren—also known as the Dunkers, from the manner in which their baptisms were performed. The brick church was completed in 1853.

GROUP III: THE WEST WOODS

III–1 through III–3 modern

Gardner's original captions invariably referred to the building as the "Tunker" Church. At first I thought this an error on Gardner's part until I learned that *tunker* means dunker in German.[35] Perhaps the photographer received his information from a local resident inspecting the battlefield at the time.

During the fighting on the morning of September 17, the church was an objective for Union attacks and was struck numerous times by both Union and Confederate artillery and small-arms fire. Visible in the photograph are a number of shell holes on the southern (left) face of the structure. The rounds that produced these scars were probably fired by Confederate batteries, most likely during either the repulse of Sedgwick's division or later when Union general Greene's forces made an advance over this ground and for a period held the section of woods at the church.

Two days after the battle, at the time Gardner's photographs were recorded, the Dunker Church was serving as a field hospital. On September 28, 1862, Sgt. Nathan F. Dykeman of Company H, 107th New York, happened to walk inside and noticed that the large pulpit Bible was still there. When Dykeman left, he took the Bible with him as a souvenir. In 1903, the aging veterans of the 107th New York secured the Bible from Dykeman's sister (Dykeman had by that time died) and returned it to the Dunkers. The Bible is today owned by descendants of the original congregation.[36]

The Dunker Church was destroyed during a storm in 1921, but the bricks and other materials were saved, and from them the building was reconstructed on the old foundation in 1962. Today it looks virtually unchanged from its basic Civil War appearance. Most of the land behind it, where the West Woods once stood, is currently in private hands.

The tall monument seen directly across the Hagerstown Pike in the single modern photograph I have included to accompany views 1 through 3 commemorates the three Ohio regiments of Lt. Col. Hector Tyndale's brigade, Greene's division. At Antietam Tyndale's brigade consisted of the Fifth, Seventh, and Sixty-sixth Ohio, together with the Twenty-eighth Pennsylvania.

III–4 Near the Dunker Church, view looking north, Gardner, stereo #568, September 19, 1862 (LC).

III–5 Dead artillery horses, view looking southwest toward the Hagerstown Pike, Gardner, stereo #564, September 19, 1862 (Miller).

Both of these views were recorded within several yards of the preceding three photographs. View 4 may also be considered a companion to the photograph of Knap's Battery (II-1), since both views, though taken some 230 yards apart, were recorded in the same general area, with the camera pointed in the same northerly direction.

View 4 is linked to views 1 and 2 of the Dunker Church by the presence in all three of the abandoned limber chest with the hole in it. Furthermore, close examination of view 4 reveals that the group of bodies to the right of the limber chest is identical to the group in the foreground of 1 and 2. (Because of the camera angle for views 1 and 2, the bodies visible to the left of the limber chest in view 4 are outside the camera's field of vision.)

Although the bodies and limber chest matched precisely, before I discovered a print made from the right half of the stereo negative for view 2, I could not explain the fact that the horse just beyond the chest in view 4 had his leg in the air, whereas the horse attached to the chest in view 1 did not. My guess that there was a second horse located beyond the one attached to the chest was confirmed as fact by the lesser known right-hand version of view 2.

View 4 reveals that in addition to the eight bodies depicted in views III-1 and III-2 there were at least six more dead Confederates located nearby, making a total of fourteen dead soldiers. Given the fact that only eleven men of S. D. Lee's entire artillery battalion were killed at Antietam, many, if not most, of the Confederate dead in view 4 must have been infantrymen and not artillerymen.

The Confederates made three counterattacks into this field, all of them following Sedgwick's repulse from the West Woods. (A portion of those woods appears to the left in view 4.) The first of these occurred at approximately 9:45 A.M. and involved Gen. Joseph B. Kershaw's South Carolina brigade. Kershaw's men, after having taken an active part in shattering the left flank of the Union line in the West Woods, pushed out from the woods and crossed the Hagerstown Pike. The advance of two of Kershaw's regiments, the Second and

III–4

III–4 modern

GROUP III: THE WEST WOODS

Seventh South Carolina Infantry, continued across the field in view 4 until stalled by Union artillery and the presence of Greene's two infantry brigades, which by then had been resupplied with ammunition.

The South Carolinians were forced to retire, but a short while later the Confederates made another attempt to push the Union line back from its position on the high ground east of the pike. This second attempt was made by Col. Van H. Manning's brigade of Arkansas, North Carolina, and Virginia regiments. Although the Forty-eighth North Carolina Infantry was posted in a position that would have covered the area depicted in the foreground of view 4, it is not believed that the regiment was able to advance as far as the dead men in the photograph.

Greene's two brigades counterattacked, securing a position in the West Woods beyond the Dunker Church, which they held for nearly two hours. A section of Knap's Battery was dispatched to the woods to provide Greene with close artillery support. Later, at about noon, Greene's men, threatened by an enemy buildup on their flanks, were ordered to retire from their salient position in the woods. Within moments there occurred a bold Confederate counterattack spearheaded by the Third Arkansas and Twenty-seventh North Carolina regiments of Manning's brigade, both of which advanced across the open ground in view 4 and penetrated deeply the Union-held territory on the Mumma farm but were soon repulsed.

Therefore, it seems most likely that a number of the fourteen Confederate dead visible in Gardner view 4, together with views III-1 and III-2, were members of either the Second and Seventh South Carolina of Kershaw's brigade or the Third Arkansas and Twenty-seventh North Carolina of Manning's brigade, or a combination thereof. The latter two regiments, however, sustained most of their casualties farther eastward on the Mumma farm. (It is possible that at least some of the dead of the Twenty-seventh North Carolina are present in the long line of bodies portrayed in view II-3.)

Today the ground over which these units charged appears much as it did in 1862. According to official maps, the rails scattered about the foreground in view 4 marked a fence line. The land in the foreground is today owned by the National Park Service.

Visible in the left background of the modern version, near the Smoketown Road, stands the monument to Maryland soldiers who fought at Antietam. Although Maryland, a border slave state, supplied soldiers to both sides during the war, the vast majority of those engaged at Antietam were with the Union army.

Visible to the left in Gardner's photograph (view 4) is a second limber chest, distinctive because the wheels have been removed. Two dead horses can be seen lying immediately in front of the chest, one on either side. This grouping is identical to that seen in view 5, previously unidentified except for Gardner's original caption, "Demolished Confederate Battery near Sharpsburg, September 19, 1862."

The negative for this Antietam photograph has not survived, and I have never been able to discover a contemporary print. In fact, the only known photographic reproduction currently available is that which appeared in

III–5

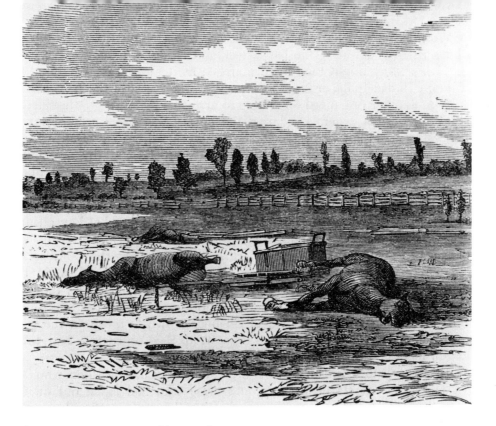

Woodcut, *Harper's Weekly,* **October 18, 1862**

III–5 modern

Francis Miller's ten-volume *Photographic History of the Civil War* (1911), the source of the version reproduced here.[37]

I did, however, come across a woodcut based on this photograph that appeared in the October 18, 1862, issue of *Harper's Weekly*. From the woodcut, also included here, it is evident that the version in Miller's history was heavily cropped, especially on the right.

Gardner recorded this photograph looking southwest toward the Hagerstown Pike. Had he directed his camera slightly to the right he would have caught the extreme southern edge of the West Woods.

It was from the area beyond the pike in the background of view 5 that the Third Arkansas and Twenty-seventh North Carolina regiments of Manning's brigade launched their assault toward the camera position and beyond. Fifteen minutes later the two regiments were retiring across this same ground.

The scattered rails visible just beyond the dead horses in view 5 are an extension of the fence line in the foreground of view 4. In view 4 the lid to the limber chest to the left is partially open, whereas it appears to be closed in view 5. In actuality, the lid is also partially open in the latter scene, but because of the poor quality of the photograph, the open space is camouflaged by the grass in the background. Only by looking closely at the right base of the handle can one see that the lid is indeed open.

The presence of several postbattle structures on ground that is today privately owned robs the area depicted in Gardner's photograph of much of its Civil War appearance. If one were to walk due southwest from the camera position, beyond the house in the background of the modern version, and continue over the distant ridge, one would eventually come to the site of David Reel's barn, the subject of a Gardner photograph discussed later (VI-4).

GROUP III: THE WEST WOODS

III–6 The grave of John Marshall, Company L, Twenty-eighth Pennsylvania, Gardner, stereo #570, September 19 or 20, 1862 (LC).

Since the time it was recorded, this photograph has been known only by Gardner's original caption, "A Lone Grave, on Battle-field of Antietam." At first glance there is little or nothing in the scene itself that would provide a clue as to where the subject was located. Nor have I ever seen a published version or contemporary print crisp enough to decipher the writing on the headboard.

Fortunately, the original negative of this photograph has survived and is today in a remarkably good state of preservation—good enough to decipher, under magnification, the name on the headboard. It reads "John Marshall." The company and state designation of the regiment cannot be deciphered, but the regimental numeral is clearly 28. Further investigation into Antietam casualty lists and burial records, concentrating on units numbered 28, eventually supplied the missing information and identified the soldier as Pvt. John Marshall, Company L, Twenty-eighth Pennsylvania Volunteers.

With this information I was able not only to research the story behind the soldier in the grave but also to solve the mystery of where the photograph was taken as well, for the various positions occupied by the Twenty-eighth Pennsylvania at Antietam are a matter of record. Because the unit was almost constantly within sight of the North, East, and West Woods, and since none of those woods were visible from the location and direction of Gardner's camera, potential sites were limited in number, thereby facilitating my field investigation.

In retracing the movements of the Twenty-eighth Pennsylvania, I was led to a point on the high ground of Samuel Mumma's farm, some three hundred yards east of the Dunker Church, where the rise would have been steep enough to block completely from vision at least one of the woods (in this case the West Woods). It was the only point known to have been occupied by the Twenty-eighth Pennsylvania that matched Gardner's photograph. The exact camera position was further refined upon discovery of the rock outcroppings visible at the base of the tree in the original scene.

Here, on the eastern slope of the hill directly across from the Dunker Church, two Union brigades of Greene's division of the Twelfth Corps lay hidden as the shattered remnants of Sedgwick's division fled in confusion from the West Woods. Greene's forces, comprising Tyndale's and Col. Henry J. Stain-

III–6

III–6 modern

rook's brigades, had reached this area prior to the arrival of Sedgwick's division, but they were unable to assist Sedgwick because they had nearly exhausted their supply of ammunition at the East Woods. By the time Kershaw's South Carolina brigade emerged from the West Woods in pursuit of retreating Union forces, ammunition wagons had reached Greene's men, who were now ready to meet the Confederate onslaught. The two Union brigades rose to their feet and advanced in line of battle up to the crest of the hill and onto the ground depicted in views III-1 through III-5.

Sometime during the fighting that followed, Pvt. John Marshall of Company L, Twenty-eighth Pennsylvania, Tyndale's brigade, received his fatal wound. Whether he crawled back to the protection of the eastern slope or was carried there by comrades can only be conjectured. Whatever the case, his condition was hopeless and within a short while he was dead.

At the age of fifty, John Marshall was one of the oldest privates in the ranks of the Army of the Potomac at Antietam. Born in Ireland in 1812, Marshall eventually immigrated to the United States and took up residence in Allegheny City, Pennsylvania. He was a stonemason by trade and lived with his family at 60 Lacock Street. The Marshalls attended the Second Presbyterian Church.

John's first wife, Elizabeth, died of consumption in March 1855. This first marriage had produced at least one child, a son, William, who was delivered by the family physician, Dr. Thomas Elliot, on July 21, 1852. In 1856, the year following Elizabeth's death, John was remarried by the Reverend John Rogers to a woman named Mary, eighteen years younger. Two additional children resulted from the second marriage, a son, Samuel, born on New Year's Day 1859, and another boy, John, born in June 1861.

Allegheny City, located directly across the Allegheny River from Pittsburgh, was already considered a suburb of Pittsburgh by the time of the Civil War. The two cities were connected by a bridge and a ferry. Allegheny's population in 1860 was more than twenty-eight thousand. Contemporary accounts described the area as being dingy in appearance because of the high concentration of industry, especially iron manufacturing.

Approximately three months after the surrender of Fort Sumter, John Marshall made his decision to enlist. News of the disaster at Bull Run had just reached Allegheny City when, on July 27, 1861, Marshall joined Company L of the Twenty-eighth Pennsylvania. Bull Run may have played a part in his decision. At any rate, Marshall's feelings concerning the Southern rebellion were obviously strong, for his decision entailed the difficult task of leaving his wife Mary, then thirty-one, and his three young sons, William, nine; Samuel, three; and the infant, John, Jr., who was only one month old.

With a group of other recruits, Marshall was shipped by rail to Philadelphia, where, on August 5, 1861, he was formally mustered into the Twenty-eighth Pennsylvania. One of the men who accompanied Marshall on his journey across Pennsylvania was a young officer, also of Company L, named Joseph M. Knap, of Pittsburgh (see view II-1).

During the months that followed, Pvt. John Marshall received his training and took part in the various campaigns of the Twenty-eighth. More than likely he received frequent letters from his wife, telling him all the latest news at home and of course the progress of his three boys. Perhaps there was even a letter or two, written in childish script, from William, who turned ten on July 21, 1862.

On September 21, four days after Antietam, the various units of the Army of the Potomac received their first mail call since arriving in the vicinity of Sharpsburg. Those who had survived the battle would never forget the sadness of that event, for many of the letters were addressed to men no longer there to answer their names. Such was the case with John Marshall, who on that day lay buried at the foot of a dead tree on the hill opposite the Dunker Church.

Marshall was probably buried by comrades during a truce period on September 18 or early on September 19, before the Twelfth Corps departed the battlefield for Harpers Ferry. After the war (1866–67) the bodies of all Union soldiers still buried on the field were exhumed and reburied in the Antietam National Cemetery. The body of John Marshall was placed in grave 19, lot A, section 26, where his remains rest today.

GROUP III: THE WEST WOODS

HARRISON WHITE, photographer unknown, retouched copy of unknown type original, original ca. July 1861 (Fredericksburg NMP).

An exhaustive search to uncover a portrait of John Marshall proved futile. During this search, however, I came across a heavily retouched copy of a photograph of another member of the Twenty-eighth Pennsylvania Volunteers who fell at Antietam. He was Pvt. Harrison White, whose story and portrait are here published for the first time.

Although the story of Harrison White is in many respects typical of the thousands who fell on September 17, 1862, White's case is made unique by the fact that according to the inscription on the back of his photograph he was a first cousin of Maj. Gen. George Brinton McClellan, commander of all Union forces at Antietam. Research into White's background verified that the inscription was correct.

Four days after Christmas 1839 William White, Jr., and Sarah Frederica Brinton were married at Christ Church in Philadelphia. Undoubtedly, Sarah's sister, Elizabeth Brinton McClellan, Elizabeth's husband, George, and their thirteen-year-old son, George Brinton McClellan, attended the ceremony.

The Whites eventually had eight children, one of whom, Harrison, was born in 1843. In early 1858 Harrison's father died, necessitating the boy's removal from school to help support the family, then living at 1336 Pine Street in Philadelphia. At the time Harrison was fifteen.

Three years later, on July 11, 1861, Harrison enlisted at Philadelphia as a private in Company H of the Twenty-eighth Pennsylvania Volunteers. He was transferred to Company B of the same regiment on the following day. In the photographic portrait shown here (the reversed insignia on the belt buckle indicates that the original photograph was probably either an ambrotype or a tintype), Harrison is seen wearing the first uniform issued to the regiment that summer. Gray in color, it was later exchanged for the regulation blue uniform of the Union army, to avoid confusion in battle.

Harrison White served with the Twenty-eighth Pennsylvania throughout the next thirteen months, religiously sending home to his mother the greater portion of his pay. Sometime on the morning of September 17, 1862, probably near the Dunker Church, he was struck by a bullet that passed through his body. He was eventually carried to a field hospital in the rear where at midnight the same day he died of his wound, at the age of nineteen. Whether or

HARRISON WHITE

not General McClellan had an opportunity to visit his cousin at the field hospital or was even aware at the time that Harrison had been mortally wounded cannot be determined. Indeed, the fact that McClellan lost a cousin at Antietam has remained obscure until now.

Harrison White was initially buried in the vicinity of the hospital where he died, on the Hoffman farm. After the war his remains were transferred to the Antietam National Cemetery, where they today lie in lot B, section 26. His tombstone correctly identifies his unit as the Twenty-eighth Pennsylvania.

III–7 a and b   Scene of Sedgwick's advance and the grave of Lt. John A. Clark, Seventh Michigan, view looking toward the West Woods from Miller's fields, Gardner, stereo #551, September 19, 1862 (LC).

As was the case with Gardner's photograph of the "lone grave," the view shown here has never before been identified beyond the scant information provided by Gardner's caption, "A Contrast: Federal buried, Confederate unburied, where they fell, on Battle-field of Antietam." And as was the case with the "lone grave" photograph, the key to identifying both the soldier in the grave and location of this scene rested in the name on the headboard.

Prints from both halves of Gardner's original stereo negative are presented here. The right half (b) has survived intact and shows the total image area then visible through the right lens of the stereo camera. In this version, however, the writing on the headboard cannot be deciphered.

The left half of the double negative (a) was broken sometime during the past century and only the section shown here has survived, but it was this section that led to the positive identification of the entire scene.

There are several items of interest in this half that do not appear in the other. To the far left can be detected a dead horse and a group of civilians apparently inspecting some bodies. In the distant woods, visible above the civilians, stand two large trees that would later help confirm the identification of another photograph (II-5). But the most important feature is that both the name and unit of the soldier in the grave are readily decipherable on the original negative. The writing on the headboard reads "J. A. Clark, 7th Mich.," referring to 1st Lt. John A. Clark, Company D, Seventh Michigan Infantry, who was killed in action at Antietam on the morning of September 17, 1862.

At Antietam the Seventh Michigan was with Gen. Napoleon J. T. Dana's brigade of Sedgwick's division and took part in the disastrous action at the West Woods. The regiment was located on the left flank of the brigade (on the same line, three units to the right, was Capt. Oliver Wendell Holmes's regiment, the Twentieth Massachusetts), and it suffered all its casualties at the West Woods and in the fields east of those woods. I thus knew that the timber appearing in the background of Gardner's photograph had to have been either the East, West, or North Woods.

Through a modern investigation of all the ground covered by the Seventh Michigan, I was able to locate the exact site from which the photograph was recorded as well as identify the timber in the background as the West Woods. The camera was situated at a point where the Seventh Michigan attempted to regroup after falling back into the open ground east of the Hagerstown Pike. The regiment's position at this point was at an angle to a fence line, seen in the photograph, and faced obliquely to the southwest, or left. All the land in the photograph is today owned privately.

The maps currently used by the National Park Service do not show a fence line in this immediate area at the time of the battle. But that one existed here in 1862 is supported by ample evidence, including two contemporary maps of the field and at least two independent, detailed descriptions of the Miller farm as it appeared during the battle, both written by veterans of Antietam.[38]

Here then fell Lt. John A. Clark, who was hit probably by either small arms or artillery fire during the confused retreat from the West Woods. In my search to learn more about Clark, I hoped to uncover a photographic portrait. Because he was a junior officer, there was a chance that if the veterans of the Seventh Michigan had written a history of their service, a portrait of him might have been included.

Unfortunately, I discovered that the veterans of the Seventh left no such study, and it became clear that the odds of finding out what the soldier in the grave looked like were very poor. Portraits of almost all the high-ranking leaders from both sides have been gathered, categorized, and indexed over the years. But in the absence of even a regimental history, trying to locate a portrait of a common individual, one of literally millions of enlisted men and junior officers who served in the war, is a hopeless task.

Clark's military records showed that he enlisted at Monroe, Michigan. Checking a directory of museums and historical societies in the United States, I came across the Monroe County Historical Commission, Monroe, Michigan, to whom I wrote for any information concerning Lieutenant Clark. In reply, I was informed that they were sorry but they had little information on him other than the basics of his service record, to which I already had access.

But their letter continued by mentioning that "we do, however, have a picture of him (head and bust) in his army uniform. If you would be interested in a copy of the photograph, please contact me."

For the author it was a researcher's dream come true. Published here for the first time is a portrait of John A. Clark, the man whose previously anonymous grave formed the subject of Gardner's battlefield photograph.

III–7a

III–7b

III–7 modern

ANTIETAM

JOHN A. CLARK, photographer unknown, album card, ca. summer of 1862 (Monroe Co. Hist. Comm. Archives).

From the scattered bits of evidence that have survived, I learned that John A. Clark, son of Thomas L. and Lovonia Clark of Ida Township, Monroe County, Michigan, was born on his father's eighty-acre farm in 1841.

Ida Township was located along the Michigan Southern Railroad thirteen miles west of the city of Monroe. Contemporary accounts describe Ida as having a rolling landscape with soil, mostly sandy loam, that was excellent for grazing cattle and hogs and producing crops, particularly corn and wheat. The township's total population in 1860 consisted of 673 persons, none of whom were black.

The nearby city of Monroe, situated on Lake Erie, was an important junction on the east–west thoroughfare across the northern part of the nation. The eastern terminus of the Michigan Southern Railroad connected here with steamers for all the lake ports; hence commerce and manufacturing were considerable. Monroe is perhaps most famous as the home of George Armstrong Custer.

John Clark's father, Thomas, had emigrated from New York State in the early 1830s, and in 1834 he became one of the first landowners in Monroe County, having purchased forty acres at that time. He acquired a second forty acres in 1836, the year before Michigan was admitted to the Union.

In 1838, Thomas and Lovonia's first child, a girl named Ellen, was born. Two years later a son, Edward, was born, and the following year saw the birth of their third and last child, John.

Growing up in rural Ida Township during the 1840s and 1850s, all three Clark children attended school and certainly assisted their parents around the farm; the boys helping their father with the crops and livestock, Ellen helping her mother with the cooking, dishes, washing, and mending.

On June 23, 1860, a census taker visited the Clark farm and recorded the names of the six people living there, including Thomas and Lovonia, their daughter, Ellen, two sons, Edward and John, and Thomas Clark's sister, Eleanor. The total value of real estate and personal property was estimated at seven thousand dollars, indicating by mid-nineteenth-century standards that the Clark farm was a moderately thriving one.

Ten months later, in April 1861, the Clarks heard the electrifying news that

Liut John Clark.
7th Mich Inftry D. Co.
Monroe Mich

JOHN A. CLARK

armed rebellion had broken out in far-off Charleston, South Carolina. Two months after that, on June 19, 1861, Thomas Clark's youngest son, John, at age twenty enlisted as a sergeant in Company D, Seventh Michigan Volunteer Infantry. It was a war to preserve the Union and in the swirl of patriotic excitement John Clark could not stand idly by as the Southern "traitors" defiled the flag he had learned to honor since the days of his childhood.

Sgt. John A. Clark was a bright young man with definite leadership capabilities. On March 18, 1862, he was promoted to the rank of second lieutenant in Company D and was advanced again on April 22, 1862, to the rank of first lieutenant. With the Seventh Michigan he saw considerable action during McClellan's Peninsula campaign, but apparently he contracted some sort of ailment in the swampy country south of Richmond, for his military records show that, though unwounded, he was on sick leave during the months of July and August 1862. As there are no hospital records on file, it is almost certain that Clark returned home to recuperate during this period.

It is not hard to imagine the great pride experienced by John Clark's parents during the summer of 1862. Their twenty-one-year-old son had risen through the ranks and was now a commissioned officer in his company. He had been through combat and undoubtedly had many hair-raising stories to tell. But the war was not over, and along with their pride Thomas and Lovonia Clark must have felt a deep-seated uneasiness when John's sick leave expired and he left to rejoin his unit in August. From the newspaper accounts in the *Monroe Commercial* and the *Free Citizen* there was more heavy fighting yet to come.

During the early days of September 1862, the local newspapers began to fill with accounts of the Confederate invasion of Maryland and the pursuit of the Army of the Potomac. For the citizens of Monroe County, apprehension intensified with the knowledge that their local unit, the Seventh Regiment, was involved in the campaign.

Then came word that a great battle had been fought along the banks of Antietam Creek, at an obscure village in Maryland called Sharpsburg. Anxiously, the newspapers were pored over for lists of casualties. Soon telegrams and letters began arriving at various households throughout the county. And then, one day during the week following the battle, a message was received at the Clark farmhouse.

Whether it was a newspaper casualty list, a telegram, or a letter is not known. But the message, in whatever form it came, was as definitive as it was irrevocable, for somewhere in its contents was the name of their son and the words "killed in action."

During the fall of 1862, members of the Clark family, most likely Thomas and his eldest son, Edward, made the sad journey of nearly four hundred miles by rail from Monroe through Pittsburgh to Hagerstown, and thence by wagon to the Antietam battlefield to locate and recover the body of John A. Clark. Eventually, John's grave, inadvertently depicted in Gardner's heretofore unidentified photograph, was found and his remains recovered.

The final resting place of John A. Clark today lies forgotten in Woodlawn Cemetery, Monroe, Michigan, close to the graves of the other members of his family, including that of his father, who died on August 28, 1879, and his mother, who died February 10, 1880.

The dead Confederate soldier, apparently quite young, seen to the left of Clark's grave was probably killed during earlier fighting on the morning of September 17, 1862. A number of Confederate units crossed this ground prior to Sedgwick's arrival on the field, particularly Hays's Louisiana brigade and the right-flank regiments of Ripley's brigade, namely the First and Third North Carolina. There is no way of identifying by name the Confederate soldier who lay dead next to the grave of John Clark, but somewhere in the South his family too received word that he had not made it through the great battle in Maryland. For the members of that family, like the Clarks of Ida Township, Michigan, the words "Antietam" and "Sharpsburg" would evoke painful, haunting memories for years to come.

III–8 Col. Turner G. Morehead, 106th Pennsylvania Volunteers, on the Antietam battlefield, Gardner, stereo #586, September 19, 1862 (LC).

When I began research on this photograph, I did not anticipate any difficulty in locating the distinctive limestone outcropping on which Colonel Morehead sat as he posed for Alexander Gardner.

Gardner's caption mentioned that the view was recorded on the battlefield, specifically on September 19, 1862. Because Gardner's efforts that day centered on the area bounded by the East, West, and North Woods, it appeared reasonable that the timber in the background was a portion of one of those three woods. I thus felt certain that this particular outcropping could be located today by searching through the open fields adjoining the original wood lines.

Unfortunately, after an extensive search I was unable to locate this outcropping on the northern portion of the battlefield—or on any other portion of the twelve square miles at Antietam. The specific site of the Morehead photograph remains elusive and will not be found marked on the map for this group.

I am convinced, however, that this scene was recorded somewhere between the East and West Woods, with one of those woods appearing in the background. Not only is this the area in which Gardner is known to have worked on September 19, but it is likewise the area in which Morehead's unit, the 106th Pennsylvania, was located that same day.

Given my failure to discover the outcropping on any portion of the battlefield, I can conclude only that the outcropping no longer exists in its original state. Perhaps it was broken up sometime during the late nineteenth century by a local farmer who used the limestone as building material. Or perhaps it was leveled to become the foundation for one of the battlefield monuments; the Maryland monument, for example, was erected near the Dunker Church on just such an outcropping.

On September 17, 1862, the 106th Pennsylvania was one of four regiments, all from Philadelphia, that composed Gen. Oliver O. Howard's brigade of Sedgwick's division of the Second Corps. The other two brigades of the division were Gen. Willis A. Gorman's and Dana's. The disaster met by Sedgwick's men at the West Woods, already mentioned several times, will now be discussed in more detail as it related specifically to Colonel Morehead and the 106th Pennsylvania.

III–8

By approximately 9:00 A.M., when Sedgwick's division was arriving at the East Woods, the fighting on the battlefield had reached a standstill. The First Corps was out of action and the Twelfth had already spent the greater part of its energy. Greene's division, at an advanced position just behind the high ground on the Mumma farm, was awaiting a resupply of ammunition while the 125th Pennsylvania stood by itself in the West Woods, near the Dunker Church.

Sedgwick's division, roughly five thousand strong, emerged from the East Woods in three lines of battle, with Gorman's brigade on the front line, followed in succession by Dana's brigade, then Howard's "Philadelphia" brigade. The 106th Pennsylvania, commanded by Colonel Morehead, was at the right center of the rear brigade. Contemporary accounts described the division's westward advance across the corpse-strewn fields between the East and West Woods as majestic, with colors flying, bayonets gleaming in the sun, and mounted officers riding up and down the lines shouting encouragement.

Enemy infantry, save for the dead and dying, were nowhere to be seen, but Confederate artillery fire told Sedgwick's men that the enemy was still active. Union batteries responded, instilling confidence in the blue lines as the rounds droned through the air from behind, passing safely overhead and exploding in enemy territory.

Straight ahead was the Hagerstown Pike with its parallel rail fences and beyond that the West Woods, the objective of the advance. The Union forces hoped to brush aside whatever enemy resistance remained in the woods, allowing Sedgwick's division to swing to the left and drive southward along the Confederate left flank toward the village of Sharpsburg, thereby defeating Lee's army and perhaps ending the war.

With little opposition the lead brigade, Gorman's, scaled the double fencing along the pike and entered the woods, followed closely by Dana and Howard. Upon approaching the western edge of the woods, Gorman's men encountered their first significant resistance, mainly from Gen. Jubal A. Early's Virginia brigade and remnants of other units that had been decimated during prior action that morning.

Gorman's brigade immediately opened fire on the Confederates to the front, but the two Union brigades to Gorman's rear could do nothing but wait, since friendly forces stood between them and the enemy. Most of the members of Sedgwick's division were veterans who had been in combat before, and during this period of waiting soldiers in the two rear lines stood chatting casually and resting on their rifles while several officers were seen to light up cigars and pipes. General Sumner, commander of the Second Corps, had accompanied the division into the woods and was observing the action from near the front line. Everything appeared to be going well and it seemed only a matter of time before Gorman's brigade would force the enemy to retire.

But unbeknownst to Sumner, Sedgwick, or any Union commanders, heavy Confederate reinforcements were at that very moment closing in rapidly on—and behind—the exposed Union left flank. They were Gen. Kershaw's, Gen. Howell Cobb's, Gen. Paul J. Semmes's, and Gen. William Barksdale's brigades of McLaws's division, followed by G. T. Anderson's brigade of D. R. Jones's division and Manning's and Gen. Robert Ransom, Jr.'s, brigades of Walker's division. For Sedgwick's division it was a tactical nightmare.

There are a number of graphic accounts written by Union veterans recalling the moment they first realized what was happening. A member of the Nineteenth Massachusetts of Dana's brigade, second in line, remembered noticing that several men on the extreme left of their position began firing to the rear and left. The commander of the regiment, Col. Edward Hinks, hastily scolded the men, shouting, "What are you doing? Don't you know any better than to fire into our third line?" One of the soldiers called back to the colonel, "You had better look back and see if they are the third line." Hinks peered carefully through the trees and saw a sight he would never forget—a strong line of enemy infantry moving against his left and rear.[39]

At that same moment, General Sumner was talking to Lt. Col. John Kimball, commander of the Fifteenth Massachusetts of Gorman's brigade, when a junior officer shouted out, "See the rebels!" pointing to the left and rear. Sumner turned in his saddle and with a start exclaimed, "My God, we must get out of this!"[40]

But there was no time to shift the brigades to the left. The lines were too close together, only thirty paces apart, and the enemy was already upon them. The first Union regiments hit by the surprise flank attack were the Thirty-fourth New York and the 125th Pennsylvania.

A member of the 106th Pennsylvania remembered seeing General Sumner, his eyes flashing and white locks blowing in the breeze, riding from left to right along Howard's third line, frantically waving his hat and shouting,

"Back Boys, for God's sake move back; you are in a bad fix." Confusion quickly turned to panic.[41]

Although several Union regiments, mainly those located on the right flank, were able to retire northward in relatively decent order, the majority of units on the left broke ranks and fled eastward toward the East Woods; those in the center fled northward toward the Miller and Nicodemus farm buildings. Scattered attempts were made to rally, but they proved futile amid the volleys of well-directed Confederate infantry fire then coming from three directions—front, left, and rear.

As the 106th Pennsylvania retreated northward across the open fields between the West Woods and the Hagerstown Pike, a bullet struck Colonel Morehead's horse, sending both mount and rider sprawling to the ground. Morehead was pinned under his horse when three members of the regiment, seeing his predicament, returned to free him.

Badly bruised, the colonel was making his way northward when he realized that he had lost his sword. Those by his side at the time tried to persuade him not to return for the cherished possession, but his reply was, "Yes I will, that sword was given to me by my men and I told them I would protect it with my life and never see it dishonored, and I am not going to let them damned rebels get it."[42]

Morehead rushed back to where his horse lay and recovered the sword. The enemy, by then only yards away, ordered Morehead to surrender. He refused and fled northward amid a volley of enemy rifle fire. None of the bullets hit its mark, and the colonel made it safely to friendly lines in the vicinity of the Miller house.

Eventually, the 106th Pennsylvania managed to regroup and spent the remainder of September 17 supporting artillery batteries at the East Woods. Of the 5,000 members of Sedgwick's division, 2,210, or nearly half, were lost during the twenty-minute slaughter at the West Woods. Two days later, Colonel Morehead met Alexander Gardner on the battlefield and agreed to pose for the photograph shown here.

Turner Gustavus Morehead was born on March 18, 1814, and was forty-eight years old at Antietam. His association with the military began in 1835, when he joined the "Washington Grays," a Philadelphia militia unit. Rising through the ranks, he became a captain and was present at the Philadelphia riots of that same period.

When the Mexican War erupted, Morehead's company voted not to partici-
pate. Disappointed, Morehead resigned to become a captain in the First
Pennsylvania Regiment and served with that unit in Mexico at Vera Cruz,
Cerro Gordo, Puebla, and other locales.

After the Mexican War he returned to Philadelphia to become the colonel of
another militia unit, the "Philadelphia Blues." When the Civil War broke out
in 1861, he helped raise the 106th Regiment and served as its colonel at Fair
Oaks, Savage's Station, Malvern Hill, Antietam, and later at Fredericksburg.
Because of illness, Morehead saw no action in 1863 and was forced to retire on
April 5, 1864.

Returning again to Philadelphia, he went into the wholesale shoe business
until appointed Weigher of the Port of Philadelphia. In 1882 he moved to As-
bury Park, New Jersey, where he died on May 28, 1892, at the age of seventy-
eight.

CHARLES E. KING, photographer and type unknown, ca. 1861 (Westbrook).

At about noon on September 17, the first elements of the Union Sixth Corps began arriving on the field to strengthen positions in the vicinity of the East Woods. Immediately, Col. William Irwin's brigade of Gen. William F. Smith's division was thrown forward to the high ground across from the Dunker Church to help repulse the attack of the Third Arkansas and Twenty-seventh North Carolina. Irwin's men secured the high ground and held that salient point throughout the remainder of the day.

Generally speaking, however, the Sixth Corps played little more than a supportive role at Antietam. At that time it was deemed inadvisable to make yet another potentially futile attempt to carry the West Woods. Thus, aside from Irwin's brigade, the Sixth Corps escaped the bloodiest day of the war with relatively few casualties.

Despite the Sixth Corps' secondary role at Antietam, I have chosen to include in this study a vignette biography of one of that corps' younger members, Charles E. King, drummer boy with Company F, Forty-ninth Pennsylvania Volunteers of Gen. Winfield S. Hancock's brigade.

When I came across King's portrait in his unit's regimental history I was at first hesitant to use it, because of its inferior photographic quality. But King did serve at Antietam and I was struck by a notation under his portrait stating that he was "12 years 5 Mo. and 9 Days old when he enlisted." Just as John Marshall was one of the oldest enlisted men at Antietam, surely Charles King was one of the youngest soldiers from either army present on the field that day. Subsequent research into King's background convinced me that his story must be told.

Charles E. King, known to his family and friends as Charley, was born in the borough of West Chester, Chester County, Pennsylvania, in April 1849. He was the oldest child of Pennell and Adaline King, who, according to the 1860 census, had five other children. The census taker who visited the King household on June 11, 1860, recorded the members of the family as follows: Pennell King, aged thirty-three, a merchant tailor; his wife, Adaline, also thirty-three; and their six children, Charles, aged eleven; Lewis, nine; Theodore, six; Ella, four; William, two; and Anna, an infant of two months. The three oldest children were attending school at the time.

Located twenty-three miles west of Philadelphia, West Chester was incorpo-

12 YEARS 5 MO. AND 9 DAYS. OLD WHEN HE ENLISTED.

CHARLES E. KING

rated in 1799 and had a population of 4,757 on the eve of the Civil War. Contemporary gazetteers mention that the borough streets were laid out in a regular pattern, the citizens were noted for their "enterprise and intelligence," and the borough was the seat of considerable trade and manufacturing.

As a diversion from schoolwork young Charles had taken up the drums sometime prior to 1861 and had apparently learned to play them quite well. When the war broke out shortly after his twelfth birthday, Charles begged his parents for permission to enlist in the army as a drummer boy. His father would hear nothing of it and refused to allow his son to become involved. Charles was extremely disappointed at his father's seemingly callous decision and persisted in his nagging. A local newspaper article mentioned that at nighttime Pennell King frequently found his son "setting up in bed 'marking time' on the head-board of his bed."[43]

During the late summer of 1861, when Company F of the Forty-ninth Pennsylvania was being recruited in the vicinity of West Chester, Charles made a habit of hanging around the recruiting station and so impressed the man in charge, Capt. Benjamin H. Sweeney, with his drumming skills and eagerness to enlist that the captain agreed to intercede on the boy's behalf.

In early September, Captain Sweeney visited the King home and discussed the matter with the boy's father, explaining that drummer boys did not actually go into combat but rather stayed behind the lines to help with the wounded. Sweeney concluded by stating that he would take personal responsibility for the boy and that Charles would be well guarded against danger.

Reluctantly, and undoubtedly after considerable contemplation, Pennell and Adaline gave permission for their son to join the army. On September 9, 1861, at the age of twelve, Charles King enlisted in Company F, Forty-ninth Pennsylvania Volunteers.

During the following year Charles became one of the favorites in the regiment. So impressed were the men with his drumming that he was eventually made drum major of the Forty-ninth. Receiving a salary for the first time, Charles would send his pay home to be deposited by his parents in his name at the family bank in West Chester. He participated with the regiment in the Peninsula campaign and, by the summer of 1862, could justifiably call himself a veteran. It was a distinction few of his age group could claim, and it must have given him great pride.

Although his parents and younger brothers and sisters most likely shared in this pride, Pennell and Adaline King must have suffered great anxiety each time they picked up the local newspaper and pored over the reports and casualty lists related to the campaigns of the Army of the Potomac and specifically to the Forty-ninth Pennsylvania.

At Antietam, the Forth-ninth Pennsylvania was placed in support to the immediate right of Capt. Andrew Cowan's First Battery, New York Light Artillery, on the Miller farm just north of the East Woods. There was little going on at the time the unit reached the field (shortly before 1:00 P.M.) and several members of the Forty-ninth took the opportunity to talk with members of the 125th Pennsylvania, remnants of which were located nearby. The two units had been recruited from the same part of the state and many of them were old friends.

The fighting, for all practical purposes, had ended on the northern portion of the battlefield by the time of the arrival of Hancock's brigade and the Forty-ninth Pennsylvania, but the men were occasionally subjected to scattered artillery fire. Essentially, the Southern gunners wanted to show Union forces that they were still ready to meet any renewed attacks against the Confederate left flank.

During one of these artillery salvos, a shell exploded amidst the ranks of the Forty-ninth Pennsylvania, wounding several soldiers, including thirteen-year-old Charles King, who was hit "through the body" by a piece of shrapnel. With great care and affection, members of Company F carried the bleeding boy back to a field hospital where, three agonizing days later, on September 20, 1862, he died from his wound.

Although his name has remained obscure, Charles E. King was the youngest soldier from either side to die as a direct result of combat during the Civil War. Considering that more than six hundred thousand American soldiers died during the four years of warfare, it is indeed a tragic distinction.

But for the boy's parents, that distinction would provide no consolation. Against their better judgment they had granted permission for their immature twelve-year-old son to join the army. That decision would torment them for years to come. It is not difficult to imagine the thoughts and memories that must have crowded Pennell King's mind during the fall of 1862 when he journeyed to Antietam to recover the lifeless body of his oldest child, whose grave today lies somewhere in West Chester, Pennsylvania.

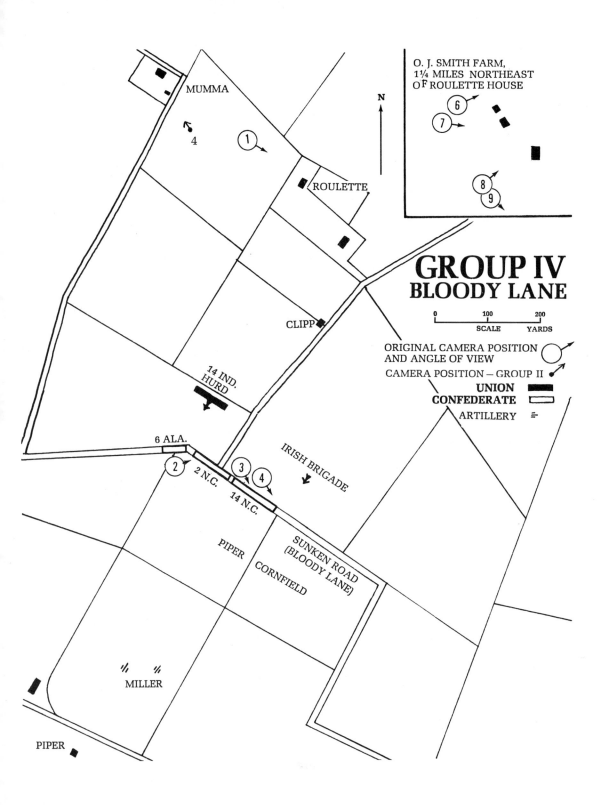

O. J. SMITH FARM, 1¼ MILES NORTHEAST OF ROULETTE HOUSE

N

MUMMA

4

1

ROULETTE

6

7

8

9

CLIPP

GROUP IV
BLOODY LANE

0   100   200
SCALE   YARDS

ORIGINAL CAMERA POSITION
AND ANGLE OF VIEW

CAMERA POSITION – GROUP II

UNION
CONFEDERATE
ARTILLERY

14 IND.
HURD.

IRISH BRIGADE

6 ALA.

2

2 N.C.

3

4

14 N.C.

PIPER

SUNKEN ROAD
(BLOODY LANE)

CORNFIELD

MILLER

PIPER

9

GROUP IV: BLOODY LANE

IV–1 The Roulette house, Gardner, stereo #575, September 19 or 20, 1862 (LC).

The residence portrayed here, the home of William Roulette, was located only three hundred yards southeast of the Mumma house (II-4). Because Gardner photographed both buildings from the same field, it is probable that the two scenes were recorded at roughly the same time. Yet despite the proximity of the two houses, each figured in distinctly different phases of the battle—the Roulette farm being involved in the Union efforts to dislodge Confederate forces at the sunken road, or as it would be called later, Bloody Lane.

Unlike Samuel Mumma, William Roulette chose to remain at home when urged to leave by Southerners on September 15, 1862. At the time of the battle, the Roulette family consisted of seven members, including thirty-eight-year-old William; his wife, Margaret, thirty-one; and their five children (three boys and two girls, ranging in age from two to thirteen). For safety's sake the family fled to the basement when the fighting erupted.

Gardner's photograph was recorded looking southeast, in the direction of Antietam Creek. A portion of distant Elk Ridge can be seen in the background to the right of the house. From Elk Ridge, men of the Union Signal Corps were able to observe enemy movements and communicate with various stations on the battlefield. For a time, Lt. Frederick W. Owen operated a signal station in the vicinity of the Roulette farm (see I-3a).

It was across the low ground visible to the far left of the Roulette house that Sedgwick's division of the Second Corps advanced onto the battlefield after fording Antietam Creek. Sedgwick was followed closely by another division of the Second Corps, that commanded by Gen. William H. French.

Several regiments of French's division, like a number of those in the Twelfth Corps, had been recruited just weeks before and were seeing action for the first time at Antietam. Lt. Frederick L. Hitchcock, adjutant of the newly formed 132d Pennsylvania Volunteers of Gen. Nathan Kimball's Brigade, recalled in later years the oppressive anxiety that mounted with each step as his unit advanced inexorably toward the battleground.

> We ... moved, as I thought, rather leisurely for upwards of two miles, crossing Antietam Creek, which our men waded nearly waist deep, emerging, of course, soaked through, our first experience of this kind. It was a hot morning and, therefore, the only ill effect of this wading was the discomfort to the men of marching with soaked feet. It was now quite evident that a great battle was in progress. A deafening pandemonium of cannonading, with shrieking and bursting shells, filled the air beyond us, towards which we were marching. An occasional shell whizzed by or over, reminding us that we were rapidly approaching the "debatable ground." Soon we began to hear a most ominous sound which we had never before heard, except in the far distance at South Mountain, namely, the rattle of musketry. It had none of the deafening bluster of the cannonading so terrifying to new troops, but to those who had once experienced its effects, it was infinitely more to be dreaded. . . .
>
> These volleys of musketry we were approaching sounded in the distance like the rapid pouring of shot upon a tinpan, or the tearing of heavy canvas, with slight pauses interspersed with single shots, or desultory shooting. All this presaged fearful work in store for us, with what results to each personally the future, measured probably by moments, would reveal.
>
> How does one feel under such conditions? To tell the truth, I realized the situation most keenly and felt very uncomfortable. Lest

IV–1

IV–1 modern

there might be some undue manifestation of this feeling on my conduct, I said to myself, this is the duty I undertook to perform for my country, and now I'll do it, and leave the results with God. My greater fear was not that I might be killed, but that I might be grievously wounded and left a victim of suffering on the field.

The nervous strain was plainly visible upon all of us. All moved doggedly forward in obedience to orders, in absolute silence so far as talking was concerned. The compressed lip and set teeth showed that nerve and resolution had been summoned to the discharge of duty. A few temporarily fell out, unable to endure the nervous strain, which was simply awful. . . .[44]

A short while later, the 132d Pennsylvania came under the direct fire of enemy infantry. By 1:00 P.M. the regiment had lost 30 killed, 114 wounded, and 8 missing. Lieutenant Hitchcock survived his first battle unscathed.

It apparently had been the plan for French's division to move into action on Sedgwick's immediate left, covering the ground in front of and south of the Dunker Church. Had this course been enacted, it is doubtful that Sedgwick's division would have met with disaster at the West Woods. But French's orders were vague, and upon approaching the Roulette farm, his division came under fire from Confederate skirmishers located in the vicinity of the Roulette farmhouse. Assuming that this was the force he was expected to attack, French moved his entire division to the left and proceeded to advance southward, effectively breaking all contact with Sedgwick.

The Confederate skirmishers were quickly routed, a number of them fleeing for safety into the basement of the Roulette house, where the family was then hiding. Within moments, these Confederates were captured as the Union line of battle engulfed the farm buildings.

There is a story, told many times, of how some beehives in the Roulette yard were inadvertently overturned by advancing troops, enraging the bees and sending them swarming into the ranks of the 132d Pennsylvania, causing considerable confusion.[45] What appears under magnification to be a cluster of whitewashed wooden crates in front of the Roulette house in Gardner's photograph may well be the beehives referred to by members of the 132d. According to agricultural handbooks of the period, the cratelike structure was highly recommended for raising bees.

GROUP IV: BLOODY LANE

After re-forming their battle lines, French's men continued southward toward the sunken road that divided the properties of William Roulette and Henry Piper. In this road, partially hidden from view by rises in the ground, were two Confederate brigades, Gen. Robert E. Rodes's Alabama and G. B. Anderson's North Carolina, both of D. H. Hill's division, which silently awaited the enemy's approach.

Members of the Roulette family, especially the younger children, were probably badly shaken by the experience of being imprisoned in their own cellar as the battle raged, hour after hour, about the once peaceful farmyard. On at least one occasion, however, William Roulette emerged from the safety of his basement to cheer on the Union forces. The Roulettes survived the battle and undoubtedly considered themselves fortunate that their home did not meet with the same fate as that of their neighbor, Samuel Mumma.

The original Roulette house and several outbuildings, today privately owned, are still in use and appear much as they did in 1862. Perhaps one day they will come under the jurisdiction of the National Park Service, to be preserved permanently as quiet reminders of the tragedy that befell our nation on September 17, 1862.

Unfortunately, countless unprotected historic sites such as the Roulette farm have been, and continue to be, destroyed daily through neglect, ignorance, and the self-interest of housing developers. As one gazes at the modern photograph of the Roulette house, taken from Gardner's original camera position, one can only wonder what this same scene will look like a century from now.

IV–2 Confederate dead in Bloody Lane, view looking northeast, Gardner, stereo #565, September 19, 1862 (LC).

IV–3 Confederate dead in Bloody Lane, view looking southeast, Gardner, stereo #563, September 19, 1862 (MOLLUS-Mass.).

IV–4 Confederate dead in Bloody Lane, Gardner, stereo #553, September 19, 1862 (MOLLUS-Mass.).

With battle flags waving and bayonets shining in the morning sun, the long lines of French's division advanced southward in almost perfect precision toward the Confederate position at the sunken road. G. B. Anderson's North Carolina brigade and Rodes's Alabama brigade waited in the lane, using it as a trench, while a second line of Confederate infantry (from the same brigades) was posted behind the first, on the higher ground at the edge of the Piper cornfield south of the road.

As the Union lines pressed steadily closer, hundreds of Confederates peered along the sights of leveled rifles, awaiting the command to open fire. The tension mounted with each passing moment—the Union lines being allowed to advance until the features of individual faces could be distinguished by the Southern riflemen.

Finally, with the enemy only yards away, Col. John B. Gordon of the Sixth Alabama blared out the command, "Fire!" Instantly, hundreds of fingers squeezed on rifle triggers, unleashing an earsplitting hail of deadly missiles, flame, and smoke into the first line of Union infantry. The shock was staggering, the initial volley alone bringing down scores of French's men—some say nearly the entire front rank.

Although the new regiments were badly stunned, the veteran units of French's division quickly recovered and returned fire. For the next hour the fighting along the sunken road assumed a general nature, with the opposing front lines remaining in close proximity to each other. French's men took advantage of the cover afforded by rises in the ground just north of the lane.

By 10:30 A.M., Gen. Israel B. Richardson's division of the Second Corps had arrived on the field to aid French, and Rodes's and G. B. Anderson's Confederate brigades were likewise supported by Gen. Richard Anderson's division. As the noon hour approached and the casualties continued to mount, Union forces could claim little or no progress in their efforts to dislodge the strong Confederate position at the sunken road. Then, at approximately noon, the stalemate was broken by a bold Union attack against the center of the Confederate line.

The assault was made by two Union regiments of Gen. John C. Caldwell's brigade, Richardson's division—the Sixty-first and Sixty-fourth New York—who were jointly commanded by Col. Francis C. Barlow. Barlow's men penetrated the enemy line at a bend in the sunken road where Rodes's right-flank unit, the Sixth Alabama, joined the left flank of G. B. Anderson's brigade, the Second North Carolina. Having gained a foothold in the road, Barlow's two regiments were now able to deliver an enfilading fire along significant stretches of the lane to both right and left, causing great panic and slaughter among the defenders and making the once strong position untenable.

A number of Southerners were forced to surrender, though many who survived the onslaught managed to escape onto the Piper farm, where they joined supporting elements of Richard H. Anderson's division. With the help of several artillery batteries, conspicuously Capt. M. B. Miller's Battery of the Washington Artillery (Louisiana), a new defensive line was established on the Piper farm, some six hundred yards to the rear of the sunken road. Never threatened seriously after 1:00 P.M., this second position would hold through the end of the battle.

In retrospect, the repulse of all Confederate units from the sunken road proved a hollow victory for the Union forces, especially when one considers that the diversion was in large part responsible for Sedgwick's disaster at the West Woods. Nevertheless, the sight presented by the lane after its capture would immortalize it as one of the most unforgettable features on the Antietam battlefield.

For a period of two and a half hours, Rodes's and G. B. Anderson's brigades had suffered continuous casualties along this one static line. By the time the brigades were forced to retire, Bloody Lane was at points choked with human corpses—a gruesome spectacle noted not only in numerous contemporary descriptions of the field but captured as well by the stereo camera of Alexander Gardner.

Despite Gardner's undeniable interest in photographing the dead at Antietam, he exposed only three negatives at Bloody Lane, with two of them (3 and 4) of the same subject from different distances. Because the most expansive view of the lane (view 3) shows only the one isolated cluster of bodies, it is my belief that although Gardner reached and covered the lane on September 19, he

IV–2

IV–2 modern   IV–3 modern

IV-3 above   IV-4 below

did so in the late afternoon (as evidenced by the shadows), after many portions of the lane had already been cleared of the dead.

For the most part, the task of burying the Confederate dead at Bloody Lane was delegated to the 130th Pennsylvania Volunteers of Col. Dwight Morris's brigade, French's division. Beginning their work sometime on the morning of September 19, members of the unit eventually reported interring a total of 138 enemy bodies, all of which were removed from the road and buried in trenches dug in the fields north of and adjacent to the road.[46]

Of the three Bloody Lane scenes recorded by Gardner, the first one presented here, 2, will be perhaps the least familiar to modern readers. To my knowledge, however, prior works have never located precisely any of the three.

To determine Gardner's original camera positions, I returned to the site of the lane (only a portion of which today remains sunken) and examined systematically all sections, comparing the lay of the land with Gardner's photographs. In this instance, the exact camera positions were determined with little difficulty.

For view 2, recorded at the center of the Confederate line in Bloody Lane, Gardner pointed his camera in a northeasterly direction, toward the ground over which Union forces advanced. The fields in the background were part of the Roulette farm; the large trees to the left mark the location of a lane that led from the sunken road to the Roulette farm buildings.

The portion of Bloody Lane visible in the foreground was occupied during the battle by the left-flank unit of G. B. Anderson's brigade, the Second North Carolina, and it is probable that most of the Confederate dead pictured in this photograph were members of that regiment. It was here, at the bend in Bloody Lane (where the left of Anderson's North Carolina brigade connected with the right of Rodes's Alabama brigade), that Barlow's Sixty-first and Sixty-fourth New York regiments first overran the Confederate line.

Two days after the battle, at the time Gardner recorded these photographs, details from the 130th Pennsylvania had already made headway in the disagreeable task of transferring the swollen, putrid corpses from the lane to waiting burial trenches. The group of Union soldiers seen standing along the edge of Bloody Lane to the right in view 2 are probably members of the 130th.

Because any movement would have shown up on the plate as a blur, it is conceivable that Gardner asked the burial detail to take a momentary break as he recorded this image. In any case, all the soldiers, as well as the on-looking mounted civilian, appear conscious that a negative was being exposed.

The modern version for view 2 was recorded from a point several yards to the right of the original camera position in order to show the background terrain, which is today hidden from view by foliage and a postbattle structure.

Views 3 and 4 were recorded some 125 yards farther east along the road, just beyond the intersection with Roulette's farm lane. Most of the dead at this point were probably members of the Fourteenth North Carolina of G. B. Anderson's brigade. In all likelihood, Gardner first recorded the distant view of the cluster of Confederate dead (3), then decided to move closer for a more detailed and more dramatic version of the same subject (4).

Bloody Lane ran uphill in a southeasterly direction at this point, with the Confederate line facing northward, or to the left. Visible to the right in both versions of this scene, beyond the remnant of the rail fence (fencing bordered both sides of the lane), stands the cornfield of Henry Piper, whose property adjoined Bloody Lane on the south. Along the edge of this cornfield stood the second line of Confederates who fired over the heads of their comrades in the road.

Today this section of Bloody Lane is closed to traffic and is preserved by the National Park Service. Due to the similarity of Gardner views 3 and 4, I have included a modern version for view 3 only. Visible in the left distance of modern view 3 is the monument commemorating the action of the 132d Pennsylvania Volunteers, and beyond that, partially obscured by the regimental monument, stands a stone observation tower erected after the war.

IV–5 Union dead of the Irish Brigade, Gardner, stereo #550, September 19, 1862 (LC).

From the information provided by Gardner's original caption for this photograph, together with the expansive nature of the scene itself, revealing as it does a large cornfield in the background with a distant ridge or wood line situated beyond, I anticipated little difficulty in determining Gardner's precise camera location.

One of the rarest of all Antietam photographs, this scene was identified by Gardner as being a "Group of Irish Brigade, as they lay on Battle-field of Antietam, Sept. 19, 1862." The Irish Brigade, commanded by Gen. Thomas F. Meagher, was with Richardson's division at Antietam and consisted of the Twenty-ninth Massachusetts and Sixty-third, Sixty-ninth, and Eighty-eighth New York regiments. Where the brigade fought and suffered all of its casualties at Antietam is a matter of record.

Specifically, they became engaged on the Roulette farm at about 10:30 A.M., opposite that portion of Bloody Lane defended by G. B. Anderson's North Carolina brigade. After sustaining heavy casualties in front of the sunken road, the Irish Brigade was pulled back five hundred yards to a reserve position. Later, at about 1:00 P.M., they were recalled to their former position in front of the sunken road, but by that time the fighting in this area had ended.

With a knowledge of the various positions occupied by the Irish Brigade and particularly of where the brigade was under heavy fire, I initially considered Gardner's most likely camera location to be somewhere in the fields just north of Bloody Lane, with the camera facing southward in the direction of the Piper cornfield. It seemed simple enough—until the hypothesis was completely shattered by subsequent field investigation. Nowhere in the fields occupied by the Irish Brigade could I find a distant view of the Piper cornfield that even approached the scene depicted by Gardner's photograph. The lay of the land, especially that in the foreground, clearly did not match. Additionally, there were no ridges or large bodies of woods present in the southward view from the vicinity of the sunken road.

Next I considered the possibility that Gardner's camera might have been facing westward, toward Elk Ridge. But the terrain did not match. Subsequently, I considered all conceivable camera angles from the field adjoining Bloody Lane—with no success.

IV–5

My search then broadened to other points occupied by the Irish Brigade, including their reserve position. Again meeting with failure, I was forced to hypothesize that perhaps Gardner's Irish Brigade identification was in error, and I expanded my search to include the entire battlefield. My efforts centered around some one dozen original cornfield sites, at least one of which, I hoped, could be matched to the terrain and background configurations of Gardner's photograph.

Although I did find one or two sites of a vaguely similar nature, none could be termed convincing. Therefore, the precise location of view 5 remains unknown. Furthermore, I am hard pressed to explain why the view cannot be located. I can find no reason to doubt Gardner's original caption. He *was* in the vicinity of Bloody Lane on September 19, 1862, and he definitely would have had access to a subject such as this. Indeed, the only logical explanation I can think of is that there is something about the image itself that is visually deceptive. Unfortunately, the original negative for this photograph no longer exists, the version reproduced here having been made from a copy negative on file at the Library of Congress.

In this instance, it appears that the copy negative was made from a contemporary print, probably an album card, which in turn was most likely cropped. And because there is a good chance that the contemporary print from which this negative was made was probably faded when copied, the odds are great that the original negative possessed considerably more detail, especially in the background, than the copy negative. Without access to the original negative, and because I cannot link this scene visually with any other Antietam photographs, we can only hope that someday a more revealing version will be uncovered.

WILLIAM S. PARRAN, photographer unknown, ambrotype, ca. 1860 (Mus. of the Confederacy).

Sometime during the mid-1850s, William S. Parran, then a recent graduate of medical school, established his physician's practice in Barboursville, Virginia, a small Orange County farming community located near the foothills of the Blue Ridge Mountains some fourteen miles northeast of Charlottesville. It was a scenic area with soil well suited for the production of corn and tobacco.

Ably serving the medical needs of villagers and local farmers, Dr. Parran took an active role in community affairs and about the year 1859 helped organize a militia company known as the Barboursville Guards. As was typical for such militia units, the officers were chosen by unit members through an election. Thus it was that William Parran was chosen company commander with the rank of captain.

Many communities both large and small throughout the United States had their militia companies—a national tradition going back to colonial days. Undoubtedly, most such units prided themselves on being descendants of the Minutemen of 1775. Generally speaking, however, the militia of the antebellum period was as much a social institution as it was military in nature. Usually outfitted in ornate uniforms, these companies provided their communities with colorful holiday parades, and drills, meetings, and picnics gave the citizens an excuse for getting together on a periodic basis.

As a rural physician, Dr. Parran would have spent much of his time making house calls, in addition to receiving patients during regular office hours. There would have been children with mumps to treat, babies to be delivered, broken limbs to be mended, prescriptions to be given covering everything from consumption to constipation.

In mid-April 1861, Dr. William Parran was twenty-eight years old. He had a wife, Mary Virginia Parran, two years younger, and one child, an infant daughter named Emma Camilia Parran. As the commander of the local Barboursville Guards, Parran undoubtedly followed closely the ominous events then transpiring in Charleston, South Carolina. His native Virginia had not yet seceded from the Union, and all eyes were turned toward Fort Sumter. Once the first shots were fired, on April 12, 1861, events moved swiftly. Within three days, Lincoln called for seventy-five thousand volunteers to put down

WILLIAM S. PARRAN

the insurrection. Taking this as a signal for a Northern invasion of the South, Virginia voted on April 17, 1861, to join the Confederate States of America. And as Virginia went, so too did the Barboursville Guards, which was shortly thereafter accepted into the service of the Confederate States Army as Company F, Thirteenth Virginia Infantry.

Hence William Parran went off to war and served as the commander of Company F through the following winter. In early December 1861, Parran contracted jaundice and was admitted to a general hospital, where he remained for some time until the illness forced him to resign his commission. On April 26, 1862, he was dropped from the rolls of the Thirteenth Virginia and saw no further service with that unit.

Returning home to his wife and infant daughter, Parran remained in Barboursville for an unknown period of time. Although we can assume that he was glad to be with his family, he must have been increasingly bothered by the fact that he was a physician and that his services were greatly needed at the front. Consequently, after regaining his health he rejoined the army and was assigned to Maj. A. R. Courtney's Artillery Battalion as an assistant surgeon.

Parran's military file does not specify the date of his reenlistment, but it is known that he was with Courtney's battalion during the Maryland invasion. On September 15, 1862, that battalion took part in the capture of Harpers Ferry. Unlike the vast majority of Confederate units, it was left behind there (with the exception of Capt. John R. Johnson's Battery) to guard the booty surrendered by Union forces.

However, Asst. Surgeon William Parran was apparently detached from the battalion immediately after the surrender of Harpers Ferry, and he accompanied the bulk of the Confederate forces northward. The unit he was formally attached to remains unknown. What is clear, though, is that Parran was on the field during the battle of Antietam and was in the vicinity of a battery of the Washington Artillery (Louisiana) during a critical stage in the fighting. As indicated by the records, this undesignated battery was in a desperate situation when, having lost many of its members, Assistant Surgeon Parran pitched in to help man the field pieces.

Four batteries of the Washington Artillery saw action at Antietam, only one of which, Capt. M. B. Miller's, found itself in a situation approaching the desperation just described. The action took place shortly after Barlow's breakthrough at Bloody Lane.

Remnants of Confederate units were streaming back through the Piper cornfield while elements of Richardson's division followed in pursuit. Miller's battery had already sustained heavy casualties and could barely muster enough men to operate two of the battery's four twelve-pounder Napoleons. Help was desperately needed to stem the Union advance—and it was quickly found.

According to official accounts, a number of nearby Confederate infantrymen, together with several members of General Longstreet's staff, assisted in manning the guns, Longstreet himself observing the action.[47] Firing canister at close range, the battery was able to check the Union advance long enough for the Confederates to establish a defensive line on the Piper farm.

Although William Parran's name is found nowhere in the official Confederate reports of the battle, it is believed that he was one of those who volunteered to man Miller's guns. But whichever battery of the Washington Artillery he volunteered to aid, the decision would be his last, for on September 17, 1862, while serving as an impromptu gunner, William S. Parran, the physician from Barboursville, Virginia, was hit by enemy fire and fell dead.

His body probably lay on the battlefield for two or three days until interred by Union burial details in an anonymous grave. Today his remains most likely rest with those of hundreds of other unidentified Southern dead who were removed from the battlefield after the war to the Confederate cemetery in Hagerstown, Maryland.

IV–6 a and b Dr. Anson Hurd, 14th Indiana Volunteers, attending Confederate wounded at the field hospital of French's division; Gardner, stereo #588, on or about September 20, 1862; a) left half (LC), b) right half (MOLLUS-Mass.).

IV–7 The Smith house and outbuildings, used as hospital by French's division, Gardner, stereo #590, on or about September 20, 1862 (LC).

IV–8 The Smith barn at the hospital of French's division, view looking eastward toward Antietam Creek, Gardner, stereo #589, on or about September 20, 1862 (LC).

IV–9 Scene at the hospital of French's division, taken looking southeastward toward Elk Ridge, Gardner, stereo #592, on or about September 20, 1862 (LC).

Of these four views, all of which were identified by Gardner as having been taken near Keedysville on a farm owned by someone named Smith, only two—6 and 8—have been reproduced widely over the past century. The companion views have remained obscure until now.

Gardner's caption for view 6 identified the standing officer as Dr. Anson Hurd, Fourteenth Indiana Volunteers, an identification that has rightfully survived to become part of the scene's traditional caption. To my knowledge, however, no one has ever attempted to research the Smith farm series in any significant detail.

My research on these views began with a study of contemporary maps showing hospital locations in the vicinity of Sharpsburg and the nearby village of Keedysville (located east of Antietam Creek, along the Sharpsburg–Boonsboro Pike and less than a mile northeast of McClellan's headquarters at the Pry farm).

Some have assumed that Gardner's captions referred to the David Smith farm, the site of a large Confederate hospital located just west of the village of Sharpsburg. But because Gardner described the site as being near Keedysville rather than Sharpsburg, it seemed more logical that the Smith farm referred to was actually located closer to the former village than to the latter. Consequently, I was able to determine from maps that the most likely site was the farm of Dr. Otho J. Smith, whose property adjoined the west bank of Antietam Creek two miles northeast of Sharpsburg but only one west of Keedysville.

IV–6a

IV–6b

IV–7

IV–6 modern

IV–7 modern

IV–8

IV–9

IV–8 modern   IV–9 modern

This contention was further supported by the facts that Dr. Anson Hurd's regiment, the Fourteenth Indiana, belonged to Gen. Nathan Kimball's brigade of French's division and that the O. J. Smith farm served as French's divisional hospital.

Through field investigation I was able to confirm that the O. J. Smith farm was indeed the site of Gardner's four Antietam hospital scenes. As is evident from the modern versions, the terrain today matches perfectly the distinctive terrain visible in each of Gardner's views. (The O. J. Smith buildings were all torn down prior to the turn of the century.) Although these photographs were recorded fully a mile and a quarter northeast of the Roulette house and in an area distinctly separate from any of the major groupings of battlefield photographs, it is appropriate to discuss them here with the Bloody Lane group because of their association with French's division.

Exactly when the hospital series was recorded remains uncertain. Yet, judging from the subject matter, subject location, and even the negative numbers of the four hospital scenes, there is little or no doubt that all four were taken between September 19 and 22, the period during which Gardner recorded the bulk of his September series.

It is known that Gardner spent September 19 working on the Miller, Mumma, and Roulette farms. September 21 was devoted mainly to Burnside Bridge, September 22 to Antietam Bridge. Because Gardner's captions provide no indication as to his whereabouts on September 20 and since he dated none of the Smith farm hospital scenes, it seems at least likely that a portion of September 20 was spent on the Smith farm. In the absence of additional information, I have therefore dated them as on or about September 20, 1862.

Of all the many field hospitals that dotted the countryside surrounding Sharpsburg, one wonders how Gardner came to single out the one located on the seemingly out-of-the-way Smith farm. A possible explanation is that the Smith farm buildings were situated some six hundred yards west of a third stone bridge over the Antietam, known to history as the Upper or Hooker Bridge. It was over this bridge (which still stands), on the late afternoon of September 16, 1862, that a portion of Hooker's First Corps crossed the creek, followed later that night by the Twelfth Corps, elements of which also used the same bridge.

After the battle, anyone traveling the direct route from Keedysville to the northern part of the battlefield via the Hooker Bridge would have passed by the sprawling Smith farm hospital. It seems plausible, therefore, to conjecture that this was the route used by Gardner, perhaps more than once.

The battlefield reeked with the offensive odors of decaying men and horses for days after the fighting. Since this was Gardner's first experience in photographing a freshly scarred battlefield and because there existed no pressing need for him to camp amid all this decay after concluding work on September 19, it is possible that he retraced his steps that evening and sought a less offensive campground on the opposite side of the Antietam and closer to Keedysville. Because of the large quantity of views recorded on the northern portion of the field, it is likely that he returned to the vicinity of the East Woods the next day.

In essence, Gardner may have "commuted" to the northern battlefield on both September 19 and 20, passing the Smith farm hospital more than once and eventually stopping to record these four photographs.

A close examination of the Smith farm photographs reveals that they were taken in pairs, each pair being panoramic in nature. Views 6a and 7 were taken from nearly the same camera position, and they may be joined by the right half of the stereo for 6, presented here as view 6b. Connecting views 6b and 7 is the partially whitewashed farmhouse of Dr. O. J. Smith.

Likewise, views 8 and 9 may be joined by the presence of the large haystack and distant tents appearing both to the right in 8 and to the left in 9. Furthermore, from my investigation of the original camera sites (working primarily with the backgrounds), I was able to establish that the thatch-roofed barn visible in view 8 is identical to the barn appearing to the far right in view 7.

Although this farm was owned by Dr. Otho J. Smith at the time of the battle and is listed under his name on contemporary maps, it is doubtful that he actually resided here in 1862. At the age of fifty-two Dr. Smith, a prominent local physician as well as a Southern sympathizer, was quite wealthy and owned considerable property in the area, much of it in the nearby village of Boonsboro. According to the 1860 census, his total holdings were valued at $42,000. Apparently a widower, he had a home in Boonsboro that he shared with his twenty-two-year-old daughter, Jeanette; a twenty-year-old son, Francis (listed in the 1860 census as an eighteen-year-old medical student but probably in the Confederate army by 1862), and two female housekeepers.

But it is Dr. O. J. Smith's Antietam farm that concerns us most in relation to Gardner's photographs. Whoever the tenants were in September 1862, the house and adjacent outbuildings were most likely occupied by the medical staff of French's division at about the time that division began sustaining its first casualties in the vicinity of Bloody Lane.

In his pension records, it is stated that Dr. Anson Hurd, as a regimental surgeon, initially accompanied the Fourteenth Indiana to the front lines, establishing a temporary field hospital in the vicinity of the Roulette farm buildings. The advanced position proved to be a dangerous one, Hurd himself coming under fire. Sometime, probably on either the afternoon of September 17 or on September 18, Dr. Hurd moved his operation back a mile and a quarter to the main division hospital previously established on the Smith farm.

At this time Hurd was temporarily assigned to a portion of the division hospital then caring for Confederate wounded while other surgeons of French's division tended to wounded Union soldiers. Contemporary records show that at its peak the Smith farm hospital was treating 1,396 wounded men from both sides.

Following any battle the size of Antietam, government surgeons as well as civilian medical volunteers were quickly dispatched to the battlefield to aid and eventually replace regimental surgeons, who were needed with their respective units in case of another battle or skirmish.

On September 22, 1862, the Fourteenth Indiana departed the Sharpsburg area en route to Harpers Ferry. Although it is true that Dr. Hurd may have remained behind at Antietam for an indefinite period of time, the chances are greater that if anyone from the Fourteenth was thus detached it would have been an assistant surgeon rather than a chief surgeon such as Hurd. Furthermore, from Hurd's records it appears that he was with the regiment in Harpers Ferry and accompanied the unit when it departed from there in late October 1862.

Anson Hurd was born about the year 1825, and nothing is known of his youth. In July 1861, at the time he first joined the Union army, Hurd was listed as a physician living in Oxford, Indiana, seventy-five miles northwest of Indianapolis. He had a wife, Amanda, whom he had married in Oxford on June 17, 1853, and a seven-year-old daughter with the biblical name of Huldah, born June 18, 1854.

In 1861, Anson Hurd's hometown of Oxford, then the seat of Benton County, had a population of slightly more than three hundred, all of whom were white. The area was predominantly level; in fact, contemporary gazetteers referred to it as prairie, with wheat, corn, and oats being the major crops. Like Dr. William S. Parran of Barboursville, Virginia (and indeed, like Dr. Otho J. Smith), Anson Hurd spent most of his working hours before the war serving the medical needs of neighboring villagers and local farmers.

On July 23, 1861, Anson Hurd enlisted as an assistant surgeon in the Twentieth Indiana Volunteers. He was thirty-six years old, five feet eleven inches tall, with a fair complexion, black hair, and brown eyes. After serving with the Twentieth for slightly more than five months, Anson was forced to retire early in January 1862 because of poor health.

Eventually recovering from his ailments, he again joined the army on April 21, 1862, and was mustered in as the surgeon of the Fourteenth Indiana Volunteers. But health problems continued to plague him throughout the spring and summer of 1862. In July 1862 he was at Harrison's Landing, Virginia, suffering from rheumatism, asthma, piles, and chronic diarrhea. Treating himself for these ailments, he remained with the regiment and took part in the Maryland campaign that September.

At the time Gardner photographed Anson Hurd on the Smith farm, the surgeon's health was again failing, due primarily to the rigors of the campaign and battle. Chronic diarrhea had redeveloped and though Hurd managed to stay with his unit through the battle of Fredericksburg on December 13, 1862, he was subsequently forced to retire from the service a short while later (December 28, 1862). The official reasons were stated as bleeding of the lungs, a severe cough, and chronic diarrhea.

Anson Hurd never again attempted to rejoin the army. After resigning his commission he moved his family to Findlay, Ohio, where, continuing his practice as a physician and surgeon for many years, he died in 1910 at the age of eighty-five.

The land on which Dr. Anson Hurd was photographed more than a century ago is today privately owned, and the original Smith farm buildings were razed prior to the twentieth century. Since both pairs of original Smith farm views were taken looking in the same easterly direction and from camera positions located in the same vicinity, the backgrounds for the corresponding modern versions appear quite similar. In each case, the left-hand views (6 and 8) show the same distant hill on the eastern side of Antietam Creek and the right-hand versions (7 and 9) both show Elk Ridge. The dirt lane on the ridge in the distant background of view 9 was the route used by all three divisions of the Union Second Corps during the crossing of Antietam Creek. The barn visible in the modern photograph of view 6 was erected sometime during the late nineteenth century.

In order to point out the potentially disorienting change in fence lines that has occurred on the site of the Smith farm over the years, I have sketched in the original fence lines, as well as the haystack, in the modern version of view 9. Interestingly enough, aside from such minor changes, together of course with the destruction of the original Smith buildings long ago, the site still retains most of its pastoral, nineteenth-century appearance.

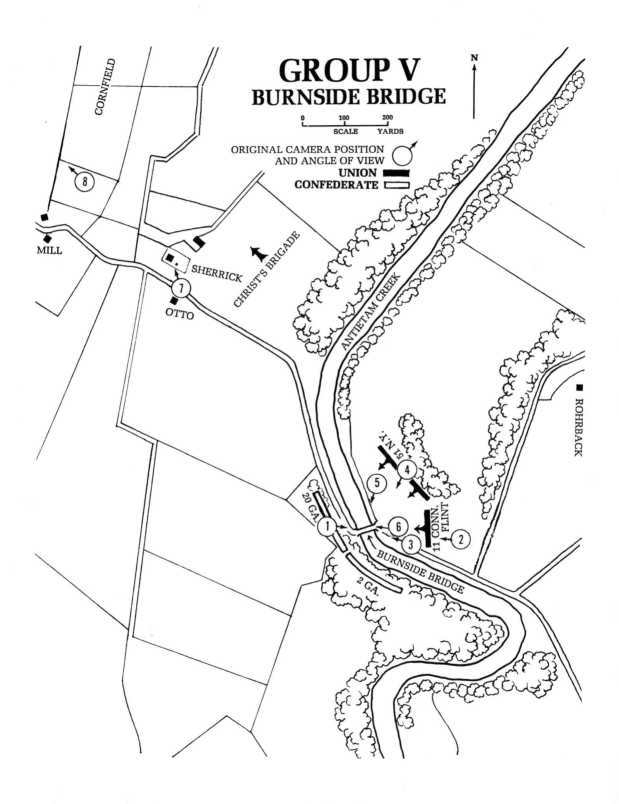

GROUP V
BURNSIDE BRIDGE

N

0   100   200
SCALE   YARDS

ORIGINAL CAMERA POSITION
AND ANGLE OF VIEW
UNION
CONFEDERATE

CORNFIELD

8

MILL

SHERRICK

CHRIST'S BRIGADE

7

OTTO

ANTIETAM CREEK

ROHRBACK

6 N.Y.

4

5

20 GA.

11 CONN. FLINT

1

6

2

3

BURNSIDE BRIDGE

2 GA.

10

GROUP V: BURNSIDE BRIDGE

V–1 Burnside Bridge, view looking eastward from the Confederate positions, Gardner or Gibson, stereo (original negative number unknown), September 21, 1862 (MOLLUS-Mass.).

V–2 Burnside Bridge, view looking westward across the ground over which Union forces charged, Gardner, stereo #600, September 21, 1862 (LC).

V–3 Burnside Bridge, view looking northwestward from the eastern bank of Antietam Creek, Gibson, stereo #584, September 21, 1862 (LC).

It was McClellan's intention to have Burnside's Ninth Corps cross Antietam Creek and advance against the Confederate right flank (south of Sharpsburg) shortly after the main Union thrust was made against the Confederate left (in the vicinity of the East and West Woods).

Had this coordination been achieved, thereby placing simultaneous pressure on both Confederate flanks, Lee would have been forced to maintain a strong line south as well as north of Sharpsburg—precluding the effective concentration of his reserve units at any given point during the morning's battle, as he was in fact able to do against Sedgwick at the West Woods.

But from faulty leadership on the part of the Union high command, the Ninth Corps did not initiate its first attempt to cross Antietam Creek until roughly four hours after the commencement of the battle. And unlike the other corps of the Union army, the Ninth encountered stiff resistance at the creek, forcing them to spend an additional three hours securing the crossing point at Burnside Bridge.

At the time the Ninth Corps launched its first assault against the bridge, the structure was defended by only a skeleton Confederate force, primarily two regiments of infantry, the Second and Twentieth Georgia, with a third regiment, the Fiftieth Georgia, guarding approaches farther downstream.

The main line of the Confederate right flank, composed of several badly understrength brigades of Gen. David R. Jones's division, was positioned on the heights south of Sharpsburg, fully three-quarters of a mile west of the bridge. The rolling nature of the terrain in this area made the bridge invisible to the main Confederate line. The two Georgia regiments, whose combined strength numbered slightly more than four hundred rifles, had the responsibility of denying enemy forces access to the bridge for as long as possible.

The Second and Twentieth Georgia were, however, immeasurably aided by the terrain in the immediate vicinity of the bridge. The west bank of the creek, on which the Georgians were posted, consisted of a high wooded bluff that commanded all approaches from the opposite bank. Cover was provided by rifle pits dug the day before, a sturdy stone wall along the crest, and numerous oak trees, many of which were occupied by snipers.

Conversely, Union forces attempting to carry the bridge were forced to cross a stretch of low, open ground on the eastern side of the creek, completely exposing them to enemy view.

At 10:00 A.M., the first Union assault was launched—spearheaded by the Eleventh Connecticut Infantry, some 440 men strong, of Col. Edward Harland's brigade, Gen. Isaac P. Rodman's division of the Ninth Corps. The Eleventh, partially deployed in skirmish order, was to secure a foothold at the bridge, which would then be crossed by support troops of Col. George Crook's brigade of Col. Eliakim P. Scammon's Kanawha Division.

Never before published, view 1 provides a unique eastward glimpse of Burnside Bridge and the ground over which the Eleventh Connecticut advanced—as seen from the position occupied by the Twentieth Georgia. Both Georgia regiments opened fire within moments after the Eleventh Connecticut emerged from the tree line visible just beyond the open field. The distant Elk

V–1

V–1 modern

V–2

V–2 modern

V–3

V–3 modern

Ridge, with a portion of the summit cleared for the use of the Signal Corps, may also be seen on the center horizon in this photograph.

Oddly enough, this stereo view was not listed in Gardner's original catalog and has remained obscure until now. There can be no doubt, however, that it was part of Gardner's 1862 series, since it was the only known series recorded at Antietam during the war and because this image was clearly taken shortly after the battle (note, for instance, the group of Union soldiers on the bridge, and especially the damaged condition of the bridge itself).

View 2 shows the same ground, this time as it appeared to the members of the Eleventh Connecticut as they dashed frantically toward the creek amid a hail of enemy rifle fire issuing from the wooded heights beyond.

The Eleventh Connecticut's left and center companies scaled the rail fence visible in view 2 and hastily established a line along the creek while the right-flank companies, unable to advance as far as the others, became pinned down in the open ground to the right.

Of special interest in view 2 is the presence of Gardner's darkroom wagon in front of the bridge. It was probably here that all the Burnside Bridge negatives exposed on the east bank were developed.

View 3 depicts that portion of the east bank occupied for but a brief time, roughly ten minutes, by the left and center of the Eleventh Connecticut. Although the creek was four feet deep at midstream, a number of the Union infantrymen, led by Capt. John D. Griswold of Company A, plunged into the waters in an isolated effort to reach the opposite bank. But the current was swift, and with scores of bullets splashing about them most of the group turned back. Griswold, who was hit midstream, reached the west bank, only to fall dead from his wound.[48]

Through some tragic misunderstanding, Crook's brigade failed to arrive at its designated position. Thus, without support and after having lost 139 men killed and wounded within ten to fifteen minutes, the Eleventh Connecticut was forced to retire.

As is obvious from the modern versions of these three photographs, the historic Burnside Bridge still stands. Constructed during the years 1836 and 1837, the bridge, along with portions of property adjoining on both banks of Antietam Creek, has since come into the possession of the National Park Service.

GROUP V: BURNSIDE BRIDGE

ALVIN FLINT, JR., photographer unknown, ambrotype, probably 1861 (McGuire Coll.).

Among the members of the Eleventh Connecticut Volunteers who advanced against Burnside Bridge at ten o'clock on the morning of September 17, 1862, was an eighteen-year-old private named Alvin Flint, Jr.

Alvin's father, Alvin Flint, Sr., was originally from Vermont; his mother, Lucy Clark Flint, from New Hampshire. On March 24, 1834, the couple was married in East Hartford, Connecticut, by the Reverend Samuel Spring, and ten years later, during the late summer of 1844, Alvin, Jr., was born.

The village of East Hartford, where Alvin, Jr., spent his childhood years, was located directly across the Connecticut River from the city of Hartford. During the antebellum period, East Hartford was both a manufacturing town and a farming community. As was typical throughout New England, most of the houses were of wooden construction painted white and in several architectural styles dating back to the eighteenth century. The main street of the village was lined with stately elm trees presenting an appearance described in contemporary gazetteers as pleasant.

Although the farms scattered about the nearby countryside were generally small, the township, which had a population of 2,951 in 1860, boasted level, fertile acreage well suited for the cultivation of a variety of crops, including maize, rye, and wheat, together with the raising of dairy cattle and horses. Especially fertile were the meadows located along the Connecticut River.

On July 23, 1860, when the census taker visited the Flint household, he recorded the members of the family as follows: Alvin, Sr., fifty; Lucy, forty-nine; Alvin, Jr., fifteen; Evaline, thirteen; and the youngest child, George, age eleven. Alvin, Sr., was listed as a papermaker by trade, so presumably he worked for a local manufacturer.

Because New England had long been noted for its superior public school systems, it is not surprising that all three Flint children were enrolled in school and attended classes daily during the school year, as each had been doing since about the age of six.

According to the financial data provided by the 1860 census, the Flint family would have been considered middle or lower-middle class by nineteenth-century standards. But generally speaking they were an average American family sharing in the universal problems and pleasures of everyday existence.

ALVIN FLINT, JR.

And like countless American families of that period, the Flints would soon find their private world disrupted by the awesome events then transpiring on the national scene and specifically, in April 1861, by the news from Charleston, South Carolina, that Fort Sumter had been fired upon.

At that time, Alvin, then sixteen, saw many of his older friends and acquaintances rush to enlist during the initial wave of excitement that spread across the country. Probably because of his age and perhaps from parental discouragement he chose to remain at home.

Then came the Northern disaster at Bull Run in July 1861 and with it the realization that the rebellion would not be easily crushed. That summer saw Alvin out of school and working on neighboring farms to supplement the family income. The prospect of joining the army must have dominated his thoughts regularly if not constantly until finally, on October 1, 1861, at the age of seventeen, he enlisted as a private in Company D of the Eleventh Connecticut Volunteers, then being formed at Hartford.

Along with the other raw recruits of the Eleventh, Alvin spent the next two and a half months in the vicinity of Hartford, training to become a soldier. It was probably during this period that the ambrotype portrait shown here was taken.

Unfortunately, at the time the Eleventh Connecticut departed (December 16, 1861) from Hartford en route to the seat of war, amid the cheers of thousands of bystanders, friends, and relatives, Alvin could hardly have shared in the festive atmosphere. His mind was preoccupied, for while he was at Hartford his mother had contracted consumption and died, on December 6, 1861. To add to Alvin's sorrow, he left Connecticut with the knowledge that his fifteen-year-old sister, Evaline, had also come down with consumption.

January 1862 found the Eleventh Connecticut at the front in North Carolina. For Alvin the initial feelings of homesickness were intensified by word from his father that Evaline's condition had grown steadily worse until finally, on January 16, 1862, she too had died from the disease.

During the months that followed, a continuous gloom hovered over the Flint home in East Hartford. Now a widower living alone with his youngest son, the father, Alvin, Sr., was constantly bombarded with household reminders of the tragedy that had taken his wife and daughter. And everywhere were reminders of his son Alvin, Jr., who was then away in the army, fighting in defense of his country.

ANTIETAM

Sometime during the mass meetings and patriotic appeals of the summer of 1862, Alvin Flint, Sr., then approaching the age of fifty-three, began to seriously consider joining the army himself. The cause was a worthy one and there was little left to keep him at home—aside from painful memories.

Undoubtedly, young George, then only thirteen, shared his father's feelings, for during the third week in August 1862, the father and son enlisted together as privates in Company B of the newly formed Twenty-first Connecticut Volunteers. On September 11, 1862, Alvin, Sr., and George were shipped out with their regiment to one of the training camps surrounding Washington.

There is no way of determining the extent to which Alvin Flint, Jr., was aware of these latest developments as he waited to go into action at Antietam on the morning of September 17, 1862. In all likelihood he was at least aware of his father's intentions of enlisting. There can be little doubt, however, that among Alvin, Jr.'s, thoughts before advancing with the Eleventh Connecticut against the stone bridge were images of his father and younger brother, memories of his mother and sister—and prayers for his own safe delivery from the battle into which he was about to be thrust.

Sometime during the fifteen-minute charge of the Eleventh Connecticut, Alvin Flint, Jr., was hit by enemy rifle fire. Sprawling to the earth, his body torn and bleeding, the eighteen-year-old private lay within sight of Burnside Bridge for an indefinite time before stretcher-bearers were able to reach him. But by then it was too late, for Alvin Flint, Jr., was dead.

A month after the battle, Alvin's father was sent by chance to Sharpsburg on detached service with the Ambulance Corps. Although Alvin's grave was probably marked (his body was later shipped home), his father failed in his necessarily brief attempt to locate the grave. The heartbroken and embittered father recorded his feelings in a letter written to the editor of the *Hartford Courant*, dated Pleasant Valley, Maryland, October 23, 1862.

> Dear Courant: You doubtless are aware that I have come to the land of Dixie, to engage in this killing business. . . . We arrived [at Sharpsburg] Saturday night, near what I call "Antie-Dam," where my boy was brutally murdered. . . . I was leaning upon that dear boy, as a prop in my declining years; but if my life is spared, I shall knock out some of the props that hold up this uncalled for, and worse than hellish, wicked rebellion. Hardly had the sadness of the

death of a dear daughter, that I lost last January worn off, when this sad, sad calamity should come upon me.

I went to hear the Chaplain preach; his text was, "How dreadful is this place, it's none other than the house of God and the gate of Heaven." Oh that I could have viewed the text as Jacob did, but to me the place was dreadful in the extreme, where my dear boy had been cut down in a moment with no one to say a word to him about the future. Oh how dreadful was that place to me, where my dear boy had been buried like a beast of the field! Oh could I have found the spot, I would have wet it with my tears! Oh how dreadful was that place to me, where I passed two long, long sleepless nights! Had it not been for this sad calamity, my sleep would have been sweet.

Monday morning we moved back five or six miles this side of Harper's Ferry, and feeling as "Lot" did on fleeing out of Sodom, I did not look behind.

My son was a member of the 11th Conn., and his age was 18.[49]

By late December 1862 the Twenty-first Connecticut was encamped at Falmouth, Virginia, across the Rappahannock River from Confederate-held Fredericksburg. Typhoid fever was rampant. Ironically, among those singled out by the disease were fifty-three-year-old Alvin Flint, Sr., who died on January 10, 1863, and his thirteen-year-old son, George Flint, who died five days later. The remains of both were eventually shipped home, perhaps by friends of the family or relatives.

It is not known who paid the expenses for exhuming and transporting the body of Alvin Flint, Jr., from Maryland to Connecticut, but today, in East Hartford's Center Burying Ground, beside the graves of his mother, father, brother, and sister, lie the remains of the eighteen-year-old private who fell at Antietam on the morning of September 17, 1862.

V–4 Burnside Bridge, view looking southwestward toward the heights occupied by Confederate forces, Gardner, plate, September 21, 1862 (LC).
V–5 Graves of members of the Fifty-first New York Volunteers killed at Burnside Bridge, Gardner, stereo #585, September 21, 1862 (LC).

Within roughly an hour and a half of the repulse of the Eleventh Connecticut, Union forces made a second effort to secure and cross Burnside Bridge—this time spearheaded by the Second Maryland and Sixth New Hampshire of Gen. James Nagle's brigade, Gen. Samuel D. Sturgis's division. Once again, after a brief but bitter struggle the assault met with failure.

Despite the repetition of Confederate success at the bridge, the odds were steadily mounting against the defenders. Union artillery fire directed at the bluff was beginning to take its toll, ammunition was running low, and a large Union force (Gen. Isaac P. Rodman's division, minus the Eleventh Connecticut) was reported moving downstream in an obvious effort to cross the creek at a nearby ford in order to outflank Confederate forces. Skirmishers of the Fiftieth Georgia were guarding the ford, but they were few in number and spread thinly. Call after call went out for reinforcements from Gen. David R. Jones's division, but they went unheeded.

At 1:00 P.M. the third and final Union assault was launched against Burnside Bridge. Foremost in the attack were the Fifty-first Pennsylvania and Fifty-first New York regiments of Gen. Edward Ferrero's brigade of Sturgis's division, who charged southwestward against the bridge from a hill to the northeast.

With ammunition left for only a few volleys, the Second and Twentieth Georgia regiments did their best to convince the attackers that another frontal assault would be as futile as the preceding two. Charging with fixed bayonets at a full run across the open ground east of the bridge, the two Fifty-first regiments (with the Twenty-first Massachusetts supporting on their left) encountered almost immediately the expected storm of enemy rifle fire. Men dropped at every step, but within a few moments both units reached the protection of the stone wall extending northward from the bridge along the eastern bank. The Fifty-first Pennsylvania was on the left, with the Fifty-first New York to their immediate right.

The ensuing firefight was at first heated. Then, unexpectedly, Union forces perceived that Confederate fire was beginning to slacken and that Confederate soldiers were withdrawing singly and in small groups. Col. John F. Hartranft, commander of the Fifty-first Pennsylvania, began yelling for the regiment to advance. Taking the initiative, Capt. William Allebaugh of Company C dashed onto the bridge. At first only five men followed, including the color-bearers of the Fifty-first Pennsylvania. Confederate fire intensified briefly, but all six Pennsylvanians crossed safely to the western bank.

It was now clear that the tide had turned. Other soldiers advanced onto the bridge and in a matter of moments both regiments were in motion, crowding the 12-by-150-foot stone structure with a mass of blue-clad soldiers, the colors of the Fifty-first New York surging forward above their heads.

Confederate snipers, posted in the trees, were now abandoning their precarious positions, sliding down trunks or dropping from low, overhanging branches as the bulk of their comrades retreated westward toward the safety of the main Confederate line. Some Georgians surrendered, waving both hands in the air, whereas others signaled capitulation by waving newspapers stuck onto ramrods.[50]

Burnside Bridge had been captured, thus opening the way for an all-out attack against the Confederate right flank. Unfortunately for the Union forces, this attack was originally designed to support the drive against the Confederate left, which by 1:00 P.M. had already ended.

Of all the photographs taken at Burnside Bridge, view 4 has been most frequently reproduced over the past century. Gardner recorded both an eight-by-ten-inch plate and a stereo version (#615) of this scene, the former being reproduced here. The camera position for this view was located on the slope of the hill from which the Fifty-first Pennsylvania and Fifty-first New York regiments began the final assault against the bridge. Visible in the foreground is the stone wall that was briefly occupied by both regiments prior to the advance across the creek, and dominating the background are the heights and woods held by the Georgians.

The next photograph, view 5, was originally captioned by Gardner as "Graves of Federal Soldiers at Burnside Bridge, Antietam, Sept. 21, 1862." Although typically the caption provided no specific information regarding the names or units of the dead buried here, it is nevertheless an important piece of evidence in that it delineates the date on which Gardner worked at Burnside Bridge.

The stretch of stone wall in the foreground of this view (with the bridge

V–4

V–4 modern

V–5

V–5 modern

visible just beyond) also appears in the preceding photograph. The identity of the soldier posed leaning against the wall remains unknown, but fortunately the original negative for this scene has survived in a remarkably good state of preservation.

Of the twelve wooden headboards, some of which appear camouflaged against the wall, I was able to read the unit designation on nine, all of which were identified as dead of the Fifty-first New York Volunteers. It can be presumed that the remaining three graves likewise contained soldiers from that unit.

Working under magnification with the nine headboards of soldiers from the Fifty-first New York, in conjunction with a list of the nineteen members of that unit who were killed at the bridge, I was further able to decipher the names on four of the headboards. They were Sgt. George W. Loud, Company C (buried at the feet of the posed soldier); Pvt. Edward Miller of Company H (three graves to the right of Loud); Pvt. John Thompson of Company B (three to the right of Miller), and Cpl. Michael Keefe, Company I (the dark headboard, second to the right of Thompson).

All four men had been with the Fifty-first New York Volunteers since its organization in New York City during the late summer and early fall of 1861. According to their military records, their ages at enlistment were Loud, thirty-nine; Miller, eighteen; Thompson, nineteen; and Keefe, twenty. Although the personal backgrounds of Miller and Keefe remain obscure, I was able to uncover from government pension records a few admittedly sketchy details pertaining to Loud and Thompson.

Born during or about the year 1822, George W. Loud was married to Mary Ann Story at Trinity Church, Manhattan, on December 5, 1844. At the time of his enlistment as a corporal in the Fifty-first New York Volunteers on October 7, 1861, Loud resided with his wife at 177 Chatham Street, New York City. The couple had no children. On September 13, 1862, four days before his death at Antietam, Corporal Loud was promoted to the rank of sergeant. If he had had time to write to his wife between September 13 and September 17, his last letter would undoubtedly have included news of the promotion. Several months after becoming a widow, Mary Ann Loud, at age forty, moved to Philadelphia.

John Thompson was the only son of James and Ellen Thompson of New York City. In 1855, when John was thirteen years old, a second child, Elizabeth, was born to the family. Sometime during the late 1850s John's father died, necessitating that he discontinue his schooling to help support his mother and young sister. At a salary of four dollars a week John worked as an apprentice bricklayer until August 25, 1861, when he enlisted in the Fifty-first New York. Through mid-September 1862 Private Thompson continued to support his mother by sending home most of his army pay.

According to the Thompson pension file at the National Archives, Ellen Thompson never recovered from the initial shock of learning that her son had been killed in action at Antietam. From the autumn of 1862 through the autumn of 1863 her health declined until finally, on November 21, 1863, she died, leaving the only remaining member of the family, Elizabeth, an orphan at age eight.

Today the body of John Thompson lies in Lot A, section 25 of the Antietam National Cemetery near the graves of other members of the Fifty-first New York, including those of George Loud, Edward Miller, and Michael Keefe.

V–6

V–6 modern

V–6 Burnside Bridge, view looking westward, Gibson, stereo #614, September 21, 1862 (LC).

The final photograph of Burnside Bridge included in this study, view 6, has never before been published. It provides an excellent close-up glimpse of the span as it appeared to the extreme left-flank members of the Fifty-first Pennsylvania Volunteers, who charged onto the bridge in response to Captain Allebaugh's initiative. Barely visible on the distant ridge line, above the center arch and amid the trees, is a portion of the stone wall occupied during the battle by the Twentieth Georgia.

One half of the original stereo negative for this view still survives in the collections of the Library of Congress. Regrettably, the emulsion was damaged many years ago, resulting in large black spots that partially obliterate center portions.

A total of five hundred Union soldiers were killed and wounded in the three-hour effort to capture Burnside Bridge. After the retreat of Confederate forces from the wooded bluff, the Union Ninth Corps began transferring over the bridge all its remaining units on the east bank (the bulk of the corps) in preparation for the attack against the main Confederate line south of Sharpsburg.

Southern artillery located near the present site of the National Cemetery fired long-range through a defile formed by the creek farther upstream, significantly delaying the crossing operation. Despite this harassment, long columns of Ninth Corps infantry, regiment after regiment, four men abreast, accompanied by supporting artillery batteries and ammunition wagons—in all, nearly ten thousand men—crossed here continuously between the hours of 1:00 P.M. and 3:00 P.M. It was a scene that could never have been envisioned by those who built the stone structure as a publicly funded roadway project more than two decades earlier.

For a time, General Burnside himself stood on the bridge that would henceforth bear his name and helped direct units to their respective staging areas along and behind the ridges on the far bank. At 3:00 P.M., five hours after the Eleventh Connecticut's initial assault against the bridge, the Ninth Corps was ready to push westward.

V–7 The Sherrick farm buildings, Gardner, stereo #598, September 21, 1862 (LC).

Aside from photographing Burnside Bridge, Gardner displayed relatively little interest in the battlefield south of the village of Sharpsburg. This neglect, though regrettable, is at least understandable in light of several factors.

By September 21, 1862, the day on which Gardner reached the scene of the struggle for the Confederate right flank, the vast majority of dead, except for a few scattered clusters of fallen Confederates, had already been buried. Since Gardner had already expended a large number of negatives on the dead at Antietam, it is doubtful that this scarcity would have bothered him to any significant degree.

The terrain on the battlefield south of Sharpsburg and west of Antietam Creek consisted mainly of vast stretches of open, rolling farmland. There were few if any landmarks of physical distinction or historical note that could match the photographic potential of the Dunker Church, the Hagerstown Pike, or Bloody Lane—especially in the absence of numerous dead to provide a dramatic touch to the foreground.

Furthermore, with the exception of the capture of Burnside Bridge, Union forces south of Sharpsburg were eventually routed at all points. Because Gardner was a Northern photographer whose photographs were sold almost exclusively to a Northern market, it is not unreasonable to assume that, where given a choice (as he was at Antietam), Gardner tended to emphasize, whether consciously or unconsciously, scenes that would evoke memories of national pride—victories, or at least heroic struggles, rather than sites reminiscent of clear-cut defeats.

Whatever his reasons, the fact remains that, with the exception of three photographs (two of which depicted Confederate dead), Gardner all but completely ignored the southern portion of the battlefield west of Antietam Creek. The first of these three scenes, view 7, was of the farm buildings owned in 1862 by Joseph Sherrick.

When it became clear that a great battle was about to be fought at Sharpsburg, the sixty-year-old Sherrick fled the area with his wife, Sarah, fifty-five. The couple apparently had no children with them at the time. Before abandoning his home, which was located along the country lane that led from Burnside Bridge to the village of Sharpsburg, Joseph Sherrick took his life

savings of three thousand dollars in gold and hid it in a stone wall in the yard. The afternoon of September 17, 1862, would find the Sherrick farm situated in the direct line of advance of the Ninth Corps' right-flank regiments of Col. Benjamin Christ's brigade, Gen. Orlando B. Willcox's division.

Christ's brigade began its westward movement from Antietam Creek shortly after 3:00 P.M., with the Seventy-ninth New York Volunteers deployed in skirmish formation and taking the lead. The main line of battle, consisting of the Seventeenth Michigan on the left (fronting the Sherrick barn), the Twenty-eighth Massachusetts in the center, and the Fiftieth Pennsylvania on the right, followed closely behind.

Moving rapidly across the open fields, Christ's brigade halted momentarily in the vicinity of the Sherrick farm buildings to allow the units farther to their left (south) to catch up. Although a ridge protected Christ's men from the fire of Confederate forces to their front, namely Gen. Micah Jenkins's South Carolina brigade together with elements of three artillery batteries, the Union brigade soon found itself pinned down by artillery fire from a Confederate battery located farther to the left. For a half hour Christ's four regiments were unable to move forward or backward.

Meanwhile, significant developments were taking place to the south. Other Ninth Corps units were pushing relentlessly westward, and as Confederate resistance began to weaken, the attention of the battery that had pinned down Christ's brigade became diverted. No longer impeded by the treacherous enfilade, Christ's men once again moved forward.

It was now approaching 4:00 P.M., and at least one Confederate artillery battery facing the Seventeenth Michigan was seen to limber up and retire. Jenkins's South Carolina brigade was also falling back, with its right flank exposed as a result of Union successes farther down the line (Confederate positions occupied by the brigades of Gen. Thomas F. Drayton and Gen. James L. Kemper had been penetrated by a Union thrust spearheaded by elements of Rodman's division).

For a brief period it seemed as if the Ninth Corps could not be stopped. The Confederate right flank was giving way and entire Southern units were retreating toward Sharpsburg.

It was at this critical juncture that Confederate general Ambrose P. Hill's veteran division, some three thousand strong, arrived on the battlefield after a seventeen-mile forced march from Harpers Ferry. For the Confederates the timing could not have been more perfect. Additionally, the direction from which Hill's division approached the field enabled his men to attack squarely upon the Union Ninth Corps' exposed left flank.

Ironically, the first Union regiment to be struck by Hill's onslaught was the newly formed Sixteenth Connecticut Volunteers. In the field for less than three weeks prior to Antietam, the members of the Sixteenth, many of whom were from Hartford, had barely learned how to fire their rifles and were in no way familiar with the disciplined art of maneuvering a line of battle in the face of an enemy flank attack.

Only a poorly conceived plan of attack can explain how an almost totally untrained unit such as the Sixteenth Connecticut found itself in an advanced position on the vulnerable extreme left flank óf the Ninth Corps. Indeed, why the corps was so blatantly unprepared to meet Hill in the first place is even more difficult to explain when one considers that at roughly 3:00 P.M., or at the same time Burnside's men began advancing westward from Antietam Creek, Union signalmen at the Elk Ridge station caught sight of Hill's division moving rapidly toward Sharpsburg. The following message was immediately relayed to Burnside's headquarters: "To General Burnside: Look out well on your left; the enemy are moving a strong force in that direction."[51]

Despite this advance warning, Burnside was unable to react in time. Not surprisingly, the Sixteenth Connecticut was thrown into a state of panic, 185 of its men falling dead or wounded in a brief period of time. The confusion quickly spread to a supporting unit, the Fourth Rhode Island.

With a snowballing effect, from left to right, the Ninth Corps line began to crumble, and though the fighting continued for more than an hour after Hill's arrival, all Union forces south of Sharpsburg were eventually forced to retire to the vicinity of Antietam Creek. Thus, by sundown on September 17, 1862, Burnside's day-long effort first to attack, then break, the Confederate right flank had ended in complete failure.

Hastily abandoned by Christ's four regiments during the withdrawal to Antietam Creek, the Sherrick farm remained between the lines from the evening of September 17 through the early morning hours of September 19. Christ's brigade had suffered 244 casualties on Sherrick's property, and both the house and barn contained many wounded Union soldiers throughout this interim period, as well as on the day Gardner's photograph was recorded.

Sometime after the battle, Joseph Sherrick returned to his farm to recover the three thousand dollars in gold he had hidden in the stone wall. With his wife, he thereupon moved to nearby Boonsboro, graciously allowing the homeless family of Samuel Mumma to occupy his battlefield dwelling until their own residence could be built anew the following spring.

The historic Sherrick farm today lies within the boundaries of the Antietam National Battlefield Site. Although the barn has undergone extensive alterations over the years, the house and at least one of the outbuildings remain virtually unchanged.

Gardner's 1862 photograph was recorded from the front yard of the neighboring Otto house, just south of the country road that ran from Burnside Bridge to Sharpsburg (note the roadway fencing in the foreground). Most of the area to Gardner's back, including the original Otto farmhouse as well as the bulk of the battlefield over which the Ninth Corps fought on the afternoon of September 17, 1862, is today privately owned.

GROUP V: BURNSIDE BRIDGE

V–8 Confederate dead near the Sherrick farm, Gardner, stereo #571, September 21, 1862 (LC).

Although this scene, one of the three known to have been recorded on the afternoon's battlefield, revealed little at first glance that would appear helpful in determining Gardner's exact camera location, a thorough study of the image, in conjuction with Gardner's original caption, uncovered a number of clues.

Gardner's contemporary identification described the photograph as a "View on Battle-field of Antietam, near Sherrick's House, where the Seventy-ninth New York Volunteers fought after they crossed the creek; group of dead Confederates." It is not known why Gardner chose to single out the Seventy-ninth New York for special mention since, as skirmishers, the Seventy-ninth covered the entire front of Christ's brigade on the Sherrick farm. But the reference supports the credibility of the most important element in the caption, that the view was recorded "near Sherrick's House."

During my research on this scene I had access to both halves of the original stereo negative as well as an original Civil War–period stereo card. From a careful study of these items and with the advantage of being able to view the scene in three-dimensional form the following information was gleaned.

The view was taken close to, and looking upward toward, the crest of a ridge or hill. The dark mass blocking out the sky on the upper left-hand portion of the image turned out to be a pile of fence rails; to the right of the rails was an opening on the horizon, showing a tree far in the distance. In stereo it is clear that this tree was situated on another, still higher ridge.

The most important clue is the field of corn dominating the right horizon. Because there is no reason to doubt the accuracy of Gardner's "near Sherrick's House" identification, it appeared that wherever this site was, it was located adjacent to a cornfield within reasonable proximity to the Sherrick farmhouse.

According to official battlefield maps, there was only one cornfield located within a radius of a third of a mile from the Sherrick house. It was an extensive field that stretched northward from a point two hundred yards northwest of the house. None of the three other cornfields on the southern portion of the battlefield could reasonably be termed near the house.

During the course of my fieldwork I eventually became familiar with the

V–8

V–8 modern

boundaries of all original cornfield sites on the battlefield, but I found only one point that appeared to match both the terrain in view 8 and Gardner's caption. This point was located along the southern boundary of the cornfield closest to the Sherrick farm, with the camera facing northwestward.

Of interest in the modern view taken from this point is the line of trees to the right, which marks the boundary of the original field of corn. We are looking uphill toward a slight ridge. In the far distance, at eye level, is a second and higher ridge. Moreover, though it is not readily apparent in the modern photograph, there is today a slight depression or gully that runs diagonally across the foreground. A similar gully, quite prominent when viewed in stereo, appears in Gardner's photograph to the immediate left of the dead soldiers.

At no other point along the more than nineteen-hundred-yard boundary of the only cornfield "near Sherrick's House" did the terrain on the battlefield match as closely that in Gardner's photograph.

The same official maps that helped lead me to this point also contained two items of information that tended to contradict my conclusion. According to the maps, a stone wall lined most of the southern boundary of the cornfield in question, whereas Gardner's photograph clearly shows a large quantity of fence rails at that point. But if one looks closely at the fence line farther uphill, he will notice what appears to be a base of stones. It is not farfetched to conjecture that the original fence was of both stone and rail, a type of fence construction common in that period, with only the stone portion remaining when the maps were made.

The second contradiction poses a more serious obstacle, for according to the maps, the field adjacent to the cornfield on its southern boundary was occupied by an orchard, but not one tree is present in Gardner's photograph. One possible explanation is that there may have been an open space between the orchard and the cornfield—a space that the mapmakers did not consider significant enough to delineate at the time. Unfortunately, I have no hard evidence to support this suggestion, and thus the problem posed by the orchard remains unresolved.

Therefore, though I found no other point on the battlefield that could be matched as convincingly to Gardner's photograph, as well as to the caption, the site indicated by the modern view cannot be considered confirmed, though it is most likely correct. If my analysis is correct, then the odds are great that the dead Confederates portrayed in the foreground were members of Jenkins's South Carolina brigade.

It is disappointing that no one thought to undertake an in-depth study of these photographs when scores of local farmers and veterans, intimately familiar with the Antietam battlefield as it appeared in September 1862, were still available for questioning. Instead, more than a century has been allowed to pass before any serious study was initiated.

The lesson is obvious, for despite the fact that it is all too easy to take for granted those things considered modern or recent, it is never too early to begin the process of documentation.

V-9 Confederate dead on the southern portion of the battlefield, Gardner, stereo #555, September 21, 1862 (LC).

Although Gardner's original caption for this view, "Confederate Soldiers, as they fell, near the Burnside Bridge, at the Battle of Antietam," clearly places the scene on the southern portion of the battlefield, countless hours of investigation have failed to uncover any point that could be matched convincingly to the terrain in the photograph, either in the vicinity of Burnside Bridge or anywhere else on the battlefield north or south of Sharpsburg.

On the other hand, and as was the case with the preceding view, there exists no valid reason for doubting the reliability of Gardner's caption, since he was known to have worked in the vicinity of Burnside Bridge on September 21, 1862, and because it is conceivable that there were still some unburied Confederates lying nearby at that time.

Unfortunately, an examination of the image itself revealed little in the way of tangible evidence that would indicate where the scene was located. The uniforms on the two fallen soldiers appear to be quite dark, bringing to mind the fact that many Confederates of A. P. Hill's division were wearing various dark blue items of Union clothing captured at Harpers Ferry. If these were some of Hill's men, it would mean that the photograph was probably recorded in the vicinity of the Harpers Ferry road. And yet it is just as likely that the clothing seen here was some shade of brown, a color commonly worn in the Confederate ranks. The latter makes more sense in light of the fact that there was apparently little or no confusion in Gardner's mind when he identified these dead as Confederates.

Both bodies have been pillaged, their pockets turned inside out, suggesting that wherever they fell, it was within enemy lines by the end of the battle. Although admittedly tenuous evidence, this at least tends to support Gardner's "near the Burnside Bridge" identification, since the bodies of Confederates killed on the heights just above the bridge fell into Union hands and remained there through the end of the battle, whereas those Confederates who fell farther west lay in friendly territory and were less likely to be pillaged.

Although I was unable to pinpoint the location of this scene, the number of potential camera angles was by no means without limit. For example, had the camera been facing in any easterly direction, Elk Ridge or an extension thereof would almost certainly have been detectable beyond the tree line in the background. An examination of the original stereo negative, only one-half of which has survived, revealed no trace of a distant ridge.

The ground depicted between the bodies and the far-off woods is disappointingly indistinct. Furthermore, the distant woods themselves raise a problem, since they cannot be linked visually with any known woods sites, and because there were no extensive woods present on the southern portion of the battlefield, aside from the trees bordering Antietam Creek.

The most reliable official maps, though comprehensive in their coverage of the battlefield proper, are invariably sketchy as to the terrain features located just off the battlefield, particularly in the area south of Sharpsburg and west of the Harpers Ferry road. It is thus possible that the distant woods in view 9 were located in this area.

Indeed, it is my educated guess that view 9 was recorded somewhere on the heights just west of Antietam Creek, with the camera facing in a generally southwestern direction. The terrain in that area was basically similar to the terrain in the photograph, i.e., open. In the absence of more definitive evidence, I can only conjecture that there is something about the image itself that is visually deceptive and that wherever this site was located it was, according to Gardner's caption, situated "near the Burnside Bridge."

The vagueness surrounding the dead portrayed here, as was the case in many of the Antietam battlefield scenes, is regrettable. Throughout this study I have sought to emphasize the more personal elements of human tragedy that lie just beneath the surface in all of Gardner's death studies. But there are other factors, strictly impersonal, that are no less vital in perceiving the total reality of these scenes—factors that were likewise incapable of being recorded by Gardner's strictly visual representations. These additional elements must be described, for otherwise the photographs become only sanitized, and hence distorted, portrayals of reality.

The reality was this: by sundown on September 17, 1862, some twenty-six thousand Americans from both North and South had become casualties at Antietam. Thousands had been killed outright; their bodies would lie strewn about the field, exposed to the elements, for a period of from one to four days. There were some temporary, scattered truce periods on September 18, primarily on the northern portions of the battlefield, during which an undetermined number of dead from both sides were buried by their respective armies. Basi-

V–9

cally, however, efforts that day were concentrated on removing the wounded caught between the lines.

Not until September 19, the day on which Union forces found themselves in possession of the entire battlefield, were burial operations begun in earnest. But by then decomposition was already well advanced. The weather during the third week in September had been generally fair, with the sun shining brightly and temperatures reaching the mid-seventies. The evenings were cool, and for roughly an hour on the afternoon of September 18 the bodies were subjected to a heavy shower. Although each corpse decayed at a different rate, the vast majority of bodies began bloating within a day after they were killed.

It is nearly impossible to describe what a battlefield such as Antietam smelled like at the time Gardner recorded his photographs. Decaying flesh and internal organs exude a disgustingly sour, pungent smell. Interspersed with the foul odors produced by decomposition was the distinctive odor of human excrement, for whenever a human dies, the contents of the bowels (which at Antietam were frequently diarrheic) are usually evacuated as a result of internal gaseous pressure and the action of death upon the muscles of the digestive system.

Obviously, if only a handful of soldiers had been killed at Antietam, the odors would have been localized and thus easily avoided. But with thousands of dead, the vast majority of whom lay unburied until September 19 and 20, combined with the presence of hundreds of horse carcasses, the smell permeated the entire twelve square miles of battlefield. In fact, by the morning of September 19, anyone approaching within a mile of the battlefield could readily detect the odor.

According to available evidence, the task of burying the dead, excluding horses, on the battlefield proper was completed sometime late on September 21, 1862.[52] Because of their size, dead horses were usually disposed of by dragging them into piles and setting them on fire.

The thousands of soldiers killed in action at Antietam were not the only ones who died as a result of the battle. Untold thousands lingered in agony for days, weeks, months, and even years before death came to their relief.

By nightfall on September 17, 1862, the field hospitals on both sides were flooded with nearly nineteen thousand wounded soldiers, men who had been hit in every conceivable portion of the human body. The hospitals were a nightmare; there were never enough attendants. Members of civilian organizations comparable in function to the modern Red Cross (for example, the United States Sanitary Commission) volunteered their services on behalf of the wounded. Although the American Red Cross was not organized until 1881, its founder, Clara Barton, was present at Antietam as a civilian nurse. But these dedicated volunteers were in the minority, and more often than not, curious civilians would gather about the field hospitals to gawk at the wounded, offering no assistance whatsoever.

Most of the soldiers who fought at Antietam had had little opportunity to wash their sweat-stained clothing or bathe during the days, and sometimes weeks, preceding the battle. Most were therefore uncomfortably soiled by September 17, 1862. Additionally, the rigors of forced marching, combined with haphazard distribution of rations, forced thousands of soldiers to eat whatever was available whenever possible. The resulting prevalence of diarrhea was extensive in both armies.

Obviously, these problems did not miraculously disappear for the wounded but were, on the contrary, invariably intensified. With so many casualties produced in one day, it is not unusual to come across firsthand accounts of wounded men, already in excruciating pain from their wounds, lying incapacitated amid the stench and misery of similarly helpless sufferers, pleading to no avail for someone, anyone, to bring an item as basic as a bedpan—to spare them from that one last humiliation they could never have envisioned on the day they proudly signed their names to the enlistment papers. Untold numbers would survive, only to find themselves horribly crippled and disfigured for life.

The battle of Antietam ended at sundown on September 17, 1862. But for the thousands of wounded soldiers and for the thousands of families, comrades, and friends of the men who did not survive the battle, the horrible memories, pain, and heartbreak did not as conveniently terminate at day's end.

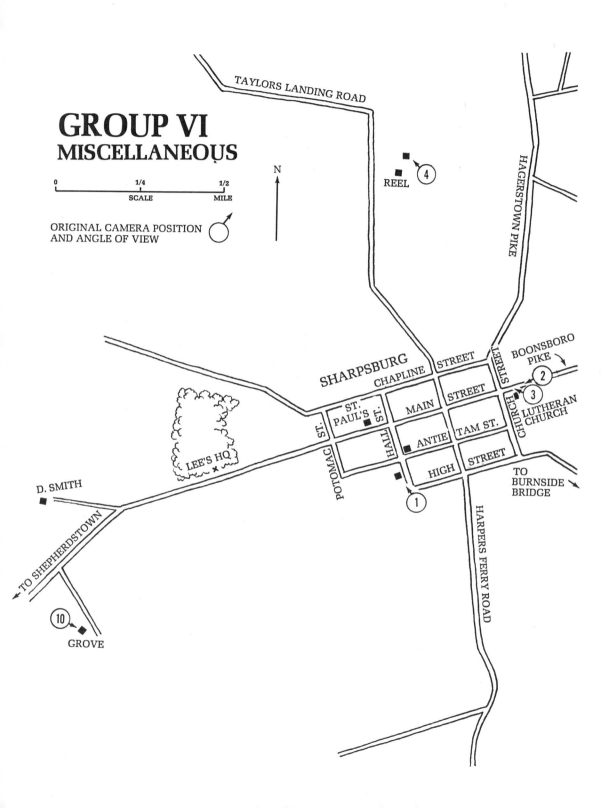

GROUP VI
MISCELLANEOUS

0   1/4   1/2
SCALE   MILE

N

ORIGINAL CAMERA POSITION
AND ANGLE OF VIEW

TAYLORS LANDING ROAD

REEL ④

HAGERSTOWN PIKE

SHARPSBURG

CHAPLINE STREET

STREET

LEE STREET

BOONSBORO PIKE

② ③

ST. PAUL'S

CHURCH ST.

MAIN STREET

LEE'S HQ

HALL ST.

POTOMAC ST.

ANTIE TAM ST.

LUTHERAN CHURCH

D. SMITH

HIGH STREET

TO BURNSIDE BRIDGE

①

TO SHEPHERDSTOWN

HARPERS FERRY ROAD

⑩
GROVE

11

GROUP VI: MISCELLANEOUS

This section discusses a number of Gardner's Antietam photographs whose subjects fall beyond the five major categories already examined. The following miscellaneous views include photographs of Sharpsburg, sundry group portraits, and Gardner's October series of Lincoln studies.

Of the twelve photographs in this section, the only five that can be located precisely were all recorded in or about the village of Sharpsburg. Hence, the accompanying map includes only those areas in which exact camera positions could be determined.

VI–1 The village of Sharpsburg, view looking northwest along Hall Street, Gardner, stereo #599, September 21 or 22, 1862 (LC).

VI–2 The Lutheran Church, Sharpsburg, Gardner, stereo #596, September 21 or 22, 1862 (LC).

VI–3 View of Sharpsburg, looking northwest along Main Street, Gardner, stereo #595, September 21 or 22, 1862 (LC).

Of the ninety-five individual negative plates exposed at Antietam in 1862, only three (all stereo) depict the village of Sharpsburg. None of the three was specifically dated by Gardner, but there can be little doubt that all were recorded prior to the completion of his September series.

Analysis of Gardner's coverage of the battlefield indicates that he would have passed through the village more than once on both September 21 and 22. Granted, he did not show as much interest in the village as he did, for example, in the two bridges, but he would not have considered his main battlefield series complete without at least token documentation of Sharpsburg. Therefore, the three scenes reproduced here were most likely recorded on either September 21 or September 22, 1862.

The first of these Sharpsburg scenes, view 1, has remained obscure for more than a century. It was recorded from a slight hill on the southern edge of the village with the camera facing northwest along the length of Hall Street. The log house dominating the foreground still stands and has since been refurbished. The white frame house appearing to the right, at the intersection of Hall and West Antietam streets, has likewise been preserved. Both structures are visible in the modern photograph.

The large building standing in the background of view 1, above and to the immediate left of the log house, was Saint Paul's Episcopal Church. Erected in 1819, Saint Paul's suffered heavily from Union artillery fire during the battle. At the time Gardner's photograph was recorded, it was being used as a hospital for Confederate wounded. The structure survived the battle in such poor condition that it was eventually razed and replaced by a new one in 1871 that is visible in the modern version.

Of additional interest in view 1 is the presence of Gardner's darkroom wagon in the foreground. Since Gardner was the actual cameraman, the possibility exists that the figure facing the picket fence in front and to the left of the darkroom wagon is his assistant, James F. Gibson. The white, blurry form at the lower edge of the photograph is a portion of a stone wall behind which Gardner's stereo camera was placed.

The remaining two Sharpsburg views, 2 and 3, were recorded at the eastern edge of the village from camera positions roughly seventy-five yards apart, with the camera facing generally westward in both. As a point of reference, the white structure visible to the right in view 2 is the residence appeaing at the extreme left in view 3. The house standing at this site today may well encompass the original building of log construction.

Gardner focused his attention in view 2 on the Lutheran Church, which, as is evidenced by the photograph, had been struck many times by Union artillery fire. Built in 1768, this church served as both a Confederate signal station during the battle and a Union field hospital at the time this photograph was recorded. Damage was so extensive that it was subsequently torn down and another structure was erected across the street. The original Lutheran cemetery, hidden by the rail fence to the left in the 1862 photograph, has been preserved and is visible above the latter-day stone embankment in the modern photograph.

In view 3 Gardner placed his camera closer to the white house adjacent to the Lutheran property in order to make a general study of the village. In the distant background is Saint Paul's Episcopal Church and beyond that, on the horizon, are the woods in which General Lee's headquarters was located during the battle (near the left-hand edge of the woods).

The village of Sharpsburg, Washington County, Maryland, was founded on July 9, 1763, and so was approaching its hundredth anniversary in 1862. Its population at the time of the Civil War was approximately thirteen hundred. Because Maryland was a border state in which slavery was legal and recognized as such by the Federal government (though the institution was not widespread in the western counties), it is not surprising to learn that Sharpsburg's residents were divided in their sympathies, with many supporting the Southern cause. However, the vast majority of its citizens remained loyal to the Union, and during the course of the war some two hundred of its men served in the Union army.

A large number of local residents fled the village in September 1862, when it appeared obvious that a major battle was about to be fought. For the most part, those who stayed behind sought shelter in their basements during the fighting.

VI–1

VI–1 modern

VI–2

VI–2 modern

VI–3

VI–3 modern

From September 15 until the predawn hours of the nineteenth, the streets were occupied by Confederate forces who were at times subjected to intense Union artillery fire, especially on September 16 and 17. As a result, only a handful of village structures survived the battle without sustaining some sort of damage, and at least one resident, a little girl whose name remains unknown, was killed.[53]

By the morning of September 19, this once peaceful community found itself destitute. Those citizens who had fled returned to find their streets and alleys littered with dead horses and dead and wounded Confederate soldiers. The village had been nearly picked clean of provisions, and what the Confederates did not consume the Union soldiers carried away when they entered the village on September 19. Before long Sharpsburg was transformed into one vast hospital.

During the weeks that followed, as the villagers struggled to recover from the shock of war, they were no doubt aided in varying degrees by sympathetic officers and men of the Army of the Potomac, elements of which were encamped west of town for the next month. One of the Union regiments, the Thirteenth Massachusetts of Hartsuff's brigade, Ricketts's division of the First Corps, had been based at Sharpsburg for nearly three weeks the year before (in August 1861) while on duty guarding Potomac fords. Many of the friendships between villagers and soldiers that were formed in 1861 were renewed in the days and weeks following the great battle of 1862.[54]

In June 1863, nine months after Gardner recorded his three photographs of Sharpsburg, the village would once again see its streets filled with Confederate soldiers as elements of the invading Army of Northern Virginia passed through en route to Gettysburg. The following month, Union forces in pursuit of Lee's defeated army also passed through the village again.

Today, more than a century later, Sharpsburg remains a small rural community appearing much as it did in September 1862. Scores of original buildings still stand and, despite its being surrounded by one of the world's best-marked battlefields, Sharpsburg has thus far escaped the commercial exploitation that has afflicted so many historic sites throughout the nation. And yet if Sharpsburg's integrity is to be maintained for future generations, the time for action at all levels is now. This village needs some form of organized protection or, with little question, it will eventually be raped.

VI–4

VI–4 modern

VI–4 The ruins of the Reel barn, Gardner, stereo #591, probably September 21 or 22, 1862 (LC).

Adjoining the village of Sharpsburg on its northern boundary was the property of a forty-five-year-old farmer named David Reel. The Reel farm buildings were situated on the eastern side of Taylors Landing Road, midway between the village and the West Woods.

At the time of the battle, David Reel lived on the farm with his wife, Sarah, aged fifty-two, and their seven children (two boys and five girls ranging in age from five to twenty-seven). In all likelihood, the Reels fled their home when the fighting became imminent, even though there is some evidence suggesting that David's oldest daughter, twenty-seven-year-old Barbara, remained behind to care for wounded soldiers.[55]

The Reel farm lay just behind the Confederate lines throughout the battle and served as a staging area for Southern attacks against the West Woods on the morning of September 17. Although hidden from the vision of Union artillery batteries by a ridge that ran just east of the barn, the farm buildings nevertheless came under severe Northern artillery fire, perhaps at the direction of signalmen stationed on Elk Ridge.

Sometime on September 17 a direct hit was scored on the barn, then serving as a Confederate field hospital. The structure immediately went up in flames, the fire and intense heat spreading so swiftly that it was impossible to remove all the wounded in time. A group of boys hunting through the ruins after the battle discovered human bones amid the ashes, all that remained of a number of the more helpless cases who had been burned alive.[56]

Due to its proximity to the village, Reel's barn was most likely photographed on the same day the Sharpsburg views were recorded, either September 21 or 22.

After the war the Reels sold their farm and moved west. The barn that currently stands on the site of the original foundation has been rebuilt twice since the battle, but it probably incorporates at least some of the original stonework. Located on private property just off the battlefield proper, the Reel farm rarely attracts visitors today, and the horror of what happened at the barn during the battle has long since been forgotten.

VI–5 Brig. Gen. John C. Caldwell and staff on the Antietam battlefield, Gardner, stereo #580, September 21, 1862 (LC).

VI–6 Union artillery officers on the Antietam battlefield, Gardner, stereo #579, probably September 21, 1862 (LC).

Although Gardner recorded a number of portraits of civilian dignitaries and high-ranking Union officers in rear areas at the time of Lincoln's visit in October 1862, only two formal group portraits were recorded during the production of the September series.

According to Gardner's original caption, the first of these, view 5, was taken "on Battle-field of Antietam, Sept. 21, 1862." It shows Brig. Gen, John C. Caldwell, commander of one of the three brigades of Richardson's Second Corps division, which, it will be remembered, fought at Bloody Lane.

Surrounding the general are members of his staff. Of the seven officers in the photograph, six can be identified: Seated, left to right—unidentified, 1st Lt. C. A. Alvord, Capt. George H. Caldwell; Standing, left to right—Capt. George W. Bulloch, General Caldwell, 1st Lt. George W. Scott, and 1st Lt. D. R. Cross. Gardner recorded two versions of the group, an eight-by-ten-inch plate and a stereo view, the latter being reproduced here.

In his official report of the battle, dated September 24, 1862, General Caldwell made special mention of several of those appearing in this photograph.

> The members of my staff were indefatigable in their efforts, and did all I could wish in the transmission of orders. Lieutenants Cross, Alvord, and Scott were all particularly brave and active. Lieutenant Alvord captured several prisoners with his own hand, and conducted to the rear those taken by Colonel Barlow. By command of General Richardson he gave orders to the Irish Brigade, and assisted in forming them into a second line. During the entire day all the members of my staff were incessantly active, and did most valuable service.[57]

Gardner's photograph is particularly interesting in light of the fact that he dated the image as having been recorded on September 21, 1862. According to

VI–5

available evidence, it seems that the Second Corps was bivouacked at the East Woods from September 19 until their departure from the battlefield, en route to Harpers Ferry, on the morning of September 22.[58]

Thus, it appears that immediately prior to terminating his photographic operations on the northern portion of the battlefield and before heading southward via Sharpsburg to spend most of the afternoon of September 21 covering Burnside Bridge, Gardner spent at least a brief period on that morning at the East Woods.

The second study, view 6, has remained little known until now and was identified only vaguely by Gardner as a "Group.—Artillery Officers on Battlefield of Antietam." But because it was recorded, like the Caldwell photograph, on the actual battlefield and in, or adjacent to, an apparently large body of woods, it can at least be surmised that the two groups of officers may have been photographed at approximately the same place and time, i.e., at the East Woods on September 21, 1862. A close examination of view 6 tends to support this suggestion.

Although none of the six men was identified by name or unit, the man seated in the center wears a numeral 4 within the crossed cannons on his hat, indicating that he was a member of one of the six batteries of the Fourth U.S. Artillery present at Antietam. (There were no state batteries designated by the numeral 4 in the Maryland campaign.)

VI–6

Lt. Alonzo H. Cushing, detail of
photograph taken during the
Peninsula campaign (MOLLUS-Mass.)

Of these six batteries of the Fourth U.S. Artillery, only two were still camped on the battlefield proper after September 19 and prior to September 22. They were Batteries A and C of the Second Corps. These two batteries fought as one unit at Antietam, having been consolidated prior to the battle under the single command of 1st Lt. Evan Thomas. Thomas's Batteries A and C belonged to the same division as did Caldwell's brigade, and on September 21 Thomas's men would have been located with the rest of the division at the East Woods, near Caldwell's encampment.

The link between the photograph and Thomas's Batteries A and C can be further supported. When I first began research on view 6, I noticed that the unidentified lieutenant standing in the center of the back row bore a striking resemblance to a young artillery officer I had known to have been associated with the Fourth Artillery. His name was Alonzo H. Cushing, a West Point graduate whose first assignment in the summer of 1861 was as commander of Battery A.

By early 1862 Cushing was temporarily detached from Battery A to serve on General Sumner's staff. During the Peninsula campaign, a photograph was taken of Sumner's staff showing Lieutenant Cushing on the far left. A detail of this photograph is shown here so that the reader may better evaluate the resemblance I have suggested.

Although Cushing was still serving as a staff officer at Antietam, assigned to General McClellan, he maintained a strong feeling of attachment toward Battery A and was with it for a time during the battle. It is therefore reasonable to assume that he paid frequent visits to the unit during free moments. By the spring of 1863, Lieutenant Cushing had been reassigned to Battery A, Fourth U.S. Artillery, with which he served as commander until his death at Gettysburg on July 3, 1863.[59]

Although the evidence pertaining to Gardner's photograph of artillery officers on the Antietam battlefield cannot be termed conclusive, it is nevertheless strong enough to suggest by way of summation that most of the men pictured were probably in some way associated with the consolidated Batteries A and C, Fourth U.S. Artillery; that the photograph was recorded at the Second Corps encampment at the East Woods on the same day Caldwell's staff was photographed, September 21, 1862; and that Lt. Alonzo H. Cushing was probably visiting with his comrades from Battery A at the time Gardner happened by.

VI–7 Forge scene at McClellan's headquarters, Gardner, plate, September 22, 1862 (LC).

VI–8 McClellan's headquarters guard, the Ninety-third New York Volunteers, Gardner, plate, on or about October 4, 1862 (MOLLUS-Mass.).

Two nearly identical versions of view 7 were recorded by Gardner, according to his captions, on September 22, 1862; one in stereo (#587) and the other on an eight-by-ten-inch plate, the version reproduced here.

Although the scene depicted, showing as it does army blacksmiths at work, is perhaps of only peripheral interest in terms of photographic documentation of the battle of Antietam, the caption itself is significant in that it places Gard-

VI–7

ner "at General McClellan's Headquarters, Sharpsburg, Sept. 22, 1862," the day on which Gardner is believed to have completed his September series of battlefield views.

The interest prompted by the caption centers around the fact that no one knows today precisely where McClellan's headquarters was located on September 22. What is certain, however, is that on the afternoon of September 20, the day after it was confirmed that Lee's army had retired across the Potomac, McClellan abandoned his position at the Pry house and moved his entire headquarters to an undesignated point somewhere close to the western outskirts of Sharpsburg.[60]

Apparently, Gardner's interest in McClellan's newly established headquar-

VI–8

ters did not extend beyond the forge scene, which in itself provides no visual clues as to where that site may have been located.

On September 27, 1862, after direct contact with the Confederate army had been broken, McClellan once again relocated his headquarters. Although locating the exact site of this third position, like that of the second, continues to elude the best efforts of historians, my research indicates that it was situated roughly two miles south of the village, along the Harpers Ferry road, and on the northern portion of the property owned by the Reverend J. Adams.[61]

This third headquarters site, occupied by McClellan from September 27 until October 8, 1862, (on which date his headquarters was finally moved out of the Sharpsburg area and into Pleasant Valley), is of some importance because it was here that Lincoln spent the nights of October 2 and 3, 1862.

Gardner visited McClellan's third headquarters during the first week in October, but aside from his now classic photographs of Lincoln and McClellan, most of the views he produced there in October were repetitious and consisted primarily of group portraits of civilian dignitaries, staff officers, and members of McClellan's headquarters guard—the Ninety-third New York Volunteers.

One of the latter studies is reproduced here. It shows the entire Ninety-third New York posing before Gardner's camera. The unit's commander, Col. John S. Crocker, may be seen seated on horseback to the immediate right of the flag. Crocker, who had been absent from the regiment since April 1862, had rejoined the Ninety-third only on October 3, 1862, just in time to be included in Gardner's group study.[62] As McClellan's headquarters guard, the unit saw no action at Antietam.

VI–9 through 12

The highlight of Gardner's October series of camp portraits was the group of four studies (consisting of seven individual negatives) that he produced showing President Abraham Lincoln. Undoubtedly, it was Lincoln's visit to the field that prompted this supplementary coverage of the Army of the Potomac as it lay idle during the third week following the battle.

Lincoln's journey began on October 1, 1862, with a railroad trip from Washington to Harpers Ferry. The Republican president was accompanied by five traveling companions, one being Gen. John A. McClernand, a past acquaintance from Illinois as well as a staunch Democrat. Lincoln's selection of McClernand was decidedly political in nature, his motivation being to display unity between the two parties, especially since he was about to deal face to face with McClellan, who, like McClernand, was a dedicated Democrat.

The remaining four companions included Ward Hill Lamon, the president's personal bodyguard and marshal of the District of Columbia; Joseph C. G. Kennedy, superintendent of the Census for 1850 and 1860 and an expert on munitions production; Ozias M. Hatch, the secretary of state of Illinois and an old friend of Lincoln's from Springfield; and, finally, John W. Garrett, president of the Baltimore & Ohio Railroad.[63]

The commander of the Army of the Potomac, General McClellan, traveled south to meet the president at Harpers Ferry on October 1, and on that same afternoon the two leaders reviewed Union troops then stationed at Bolivar Heights. Later in the day, McClellan returned to his headquarters at Antietam while the president spent the night at Harpers Ferry. After reviewing more troops in the vicinity of Harpers Ferry on the morning of October 2, Lincoln journeyed northward to pass the remainder of his visit with McClellan.

Of the four Lincoln studies recorded by Gardner, two were taken on October 3 and two on the morning of October 4. Although Lincoln visited with his commanding generals in the field several times during the war, photography would record only his October 1862 visit.

VI–9 President Lincoln, General McClellan, and others at the headquarters of the Army of the Potomac, Gardner, stereo #605, October 3, 1862 (LC).

VI–10 President Lincoln, General McClellan, and others at Fifth Corps headquarters, Gardner, plate, October 3, 1862 (LC).

The first of Gardner's Lincoln studies in the field was taken, according to the original caption, just prior to the review of Union troops on October 3, 1862. The scene was at McClellan's headquarters.

Included in the group are (from left to right) a soldier named Buck Juit; Ward Lamon (seated); Ozias Hatch (wearing the light top hat); Gen. Randolph B. Marcy, McClellan's chief of staff as well as his father-in-law; Capt. Wright Rives, an aide to McClellan; General McClernand; President Lincoln; Lt. Col. Andrew P. Porter, commissary of subsistence; General McClellan; Joseph Kennedy (wearing the light coat); John Garrett; and Col. Thomas S. Mather.

Shortly after this photograph was recorded, Lincoln and McClellan traveled northward through Sharpsburg and visited the headquarters of Gen. Fitz-John Porter, commander of the Fifth Corps. At the time, General Porter's headquarters was located about a mile west of the village, at the home of Stephen P. Grove.

After reviewing the Fifth Corps in nearby fields, the presidential party returned to the Grove house, at which time, according to a correspondent for the *New York Times*, view 10 was recorded by "an artist connected with the establishment of Brady."[64] The Brady employee was Alexander Gardner, who had apparently followed the dignitaries closely, waiting for opportunities to record the presidential party with his camera.

That view 10, one of the most famous to be produced during the war, was recorded at Porter's headquarters is further supported by Gardner's original caption, "Group.—President Lincoln . . . at Headquarters [of] Fitz-John Porter, Antietam, October 3, 1862." Consequently, there can be little doubt that the building seen beyond the tents in the background was the home of Stephen Grove, which still stands today (though privately owned and in much need of repair).[65]

The men pictured in the group are as follows (left to right): Col. Delos B. Sacket, McClellan's inspector general (during the battle, Sacket delivered McClellan's final order to Burnside to capture Burnside Bridge); Capt. George

VI–9

Monteith (background), a Fifth Corps staff officer; Lt. Col. Nelson B. Sweitzer, an aide to McClellan; Gen. George W. Morell, commander of a division of the Fifth Corps; Col. Alexander S. Webb, Fifth Corps chief of staff, later to become famous as a general in the Second Corps; General McClellan; an army scout named Adams; Dr. Jonathan Letterman, medical director of the Army of the Potomac; unknown; President Lincoln; Gen. Henry J. Hunt, McClellan's chief of artillery; Gen. Fitz-John Porter; unknown (background); Col. Frederick T. Locke, assistant adjutant general of the Fifth Corps; Gen. Andrew A. Humphreys, commander of a division of the Fifth Corps; and finally, the man standing apart from the group at the tent, Capt. George A. Custer, then serving as an aide on McClellan's staff and fourteen years later as commander of the Seventh U.S. Cavalry, to die at the battle of the Little Bighorn.[66]

According to Gardner's catalog of 1863, two versions of this scene were recorded: an eight-by-ten-inch plate (reproduced here) and a version available only as an album card (#606). Whether the album card negative was copied from the larger format view or was a separate exposure (perhaps the remnants of an unsuccessful stereo attempt) is not known.

Aside from functioning as the Fifth Corps headquarters after the battle, the

VI–10

VI–10 modern

Grove farm also served as an extensive Confederate hospital. Before departing the site on the afternoon of October 3 to review the First and Sixth Corps, Lincoln took time to visit a number of wounded enemy soldiers, who received the president with solemn respect.

VI–11 President Lincoln, Allan Pinkerton, and General McClernand at McClellan's headquarters, Gardner, plate, October 4, 1862 (LC).

VI–12 President Lincoln and General McClellan at McClellan's headquarters, Gardner, plate, October 4, 1862 (LC).

Both of these studies were recorded just prior to Lincoln's departure for Washington via Frederick on the morning of October 4, 1862. Two similar exposures were made of view 11, showing the president posed between Allan Pinkerton (left) and General McClernand (right). The less common of the two versions is reproduced here.

Allan Pinkerton, head and founder of the Pinkerton National Detective Agency, was photographed several times by Gardner during the first week in October 1862. At the outbreak of hostilities in 1861, Pinkerton volunteered the services of his agency to the Federal government, and by 1862 Pinkerton was one of McClellan's prime sources of enemy intelligence. Ironically, Pinkerton, who during the war went by the assumed name of E. J. Allen, consistently and significantly overestimated the strength of Lee's army—a factor that in turn contributed to McClellan's extreme caution. Pinkerton's military influence terminated with McClellan's removal.

The final photograph, view 12, shows Lincoln and McClellan posed sitting inside the commanding general's tent. Visible on the ground at the lower left lies one of the thirty-nine Confederate battle flags captured during the campaign. Two nearly identical exposures were made of this scene, one in the larger format (reproduced here) and the other in stereo (#602).

Lincoln spent considerable time conferring privately with McClellan from October 2 to 4. Although outwardly congenial toward McClellan throughout these discussions, the president was nevertheless extremely dissatisfied with McClellan's reluctance to pursue and engage the enemy.

Finally, on November 7, 1862, Lincoln relieved McClellan of command of the Army of the Potomac and replaced him with General Burnside. McClellan would never again be asked to serve in the field.

VI–11

VI–12

PART THREE

CONCLUSION

12

THE PHOTOGRAPHIC LEGACY OF ANTIETAM

On December 13, 1862, slightly more than a month after McClellan's replacement by a more "aggressive" general, the Army of the Potomac under its new commander, General Burnside, met with complete disaster at the battle of Fredericksburg, Virginia. Lincoln's choice had been a mistake. Burnside was eventually replaced by General Hooker, who in turn led his forces to disaster at the battle of Chancellorsville in May 1863. Hooker was subsequently replaced by Gen. George G. Meade.

As the nightmare at the front continued, photographic firms such as Gardner's and Brady's were developing a fairly good instinct for what the public wanted to see. The Antietam series had shown that sensational photographs attracted substantial attention. Unfortunately, photographers from the major firms were unable to produce any particularly outstanding series at either Fredericksburg or Chancellorsville, mainly because both battles were clear-cut Northern defeats, with the fields remaining in enemy hands.

Working independently of the major firms, however, an official army photographer, Capt. Andrew J. Russell of the U.S. Military Railroad, managed to secure several noteworthy negatives at Marye's Heights, Fredericksburg (May 3, 1863), during the Chancellorsville campaign. The views are remarkable in that Marye's Heights was in the temporary possession of Union forces for less than twenty-four hours before being recaptured by Confederate units.

One view showed dead Confederate soldiers along the famous stone wall at the base of the Heights; another view taken in the vicinity showed damaged Confederate artillery limbers and dead horses.

Not until the major Union victory at the battle of Gettysburg, Pennsylvania (July 1–3, 1863), however, would conditions once again permit the timely coverage of a battle's aftermath on any extensive scale.

Of the many firms that flocked to the Gettysburg battlefield in July 1863, including Brady's, none made as determined an effort to reach the site quickly as did Gardner's. Here was his first chance to duplicate his success at Antietam without having to see his efforts published under the Brady label. Within only two days of when the first reports of the battle reached Gardner in Washington, he and two assistants, James Gibson and Timothy O'Sullivan, were at Gettysburg recording death studies on the southern portion of the field. Gardner's group of cameramen was not only the first to reach the area but was the only one to arrive prior to the completion of burial operations. Brady arrived approximately one week too late.[67]

That Gardner's motivation to reach Gettysburg as soon as he did was prompted by a desire to record death studies similar to those taken at Antietam is evidenced by the fact that nearly 75 percent of his Gettysburg series focused on the bloated corpses of soldiers and horses.

For many months following the devastating Gettysburg campaign, neither army was anxious to initiate a major confrontation. The remainder of 1863 saw little fighting in the East, most large-scale actions during that period taking place in the western theater.

In March 1864, Lincoln appointed Gen. Ulysses S. Grant as overall commander of Union forces in both the eastern and western theaters. With the advent of the spring campaigns of 1864, obsure place names once again dominated newspaper headlines: the Wilderness, Yellow Tavern, Spotsylvania, Drewry's Bluff, North Anna, Cold Harbor. The conflict would continue for nearly one more year, and although opportunities for safely recording the human wreckage of war materialized rarely in 1864 and 1865, whenever such opportunities did surface, photographers from all the major firms made a determined effort to exploit them. Brady's men were at Fredericksburg in 1864 to photograph the dead and wounded from the Wilderness campaign. O'Sullivan, working for Gardner, was at Spotsylvania to record a series of views of burial operations the morning after the battle of May 19, 1864.

ANTIETAM

One of the most notable examples of this dramatic documentation occurred on April 3, 1865, the morning after the final Union assault at Petersburg, Virginia. Thomas C. Roche, working for E. & H. T. Anthony & Co. of New York, recorded twenty separate exposures, all in stereo, of dead Confederate soldiers in the trenches at Fort Mahone.[68] Had Gardner's Antietam series of 1862 proven a financial failure, it is doubtful that Roche, two and a half years and several similar series later, would have expended quite as much energy in securing his Fort Mahone death studies as he did.

But the Antietam series had not been a financial failure. On the contrary, based on available evidence, it appears that the sale of Gardner's Antietam views continued at a steady pace throughout the war. Many of the numerous original Antietam stereo views I examined for this study were issued on cardboard mounts dating from late in the war. Others bore revenue stamps on the back indicating that they were sold between 1864 and 1866. (Two of these were stamped with the specific date of sale, July 17, 1865—more than three months after the war had ended and almost thirty-four months after the views were recorded.)

Antietam had an impact on the course of photography during the remainder of the war. The series provided cameramen with an example to be followed, and its financial success provided the incentive to make extraordinary efforts to reach the sites of carnage before the ugliest scars had been covered. The result of these efforts was the production at Gettysburg, at Spotsylvania, at Petersburg, and at other sites of many of the most powerful war photographs ever recorded.

But the Antietam photographs and their descendants portray only the visual aspects of battlefield reality. There is much that is missing. Had the photographers somehow been able to capture the smells and the agonizing screams along with the sights, and to ensure that each time their work was displayed these sensations would be present, I venture that the photographs would have been buried as quickly as the dead they represented.

Of equal significance is the point made on October 20, 1862, by the *New York Times* reporter in one of the earliest and most comprehensive reviews of the Antietam series: "Broken hearts cannot be photographed." There is only so much a photograph can say. Anonymity is ever present, and as long as the tragedy depicted by the photograph occurred to a stranger, the emotional response on the part of an audience, though it may on occasion be high, will rarely reach a level approaching that experienced by those who knew the subject of the original scene.

By emphasizing these lost elements of personal heartbreak, pain, and repulsive sensations, it was my desire throughout this study to recapture the stark realities surrounding the scenes photographed at Antietam in 1862, all of them visual documents of one of the greatest tragedies this country has ever experienced.

NOTES

1. The *New York Times*, October 20, 1862. Regarding the subject of repulsion vs. fascination, the article made these comments: "Crowds of people are constantly going up the stairs; follow them, and you find them bending over photographic views of that fearful battle-field, taken immediately after the action. Of all objects of horror one would think the battle-field should stand preeminent, that it should bear away the palm of repulsiveness. But, on the contrary, there is a terrible fascination about it that draws one near these pictures, and makes him loth to leave them."

2. *Harper's Weekly* 6 (October 18, 1862): 663–65; Dr. Oliver Wendell Holmes, "Doings of the Sunbeam," *Atlantic Monthly* 12 (July 1863): 11–12.

3. The most authoritative source for Antietam casualty figures is Thomas L. Livermore, *Numbers and Losses in the Civil War in America, 1861–65* (Boston: Houghton Mifflin, 1901), pp. 92–93. The figures are: Army of the Potomac: killed in action, 2,108; wounded, 9,549; captured or missing, 753; total, 12,410; Army of Northern Virginia: killed in action, 2,700; wounded, 9,024; captured or missing, 2,000; total, 13,724; total for both armies, 26,134. Antietam's notoriety as the bloodiest single day of the Civil War was established prior to World War I. See William F. Fox, *Regimental Losses in the American Civil War, 1861–1865* (Albany, N.Y.: Albany Publishing Co., 1889), p. 540. But to my knowledge, no one has comprehensively compared the Antietam casu-

alty figures to those of later wars. After doing so, I found that as far as can be determined, more Americans were killed and wounded on September 17, 1862, than on any other day in our history. It must be remembered that unlike World Wars I and II, both sides who fought at Antietam were American—one of the tragic distinctions of a civil war. Additionally, the fighting during modern warfare has become increasingly campaign- rather than battle-oriented, with the casualties being distributed over periods ranging from several days to several months. The Normandy invasion of World War II, for instance, was not a one-day battle and did not begin and end on June 6, 1944. Yet the total American casualty figures for D-Day (again, for example) did not exceed 6,700 killed, wounded, and missing, whereas those for Antietam exceeded 26,000. Hence, in terms of American losses for any single day in history, including all wars and disasters, September 17, 1862, was America's bloodiest day.

4.   Currently, the best source of information concerning the Saltillo daguerreotypes will be found in Robert Taft, *Photography and the American Scene* (New York: Macmillan, 1938), pp. 223–24, 484–85. Views not reproduced in Taft's classic work (which was reprinted as a paperback by Dover Publications in 1964) may be found in James D. Horan, *Mathew Brady: Historian with a Camera* (New York: Crown, 1955), plates 86 a–c. The original daguerreotypes are at Yale University. Documented information concerning the identity of the individual who recorded the Saltillo series has been uncovered by Mr. R. Bruce Duncan of Northfield, Illinois. Although Mr. Duncan, who plans to publish his findings when his research is completed, would not share with me the name of the cameraman, he did describe the nature of his evidence and the circumstances under which the views were recorded.

5.   The most detailed account of MacCosh's work appears in Pat Hodgson, *Early War Photographs* (Boston: New York Graphic Society, 1974), pp. 13–14, 34–35. See also Clark Worswick and Ainslie Embree, *The Last Empire: Photography in British India, 1855–1911* (New York: Aperture, 1976), p. 5.

6.   The most comprehensive account available on the subject of Crimean War photography is Helmut and Alison Gernsheim, *Roger Fenton: Photographer of the Crimean War, His Photographs and His Letters from the Crimea* (London: Secker and Warburg, 1954). For further information on Crimean War photography, see A. D. Bensusan, "Crimean War Photograph, a Recent Find in South Africa," *The Photographic Journal* 102 (April 1963): 129–31; B. A. and

H. K. Henisch, "Robertson of Constantinople," *Image* 17 (September 1974): 1–11; Constantin Savulescu, "The First War Photographic Reportage," *Image* 16 (March 1973): 13–16.

7. U.S. Congress, House, *Military Commission to Europe in 1855 and 1856, Report of Major Alfred Mordecai of the Ordnance Dept.*, 36th Cong., 2d sess., 1861, pp. 11, 64.

8. Beato's photography during the Sepoy Mutiny is discussed in Hodgson, pp. 17, 48–55. See also Worswick and Embree, pp. 8, 13, 63–65.

9. D. F. Rennie, *The British Arms in North China and Japan* (London: Murray, 1864), p. 112.

10. Dr. Oliver Wendell Holmes, "Sun-Painting and Sun-Sculpture; with a Stereoscopic Trip Across the Atlantic," *Atlantic Monthly* 8 (July 1861): 27. For further information on photography during the Franco-Austrian War see Helmut and Alison Gernsheim, *The History of Photography from the Camera Obscura to the Beginning of the Modern Era* (New York: McGraw-Hill, 1969), p. 271; Hodgson, pp. 11–12, 22–23; *La Lumière*, September 10, 1859; *Photographic News*, June 17 and 24, 1859; Franz Hubmann, *The Habsburg Empire: The World of the Austro-Hungarian Monarchy in Original Photographs, 1840–1916* (Freeport, N.Y.: The Library Press, Inc., 1972), p. 62.

11. *American Journal of Photography* 4 (August 1, 1861): 120; *Humphrey's Journal* 13 (1861–62): 133; *The New York Times*, August 17, 1861; *New York World*, April 12, 1891.

12. The history of Civil War photography from 1861 to 1862, as presented in this chapter, is based primarily on an analysis of the photographic captions, dates, and credits as listed in Alexander Gardner, *Catalogue of Photographic Incidents of the War* (Washington: H. Polkinhorn, 1863), a work that is without doubt one of the most important primary sources of photographic documentation to be produced during the first half of the war. Gardner's *Catalogue* is the source of all original captions quoted in this study. See also E. & H. T. Anthony, *Catalogue of Card Photographs* (New York: 1862), pp. 13–16.

13. Frederic Ray, "Rare Photographs Identified. Show Rebel and Yankee Troops in Frederick," *Civil War Times Illustrated* 4 (April 1965): 22–24. Two other Frederick photographs, taken at a time different from the Confederate scene and possibly by a different cameraman, show Union soldiers halted on the same street. Although these views have also been linked with the 1862 Maryland campaign in past accounts, the presence of cold-weather clothing

on many of the soldiers and nearby civilians, together with the barren appearance of the trees, indicates that the additional views bear no association with the events of September and early October 1862. Because Union forces were a common sight in Frederick throughout the war, the specific occurrence depicted would be most difficult to determine.

14.   Numerous primary and secondary sources were consulted in order to reconstruct the details surrounding events as they occurred at Antietam. These sources included regimental histories, personal narratives, newspaper accounts, historical journals, official records, local histories, manuscripts, contemporary maps, autobiographies, and general histories related to the battle and campaign. However, the most important sources for the basic details of the battle were: *The War of the Rebellion: A Compilation of the Official Records of the Union and Confederate Armies* 19 (Washington: Government Printing Office, 1887), hereafter cited as *The Official Records*; and the time-related situation maps, known as the *Atlas of the Battlefield of Antietam*, prepared under the direction of the Antietam Battlefield Board from surveys by Lt. Col. E. B. Cope and H. W. Mattern, drawn by Charles H. Ourand in 1899, with troop positions by Gen. E. A. Carman, published under the direction of the chief of engineers, U.S. Army, 1904, and revised in 1908. For the reader interested in other comprehensive reconstructions of the campaign and battle, I would recommend Francis W. Palfrey, *The Antietam and Fredericksburg* (New York: Scribners, 1882) and James V. Murfin, *The Gleam of Bayonets* (South Brunswick, N.J.: Yoseloff, 1965). For a volume rich in details of the local history of the Sharpsburg area, see John W. Schildt, *Drums Along the Antietam* (Parsons, W.Va.: McClain, 1972).

15.   For biography of Alexander Gardner see Josephine Cobb, "Alexander Gardner," *Image* 7 (June 1958): 124–36. Although little is known about James F. Gibson's life, a synopsis of his career will be found in Thomas Waldsmith, "James F. Gibson, Out from the Shadows," *Stereo World* 2 (January–February 1976): 1, 5, 20. Until now it was commonly thought that Gardner's brother, James, and Timothy O'Sullivan accompanied Gardner and Gibson to Antietam in 1862. This interpretation, which I believe to be questionable, is based solely on the credits for two photographs that appeared in Alexander Gardner, *Gardner's Photographic Sketch Book of the War* (Washington: Philp & Solomons, 1866). The first of these, plate 21, shows the Dunker Church and is credited to James Gardner. Even a cursory glance at the photograph, however,

shows that the church had been completely repaired of all battle damage when photographed and that the negative was recorded long after the battle, perhaps at the war's end. Significantly, it is the only Antietam view in the *Sketch Book* that Gardner neglected to date. The view credited to O'Sullivan, plate 22 (view I-3a in this book), shows the Elk Ridge signal station, although all Elk Ridge views listed in Gardner's *Catalogue* are credited to Alexander Gardner. Because my past experience with the *Sketch Book* and the *Catalogue* has found the latter to be more accurate and because the highly comprehensive *Catalogue* made no mention of either James Gardner or O'Sullivan as having recorded any negatives at Antietam, I do not feel that either took views on that field when Gardner's 1862 series was produced.

16.   *Photographic Art Journal* 1 (1851): 138.

17.   Dr. Oliver Wendell Holmes eventually wrote a total of three extensive articles dealing with stereo views. The second and third have already been cited (see notes 2 and 10). The first, now considered a classic, was entitled "The Stereoscope and the Stereograph," *Atlantic Monthly* 3 (June 1859): 738–48. For additional information concerning Holmes's contributions toward the advancement of stereo photography, see William C. Darrah, *Stereo Views, A History of Stereographs in America and Their Collection* (Gettysburg, Pa.: Times and News Publishing Co., 1964), pp. 7–8, 10, 14, 41, 45, 74, 100, 156, 160. A comprehensive and invaluable history of world-wide stereo photography will be found in W. C. Darrah, *The World of Stereographs* (Gettysburg, Pa.: W. C. Darrah, 1977).

18.   Dr. Oliver Wendell Holmes, "My Hunt After 'The Captain'," *Atlantic Monthly* 10 (December 1862): 738–64.

19.   In order to simplify the process of documentation while at the same time inform the reader as to where I derived information concerning these soldiers, I have included at the end of these notes a brief discussion of references found most helpful in tracing the background of each soldier. A similar section will be found relating to sources of information that pertain to those farmers whose families and farms were discussed in detail.

20.   Frederic Ray, " 'No Finer Picture of an Engagement'?," *Civil War Times Illustrated* 1 (February 1963): 10–13. The exact camera site was located by Jerry Hess and Robert L. Lagemann.

21.   William A. Frassanito, *Gettysburg: A Journey in Time* (New York: Scribners, 1975), pp. 174–76, 191–92, 222–26.

22. *The Official Records* 19: Part I, 121–23; see also *New York Tribune*, October 6, 1862.

23. This photograph is in the Military Order of the Loyal Legion, Massachusetts Commandery, photograph collection at the U.S. Army Military History Research Collection, Carlisle Barracks, Carlisle, Pa., vol. 38, 1857. Personal data on the signalmen is from J. Willard Brown, *The Signal Corps, U.S.A. in the War of the Rebellion* (Boston: U.S. Veteran Signal Corps Assoc., 1896). Supplementary information on E. C. Pierce will be found in his pension records at the National Archives.

24. William Child, *A History of the Fifth Regiment, New Hampshire Volunteers, in the American Civil War, 1861–1865* (Bristol, N.H.: R. H. Musgrove, 1893), p. 132.

25. Ibid., p. 119.

26. Francis T. Miller, ed., *The Photographic History of the Civil War*, 10 vols. (New York: Review of Reviews, 1911), 2:27.

27. Ben Fitzpatrick, Wetumpka, Alabama, September 22, 1863, National Archives. Fitzpatrick was the governor of Alabama from 1841 to 1845 and served in the U.S. Senate in 1848/49 and 1853–61.

28. Abram Martin, Montgomery, Alabama, October 14, 1863, National Archives.

29. Alpheus S. Williams, *From the Cannon's Mouth: the Civil War Letters of General Alpheus S. Williams* (Detroit: Wayne State University Press, 1959), p. 130; Holmes, "My Hunt After 'The Captain'," p. 748; Holmes, "Doings of the Sunbeam," p. 11.

30. The Regimental Committee, *History of the One Hundred and Twenty-fifth Regiment Pennsylvania Volunteers* (Philadelphia: Lippincott, 1906), pp. 68, 172. See also John M. Gould, *History of the First–Tenth–Twenty-ninth Maine Regiment, in Service of the United States* (Portland, Me.: Stephen Berry, 1871), p. 253.

31. Joseph R. C. Ward, *History of the One Hundred and Sixth Regiment Pennsylvania Volunteers, 1861–1865* (Philadelphia: Grant, Faires, & Rodgers, 1906), p. 110.

32. Napier Bartlett, *Military Record of Louisiana* (Baton Rouge: Louisiana State University Press, 1964), pp. 14–15. Reprint of first edition (New Orleans: L. Graham & Co., 1875). Details concerning individual soldiers are from their official service records.

33. Robert M. Green, *History of the One Hundred and Twenty-fourth Regiment Pennsylvania Volunteers* (Philadelphia: Ware Bros., 1907), p. 105.

34. Affidavit of Joseph N. Hamilton, Federal pension records, Huntingdon County, Pennsylvania, May 3, 1888.

35. Schildt, p. 313.

36. Ibid., pp. 289–92.

37. Miller, 5: 67.

38. *Pennsylvania at Antietam: Report of the Antietam Battlefield Memorial Commission of Pennsylvania* (Harrisburg: Harrisburg Publishing Co., 1906), pp. 132–33; Isaac Hall, *History of the Ninety-seventh Regiment, New York Volunteers ("Conkling Rifles"), in the War for the Union* (Utica: L. C. Childs & Son, 1890), p. 91; map of the Antietam battlefield prepared by Lt. Wm. H. Willcox, topographical officer on the staff of Gen. Abner Doubleday, ca. 1862, Maryland Historical Society; and map of the Antietam battlefield based on a reconnaissance of the ground occupied by the First Corps, by Lt. W. A. Roebling and W. S. Long, 1862, National Archives.

39. Ernest L. Waitt, *History of the Nineteenth Regiment Massachusetts Volunteer Infantry, 1861–1865* (Salem, Mass.: Salem Press Co., 1906), p. 137.

40. Andrew E. Ford, *The Story of the Fifteenth Regiment Massachusetts Volunteer Infantry in the Civil War, 1861–1864* (Clinton, Mass.: W. J. Coulter, 1898), p. 196.

41. Ward, p. 104.

42. Ibid., p. 105.

43. *Village Record* (West Chester, Pa.), December 31, 1861.

44. Frederick L. Hitchcock, *War from the Inside* (Philadelphia: Lippincott, 1904), pp. 56–57.

45. *Pennsylvania at Antietam*, pp. 190–91.

46. "The 130th Pennsylvania Regiment Burying the Dead at Antietam," *Frank Leslie's Illustrated Weekly* 15 (October 18, 1862): 53.

47. *The Official Records* 19: Part I, 849–50.

48. Walter J. Yates, *Souvenir of Excursion to Antietam and Dedication of Monuments of the 8th, 11th, 14th and 16th Regiments of Connecticut Volunteers* (New London, Conn.: 1894), pp. 37–38. See also Eleventh Connecticut tablet on Antietam battlefield, located east of Burnside Bridge.

49. *Hartford Courant*, October 29, 1862.

50. Thomas H. Parker, *History of the 51st Regiment of P. V. and V. V.* (Philadelphia: King & Baird, 1869), pp. 233–34.

51. *The Official Records* 19: Part I, 138.

52. George B. McClellan, *McClellan's Own Story* (New York: C. L. Webster & Co., 1887), p. 614; *New York Tribune*, September 24, 1862; *Pennsylvania at Antietam*, p. 164.

53. *New York Tribune*, September 22, 1862.

54. Charles E. Davis, Jr., *Three Years in the Army, the Story of the Thirteenth Massachusetts Volunteers* (Boston: Estes & Lauriat, 1894), pp. 8, 149.

55. See Schildt, p. 187.

56. Oliver T. Reilly, *The Battlefield of Antietam* (Hagerstown, Md.: Hagerstown Bookbinding & Printing Co., 1906), p. 26. Gardner's original caption for view VI-4 was, "Real's [sic] Barn, burned by the bursting of a Federal shell at the Battle of Antietam."

57. *The Official Records* 19: Part I, 286–87.

58. Ward, p. 115.

59. Theron W. Haight, *Three Wisconsin Cushings* (Wisconsin History Commission, 1910). Reference to Alonzo Cushing's having been with Battery A during the battle of Antietam will be found on p. 55.

60. Dr. C. R. Agnew, Frederick, Maryland, September 22, 1862, *U.S. Sanitary Commission Circular No. 48* (September 24, 1862), p. 13; *New York Tribune*, September 23, 1862. These references are supported by the various movements of McClellan's headquarters guard, the Ninety-third New York Volunteers, as described in David H. King, *History of the Ninety-third Regiment, New York Volunteer Infantry 1861–1865* (Milwaukee, Wis.: Swain & Tate Co., 1895), p. 44.

61. *New York Tribune*, October 1, 1862; again supported by the movements of McClellan's headquarters guard. (King, p. 44). See also McClellan, p. 616. Although the written evidence pertaining to the location of McClellan's third headquarters position cannot be termed precise, it is my belief that the ridge in the background of view VI-9 may well be identical to a ridge on the property of the Myers family north of and adjacent to the property of the Reverend Adams, with the camera located at or near the Harpers Ferry Road, slightly less than two miles south of the center square in Sharpsburg and facing northwestward. Other photographs taken at McClellan's headquarters in

early October show what may be Elk Ridge in the background, suggesting that these views were taken in the same area with the camera facing northeastward.

62. King, p. 59.

63. Edward S. Delaplaine, *Lincoln's Companions on the Trip to Antietam* (Harrogate, Tenn.: Lincoln Memorial University Press, 1954).

64. The *New York Times*, October 12, 1862.

65. Although approached in a roundabout fashion, the same conclusion was reached by James R. Atkinson, "Mr. Lincoln Visits His Army," *Civil War Times Illustrated* 10 (June 1971): 38–39.

66. The Library of Congress's list of identified individuals in this photograph makes no mention of Captain Custer but instead identifies the officer to the far right as a Col. George A. Batchelder. That Custer was in the group, however, is amply supported by Gardner's original caption, "Group.—President Lincoln, Generals McClellan, Porter, Morell, Hunt, Humphrey [sic], Colonel Sackett [sic], Lieut. Colonels Swietzer, Webb, Locke, Dr. Letterman, Captain Custer, etc., at Headquarters Fitz-John Porter, Antietam, October 3, 1862." Based on a well-documented portrait of Custer as he appeared in 1862 (see Miller, 1:289), there can be no doubt that the man Gardner was referring to was the officer standing in front of the tent to the far right. No one else in the photograph even remotely resembles Custer.

67. Frassanito, pp. 24–38.

68. A. J. Russell, "Photographic Reminiscences of the Late War," *Anthony's Photographic Bulletin* 13 (July 1882), pp. 212–13. For a listing of most of these views see E. & H. T. Anthony & Co., *New Catalogue of Stereoscopes and Views* (New York, ca. 1867), pp. 76–77.

Sources for Vignette Biographies of Common Soldiers

Descriptions of local areas from which the soldiers came were derived primarily from Richard S. Fisher, *A New and Complete Statistical Gazetteer of the United States of America* (New York: J. H. Colton, 1859). Population figures, however, were based on the Federal census of 1860 as recorded in Joseph C. G. Kennedy, *Population of the United States in 1860; Compiled from the Original Returns of the Eighth Census* (Washington: Government Printing Office, 1864).

The more detailed census listings for individual families were examined at the National Archives. Official military service records for all Union and Confederate soldiers are also on file at the National Archives, as are pension records (Union soldiers only) for those soldiers or their families who applied for government assistance as a result of losses incurred during the war. Not all applied.

The following compilation of sources therefore varies from soldier to soldier, depending on what was uncovered and on what was considered most helpful in piecing together the biographies.

Clark, John A.: Military service records; 1860 census, Monroe County, Michigan; and records of the Detroit Public Library, "First Land Owners of Monroe County, Michigan." On the front of the photograph (Monroe County Historical Commission) was the inscription, "Lieut. John Clark. 7th Mich Inftry D. Co. Monroe Mich." On the back was written, "John Clark—E. G. Clark's brother, Monroe, Mich. Killed at Battle of Antietam."

Flint, Alvin, Jr.: Military service records; 1850 and 1860 census for East Hartford, Connecticut; East Hartford vital records; family tombstones, Center Burying Ground, East Hartford. Attached to the back of the ninth plate ambrotype (John L. McGuire collection) was a note that read, "Alvin Flint Jr., Killed at the battle of Antietam aged 18 yrs."

Gay, John T.: Military service records; 1860 census, Troup County, Georgia. His name was mentioned in *The Official Records* 19: Part I, 1028.

Hurd, Anson: Military service records; pension records.

King, Charles E.: Military service records; 1860 census, Chester County, Pennsylvania; Robert S. Westbrook, *History of the 49th Pennsylvania Volunteers* (Altoona, Pa.: Altoona *Times*, 1898), pp. 23, 125; *Village Record* (West Chester, Pa.), December 31, 1861 and October 7, 1862.

Knap, Joseph M.: Military service records; pension records; Newton M. Curtis, *From Bull Run to Chancellorsville, the Story of the Sixteenth New York Infantry together with Personal Reminiscences* (New York: Putnams, 1906), p. 181.

Marshall, John: Military service records; pension records; 1860 census, First Ward, Allegheny City, Pennsylvania.

McCarthy, John S.: Military service records; pension records.

Miller, George D.: Military service records; pension records; Green, p. 105.

Morehead, Turner G.: All biographical information from Ward, pp. 428–31.

Parran, William S.: Military service records (Parran's service with

Courtney's Battalion will be found among the unfiled papers of the Confederate Service Records, microfilm reel #306); 1860 census, Orange County, Virginia; muster roll of the "Barboursville Guards," on file in the office of the secretary of Virginia Military Records; Will Book, Orange County, Virginia, 12: 473; W. W. Scott, *A History of Orange County, Virginia* (Richmond: Everett Waddey Co., 1907), pp. 268–69.

Rushin, Thomas J.: Military service records; 1850 and 1860 census, Marion County, Georgia; Rushin family papers, Georgia Department of Archives and History. An inscription written on the back of the photograph of Evaline Rushin Lowe reads, "Wife of J. M. Lowe Member of the 2nd Regt. Ga— Vols—Now at Centerville Va—May God bless her and protect her is the prayer of her Husband. Sept. 22, 1861 Richmond Va—"

Taylor, Thomas: Military service records; New Orleans city directories for 1850 and 1858. U.S., Congress, Senate, *Biographical Directory of the American Congress, 1774–1971,* 92nd Cong., 1st Sess., 1971, p. 1796. A companion photograph of Taylor, taken at the same time but showing him standing, is in the collections of the Museum of the Confederacy, Richmond, Virginia.

White, Harrison: Military service records; pension records; obituary in *Philadelphia Press,* September 30, 1862; list of Hoffman farm graves, the *New York Times,* October 12, 1862.

Sources on Farmers and their Farms
Property boundaries as they existed in 1862 are basically as they appear on Keo and Robertson, "Map of Washington Co., Md.," 1859.

Mumma farm: 1860 census, Washington County, Maryland; Reilly, p. 26; Schildt, pp. 183–87.

Newcomer/Orndorff farm and mill: 1860 census, Washington County, Maryland; Reilly, p. 21; Schildt, pp. 32–37.

Pry farm (McClellan's headquarters): 1860 census, Washington County, Maryland; Reilly, p. 22; Schildt, pp. 173–79.

Reel farm: 1860 census, Washington County, Maryland; Reilly, p. 26; Schildt, p. 187.

Roulette farm: 1860 census, Washington County, Maryland; Murfin, pp. 241, 249; Reilly, p. 26; Schildt, pp. 124–25, 204.

Sherrick farm: 1860 census, Washington County, Maryland; Reilly, pp. 26–27; Schildt, pp. 216–17.

INDEX

INDEX